"NOT GUILTY"

"NOT GUILTY"

The Trial of Gerald Regan

STEPHEN KIMBER

Published in 1999 by Stoddart Publishing Co. Limited
34 Lesmill Road, Toronto, Canada M3B 2T6
180 Varick Street, 9th Floor, New York, New York 10014

Distributed in Canada by:
General Distribution Services Ltd.
325 Humber College Boulevard, Toronto, Canada M9W 7C3
Tel. (416) 213-1919   Fax (416) 213-1917
Email customer.service@ccmailgw.genpub.com

Distributed in the United States by:
General Distribution Services Inc.
85 River Rock Drive, Suite 202, Buffalo, New York 14207
Toll-free Tel. 1-800-805-1083   Toll-free Fax 1-800-481-6207
Email gdsinc@genpub.com

03   02   01   00   99   1   2   3   4   5

Canadian Cataloguing in Publication Data

Kimber, Stephen
"Not guilty": the trial of Gerald Regan

Includes bibliographical references and index.
ISBN 0-7737-3192-X

1. Regan, Gerald A. — Trials, litigation, etc.
2. Regan, Gerald A. — Sexual behavior. 3. Trials (Rape) — Nova Scotia — Halifax.
4. Trials (Sex crimes) — Nova Scotia — Halifax.
I. Title.

KE229.R45K55 1999   345.716'02532   C99-930939-0
KF224.R45K55 1999

Jacket Design: Angel Guerra
Text Design: Tannice Goddard

Printed and bound in Canada

*We acknowledge for their financial support of our publishing program the
Government of Canada through the Book Publishing Industry Development
Program (BPIDP), the Canada Council, and the Ontario Arts Council.*

Contents

Acknowledgments

This book has its beginnings in my long-held fascination with Gerald Regan, and with the politics and the Nova Scotia he represents. I came of age just as he came to power. One of my first major assignments as a reporter involved trying to determine if he'd bought his first election.

I have often wondered — though I have no proof — whether he may have had something to do with my firing from the CBC in 1974. If he did, I thank him now for that. If the CBC hadn't fired me, I wouldn't have gone off to Boston to visit an old girlfriend, and I would never have met her roommate, the woman who would become my wife and the mother of our three children. We bought our first bedroom suite — an old pine collectable set that didn't quite qualify as an antique — with the proceeds from a magazine article I wrote about him. It was known in our house as the "Gerald Regan Memorial Suite."

Though Gerald Regan and I eventually went our separate ways — I into academia and he into federal politics and then international business — there was always something about him that never ceased to intrigue me. When I first read, in the fall of 1993, that the RCMP had launched an investigation into allegations Regan had sexually assaulted women in the seventies — probably during the period when I was covering the legislature — I decided the time had finally come to write the book I always somehow knew I would find in the life and times of Gerald Regan.

I had no idea at the time, of course, that it would take five years for the mounties' investigation to metamorphose into criminal charges, and for those charges — or at least some of them — to be dealt with by the courts. I had no idea either how much I still had to learn about Gerald Regan, and the politics and the Nova Scotia he represented.

I had a lot of help along the way. For obvious and entirely under-standable reasons, neither Gerald Regan nor any members of his immediate family agreed to be interviewed for this book. I have done my best to overcome that obvious weakness by talking to as many other people as possible — friends, colleagues, enemies, acquain-tances — to get a fuller perspective on him. The contributions of many of these interviewees are acknowledged in the text, but those of many others — again for obvious and entirely understandable reasons — are not. I thank them all.

This book also, of course, tells the stories of many of the women who claim Gerald Regan attacked them sexually. Having sat through much of their courtroom testimony and cross-examination, I can only imagine how painful and difficult it must have been for all of them. I salute their courage.

One of the women I did talk to directly and at length — identified in the text as Mary Graham — was Gerald Regan's girlfriend during the early fifties. Her thoughtful insights into many aspects — both positive and negative — of Regan's personality and character were invaluable. I thank her for sharing them with me.

I also want to acknowledge the contributions of my son, Matthew Kimber, and two of my former journalism students — Jaime Little and Erin Greeno — who spent days and weeks sifting through archival documents in Halifax and Windsor to help me piece together the story of Regan's childhood and his rise to power.

I can't overlook the support and camaraderie, either, of the reporters who covered the preliminary hearing phase of the Regan case with me, especially Rick Grant, Dean Jobb, JoAnne MacDonald, Lisa Taylor, and Brian Ward, who sat through the preliminary hearing for their news organizations. For months, we were among the only people in the country to have heard all of the stories of all of the women who had accused Gerald Regan. Our many corridor conversations helped me make sense of what we were hearing. JoAnne, who is a colleague at the *Daily News*, also shared with me the fruits of her own research into the case. Lisa Taylor read parts of some of the early drafts of my manuscript and offered constructive advice. I am grateful to all of them.

Just as I am indebted to Dr. Shirley Tillotson, my colleague at the University of King's College, who teaches women's and social history, and who suggested many useful avenues of research that helped me better understand the relationships between the sexes in the fifties and sixties in North America and, especially, Nova Scotia.

This project would not have been possible without the support and encouragement of my agent, Anne McDermid. I thank her for her many efforts on my behalf.

The manuscript itself would have been less clear if not for the fine hand of its editor, Gerald Owen, whose helpful suggestions for structural changes helped me lay out the story more logically.

And, of course, I want to thank Don Bastian, the managing editor of Stoddart, who waited patiently for the legal processes to reach the point where this book could finally be published.

None of the projects I have taken on over the years, including this one, would have been possible without the support — and often forbearance — of my family: my children Matthew, Emily, and Michael and my wife Jeanie, a television and film costume designer. Jeanie and I learned many years ago the perils of trying to work in the same business. So we wisely went our separate professional ways, but we remain the most loyal and enthusiastic supporters of each other's careers. I couldn't have survived without it. Or her.

Stephen Kimber
Halifax
January 1999

Prologue

On the morning of December 18, 1998, Canadians woke to the shocking news that Gerald Regan, the former premier of Nova Scotia and onetime federal cabinet minister — who was on trial in Halifax on charges of rape and attempted rape involving three women — had also been accused of dozens of other sexual attacks against women. Nearly three dozen women, most of whom did not even know the others existed — babysitters, office staff, job seekers, law clients, reporters, party workers, a legislative page, even a corporate executive — had told police what often seemed to be strikingly similar stories detailing how they'd allegedly been attacked by Regan in incidents that had supposedly happened over a forty-year period between the fifties and the nineties.

The details of all those other allegations had been kept secret from the public — and the jurors — during Regan's trial. But once the jury had finally begun deliberating the afternoon before, and after the judge had refused a defence request to continue the publication ban in place, the allegations — contained in testimony during Regan's 1996 preliminary hearing and in pre-trial arguments while the jury was out of the room — came tumbling out.

"What the Jury Didn't Hear" screamed the headlines in the December 18 *Globe and Mail* as well as on the front page of the Halifax *Chronicle-Herald* and *Daily News*. "Other Stories Revealed:

The Regan Investigation Found 35 Women Who Claimed They Were Assaulted" read one headline over a story inside the *Daily News.*

"The [court] documents," wrote Kelly Toughill in *The Toronto Star*, "show that young women and teenagers complained that Regan attacked them in his car, in his office, in hotels and at political party functions throughout the 1950s, 1960s and 1970s."

"By the time you read this," added Heather Bird in *The Toronto Sun*, "there will likely only be 10 people [the jury] left in the province of Nova Scotia who haven't heard all the dirty allegations against Gerald Regan."

Or possibly in all of Canada.

If Canadians were stunned by the stories they read in their newspapers that morning, they must have been even more shocked later that day when they turned on their television newscasts and learned that the jury had acquitted Regan of every one of the charges against him.

How could this have happened?

Civics lessons niceties about innocent-until-proven-guilty aside, there had been a public presumption for some time that Regan must be guilty.

Nova Scotians had certainly heard the gossip. During his last, unsuccessful electoral campaign in 1984, in fact, a local political gadfly had even gone door-to-door in Regan's riding distributing pamphlets claiming "several women have told me of your sexual assaults upon them" and suggesting there were many more women with similar stories to tell.

In 1994, the CBC-TV current affairs program *the fifth estate* brought some of those "similar stories" to the attention of a national audience in a report entitled "An Open Secret," which featured four women making on-camera allegations that Regan had come on to them.

The publication ban prevented journalists from reporting anything of substance that happened inside the courtroom during the long and winding legal road between the filing of charges in March 1995 and the actual beginning of Regan's trial.

But, during the six-week trial itself, fifteen or more local and national, French and English, newspaper, radio, TV, and magazine reporters did show up at court each day. For six weeks, they offered

Canadians saturation coverage of the graphic, horrific details of the allegations the three women offered. "Mr. Regan was on top of me and he was trying to get my panties off"; "He had his penis near my vagina and he was attempting to penetrate me"; "I didn't know what was going to happen. He was on top of me. Then I felt this terrible pain in my vagina. He put his penis in my vagina."

Reading such testimony day after day — and probably without paying nearly as much attention to the defence's attempts to undermine their accounts of what happened — many Canadians undoubtedly assumed Gerald Regan must be guilty.

So they were understandably shocked when a jury decided he wasn't.

What happened?

This book is an attempt to lay out exactly how the Regan case evolved and try to put the story of the allegations against him in the context of his biography and the recent social and political history of Nova Scotia.

I've chosen to incorporate most of the allegations against him into the narrative chronologically at the point where they're supposed to have occurred, in order to put the women's stories into some sort of context.

With the exception of a few instances that will be clear from the text, the details in the narrative come from court testimony, or police statements and notes referred to in testimony, or the arguments made by the Crown at various pre-trial hearings.

For legal reasons, I chose not to interview most of the women who claim Regan assaulted them, relying instead on the lengthy accounts they gave to police and prosecutors, and on their responses to questions from the Crown and defence in court. I have chosen to identify all of them — even those whose stories did not ultimately result in criminal charges — by pseudonym in order to protect their privacy.

It's important to make the point that — with the exception of the rape and attempted rape charges, on which Regan was acquitted — none of the other allegations against him have actually gone to trial. Some were not even the subject of charges. So Regan's version of these events — or his denial that any such events ever happened — has never been heard in a courtroom. During the preliminary hearing into a number of charges that the judge eventually stayed, however, Regan's lawyer did raise questions about the women's versions of events. Those arguments are detailed in the sections of Chapter Nine that deal with the preliminary hearing and the trial.

It's important too to make the point that while Regan has been accused of much, he has been convicted of nothing.

This is the story of how that came to be.

1

Believe It or Not, It's Ripley

Donald Ripley didn't have the patience for small talk. "So Phil," he demanded almost before Philip Mathias had raised the telephone receiver to his ear, "how many calls did you get?"

At the other end of the line in his Toronto newspaper office, Mathias couldn't help but smile. He had been a reporter for far too long and, more to the point, had already lived through far too many disappointments over the last thirteen years on this particular story, to hold out much hope that one obliquely written column in an obscure provincial supermarket tabloid — whose chief claim to fame was that it carried the weekly TV listings, for heaven's sake — could accomplish what he and other experienced investigative journalists for some of Canada's most powerful elite media institutions had failed to do.

"Nobody called," Mathias answered simply. "Nobody."

At the other end of the telephone, there was the briefest pause as Ripley absorbed this. "Goddammit, Phil," he thundered, "that's not good enough." Then he hung up.

Though neither of them imagined it at the time, that brief June 1993 telephone conversation cocked the trigger on what would become the Revenge of Donald Ripley. Two weeks later, on July 12, 1993, Ripley took what amounted to little more than a modest dog's breakfast of facts, fiction, and frustration to his local RCMP detachment in rural New Minas, Nova Scotia. Less than a month later, following up on Ripley's vague allegations, the mounties called Mathias in Toronto to ask if he would "cooperate in an investigation." His reluctant agreement to tell some of what he knew launched what turned into one of the longest and most controversial sexual assault investigations ever undertaken in Canada.

After conducting more than 350 interviews over a period of seventeen months all over North America, the RCMP, on March 15, 1995, charged Gerald Regan with seventeen counts of rape, attempted rape, forcible confinement, and indecent assault involving thirteen different women, one of whom was below the age of consent at the time of the alleged offence. The charges were shocking. Regan was a former premier of Nova Scotia and a former federal cabinet minister; he had even, ironically, served for a time as Canada's minister responsible for the status of women. Many of the charges involved incidents that had allegedly occurred during his years in public office.

But, equally startling — and even more troubling to some people — was the reality that the RCMP's investigation of Regan had begun not as the result of a complaint from any of his alleged victims but because one of Regan's bitterest political foes, Donald Ripley, had passed on third-hand gossip to the police. The primary source for Ripley's allegations was a report — a vague, more than decade-old names-have-been-changed-to-protect-the-innocent-or-the-guilty report — prepared by a journalist named Philip Mathias. Mathias's employers at the CBC were so unimpressed with that report they told him to abandon his investigation.

On the face of it, Philip Mathias and Donald Ripley seem unlikely knights in a holy crusade against sexual predators, even less likely comrades-in-arms.

Mathias was one of the country's most respected investigative reporters, an experienced, multi-award-winning specialist in uncovering political, business, and financial jiggery-pokery.* Ripley was a

---

* In 1995, Mathias, then a *Financial Post* reporter, won a National Newspaper Award for being the first to reveal the details of the infamous letter Canadian investigators wrote to Swiss authorities, accusing former prime minister Brian Mulroney of accepting secret kickbacks in the Airbus affair.

grudge-nursing, disgraced former stockbroker and political bagman who had been drummed out of the stock business for leaking details of a federal MP's blind trust to a Liberal critic.

But in the shadowy netherworld of gossip and rumour and innuendo, the fertile swamp where the most significant investigative reporting is often spawned, Mathias and Ripley made perfectly logical allies. In fact, many investigative reporters would probably identify Ripley as an often helpful, sometimes hazardous archetype of their trade — the voluble, vindictive, and well-connected outsider/ insider who not only knows where the bodies are buried but revels in sharing this information, especially if it is damning to those he sees as his enemies. But always, of course, on a strictly confidential basis.

Donald Ripley — a colourful, controversial, larger-than-life character in the small, everybody-knows-everybody world of Nova Scotia politics — fit his role perfectly. He was a Liberal turned Tory, an insider pushed beyond the margins by events, a man who felt betrayed by those he trusted. And, perhaps most importantly, he not only knew where all the political bodies were buried in Nova Scotia but he also loved to gossip about where to go to dig them up.*

The only son of a Kentville, N.S., shoe store owner and his partly native wife, Ripley saw himself as the quintessential outsider in the close-knit old boys' network of Nova Scotia business and politics. He had dropped out of school at sixteen after he was kicked off his school's hockey team for failing a history test. He spent winters playing hockey for the Kentville Wildcats senior team — Gerald Regan was the play-by-play announcer for Kentville's down-the-highway rivals, the Windsor Maple Leafs — and summers in the United States trying his hand at semi-pro baseball.

There, largely on a whim, he joined the U.S. army, where a recruiting officer was the first to realize his academic problems were the

---

* Ripley was a key Nova Scotia source for Stevie Cameron's 1994 bestseller, *On the Take: Crime, Greed and Corruption in the Mulroney Years*. Why would Ripley, a passionate Tory, provide Cameron with derogatory information about Mulroney and other Tories? Cameron herself suggests the likely if banal reason. During the summer after his 1983 federal leadership victory, Mulroney visited Halifax several times. On one occasion, he held an intimate dinner for his "closest advisers" at Halifax's popular Henry House restaurant. "Oddly enough," Cameron wrote, "no one thought to invite Donald Ripley . . . even though Ripley had been the fundraising mastermind. Ripley was a Micmac and a bit of a loudmouth and had never attended Dalhousie or joined the Masons; he was not quite one of the boys. Ripley soon lost his enthusiasm for the Mulroney campaign."

result of dyslexia, a learning disability. "Until then," Ripley says, "everyone just thought that I was stupid." During his "three years, six months, fourteen days and five hours" in the U.S. army, he painfully and laboriously upgraded his education ("I had to copy out the textbooks in long hand so I could figure them out"), eventually earning ten university credits in police science and criminology.

But when he returned home to rural Nova Scotia with his wife and young family, Ripley couldn't seem to find a permanent job. After Ripley was turned down for nineteen different jobs, his father, a cautious but successful stock market investor, encouraged him to talk to Bill Ritchie, then the local manager at Eastern Securities. Ritchie, who later became a Regan adviser and whose stockbroking firm consequently got the lion's share of Liberal government bond business, was impressed by Ripley, "one of those energetic, smart, provocative people who took to this business easily and quickly."

Over the next decade, Donald Ripley made himself into a successful stockbroker largely by force of will and personality, and then used his corporate connections to open doors into the province's political backrooms, the place where real power resides in Nova Scotia. During the 1960s, he was a fundraiser and constituency president for the Liberals. He might have happily remained a Liberal forever except for one incident just before and another immediately following the 1970 provincial election that brought Regan to power.

At the time, Ripley was the president of the King's North Liberal constituency association. When Regan visited Kentville to speak at his association's nomination meeting, Ripley invited Regan, his wife Carole, and their new baby, Nancy, to dinner at his house before the meeting. "It soon became crystal clear," Ripley would recall later, that Regan wanted to prevent the front-runner for the nomination, Vic Cleyle, from winning. "Vic is Catholic and this is a very Protestant seat, and he's of Lebanese ancestry, which would be a liability in Waspy King's North," Ripley quotes Regan as saying. So Regan, who was a Roman Catholic himself, wanted Ripley to talk Cleyle out of seeking the nomination. Ripley, who claims he is "at heart . . . a revolutionary who believes in social justice," refused.[*]

---

[*] In the end, Cleyle withdrew his name from nomination. In the subsequent general election, Regan's chosen candidate in the riding, a local farmer named Glen Ells, lost by 242 votes.

"I decided I didn't want anything more to do with the party after that," he said in his book *Bagman*.

But after the Liberals squeaked into office in the fall of 1970 with the barest of majorities, Ripley did arrange what was supposed to be a get-acquainted meeting between the new premier and specialists from Burns Bros. and Denton, the brokerage firm where Ripley then worked. In theory, they were meeting so that the firm's experts could "advise the new premier on financial planning for Nova Scotia." In reality, it was an attempt to grease the wheels so Burns could land the patronage prize of the province's bond business.

Unfortunately for Ripley — and ultimately for Regan — "after I delivered the Burns people to the spacious country residence [of Dr. Clarence Gosse, later the province's lieutenant-governor] where Regan was relaxing, and made the introductions, [the Liberal party president] John Shaffner not too subtly instructed me as to when I should return to pick them up." Ripley was mortified. "My associates would have no illusions about my role in the halls of power with the new government of Gerald A. Regan: I was a chauffeur."

Despite later apologies from Regan and Shaffner — Ripley says they blamed each other for the slight — he was not inclined to forgive and forget. He preferred to get even. "I became a Tory." A passionately partisan Tory.

Ripley's animosity to Regan solidified in late 1971 after the new Liberal government announced plans to take over the Nova Scotia Light & Power Company, the province's largest and most profitable privately owned utility company. Like plenty of other brokers with business and personal connections to the company's powerful major stockholders, Ripley opposed the deal.

In *Bagman*, his 1993 book about his life in the province's political backrooms, Ripley claims an unnamed Liberal fundraiser stopped him on the street one rainy day during the takeover battle and threatened to torpedo his career if he didn't back off. "He told me that I was on the wrong side of the power issue, that Regan was fuming, and that the managers would adjust my firm downward in the provincial bond syndicate after the takeover was complete. Further, he said, when or if my company complained, the government would tell them it was my fault. Angry beyond reason, I walked to the Halifax Club [the city's most exclusive business club], swearing to devote my life to kicking Gerry Regan out of office."

It took seven years and two more elections, but the Tories did finally wrest control of the government — and the patronage that went with it — from Regan's Liberals in September 1978. As a reward for services rendered to his new party, Ripley's then employers, McLeod Young Weir, became one of the lead managers for provincial bond issues. A year later, McLeod rewarded Ripley, its Atlantic manager, by making him a vice-president and director of the firm.[*]

During the 1980s, Donald Ripley was one of the province's most powerful backroom politicians. His influence spread well beyond his home province: he headed up the successful 1983 "Nova Scotia for Brian Mulroney" fundraising effort that helped propel Mulroney into the federal party leadership, and also served as a behind-the-scenes adviser to provincial Tory fundraisers in Saskatchewan, New Brunswick, and Newfoundland. His political connections were good for his business career too. McLeod Young Weir was, as the author Stevie Cameron delicately phrased it, "the beneficiary of significant provincial bond business in all four provinces."

But a startling 1987 allegation that Ripley had leaked confidential information about the blind trust of Stewart McInnes, the federal Tory public works minister, marked the beginning of the end of Ripley's personal power and influence.

On June 21, 1987, the CBC-TV National News reported that McInnes's trust might not be blind after all. Under conflict of interest guidelines, McInnes, who had defeated Gerald Regan for the Halifax federal seat in the 1984 general election, was supposed to have placed his investments in what is known as a "blind trust" — an arm's length arrangement under which a third party manages a politician's investments independently while he or she holds office — but Mike Duffy, the reporter, showed off documents that night which included details about the trust that appeared to have come from McLeod Young Weir's Halifax office. The next day, the Liberal MP Sheila Copps rose in the House of Commons to ask more questions about the true nature of the trust administered on behalf of the minister. Copps too had confidential documents from McLeod

---

[*] As if to underline the connection between Ripley's work for the Tory party and the bond business, the province pointedly dropped McLeod Young Weir as a manager shortly after he was fired.

Young Weir she said had been sent to her in a plain brown envelope.

Since McInnes's trust was administered by a stockbroker in McLeod Young Weir's Halifax office — the office Ripley managed — attention quickly focused on what role, if any, Ripley himself might have played in leaking them.

Although Ripley denied any involvement whatsoever,* the Investment Dealers' Association, the professional organization that regulates the activities of brokers, launched a formal investigation. On July 7, McLeod Young Weir flew six officials from its Toronto office to Halifax in a private plane to fire Ripley, change the locks on his door, and post a security guard to keep him from returning to get even his personal belongings. Six months later, in January 1988, the IDA filed six charges against him, including allegations he'd given the confidential information to Copps† and that he'd been involved in side deals: off-the-books financial transactions in which employees issue securities without notifying head office.

On February 5, 1990, after two years of IDA investigations and hearings, and a flurry of counter attack lawsuits by Ripley — against the IDA for what he called its "oppressive, unfair, and unwarranted investigation"; against his former employer for wrongful dismissal; and against a former colleague at McLeod Young Weir for defamation of character — the Investment Dealers' Association found Ripley guilty of what it described as "reprehensible, . . . deceitful, . . . and unethical" conduct.

All of this intrigued the *Financial Post* reporter Phil Mathias. What piqued his interest was not so much the question of whether Ripley was guilty of the charges against him — Mathias says he was never able to determine that — but whether Ripley could ever get a fair hearing from an incredibly powerful, self-regulating agency like the IDA.

Mathias spent several months poring over the sixteen volumes of transcripts of the hearings and interviewing all the various officials, experts, lawyers, and participants involved in the affair. During that

---

* Why would Ripley be involved in a plot to expose a supposed Tory ally? Once again, the answer may have more to do with personality than politics. In her book, Stevie Cameron noted that Ripley was also conspicuously not invited to a lavish barbecue for key Nova Scotia Mulroney advisers to celebrate their candidate's 1983 leadership victory. The event was held at Stewart McInnes's home.

† Copps testified during the IDA hearing that she didn't believe Ripley was her source.

process, he naturally spent a good deal of time with the scandal's central figure.

Mathias and Ripley weren't complete strangers. Their paths had crossed briefly in 1980 when Mathias, then a producer with a CBC-TV program, *the fifth estate*, first began looking into allegations of sexual misconduct by Gerald Regan. Ripley was just one of many — disaffected Liberals, Tories, NDPers, journalists, and others* — who provided Mathias with the names and leads and gossip that eventually convinced him there could be fifty or more victims of unwanted sexual advances by the former premier. But before he could complete his research, the CBC ordered him to abandon the project.

"How did I feel?" Mathias asks rhetorically. "Just imagine that you have come up with fifty allegations of sexual assaults involving the premier of a province and someone suddenly tells you to stop and forget about it. It was very upsetting."

In 1986, for reasons unrelated to the Regan case, Mathias left the CBC to return to *The Financial Post*. But he continued to nurse his unhappiness at the blocked investigation and tried from time to time — though "not with any furious interest" — to get the story published. "There were a number of women who were very distraught and had trusted me with their stories," he explains. "I felt I owed it to them."

In 1980, during the original internal battle over whether he would be allowed to continue with his investigation, Mathias had prepared what he called "The John Doe File," a detailed report for CBC lawyers and senior officials that outlined the allegations against Regan without identifying him or his alleged victims.† Over the years, Mathias had shopped this file around to reporters and editors he knew in other media, including *The Toronto Star* and *The Globe and Mail*, hoping one of them might pursue the story. No one did.

Given that Ripley knew about Mathias's original Regan investigation, it wasn't surprising that he was curious to know what had happened to it. When Mathias came to see him again in 1990 to talk to him about the IDA, they spent some time talking about the

---

*   Full disclosure: I was one of those Mathias spoke to at the time.
†   Mathias says he gave the complainants as well as Regan different identities in his report because he was afraid someone in the CBC hierarchy might "slip a copy" to Regan and the complainants might then be open to influence.

investigation, and about Mathias's frustrations in getting the story published or broadcast.

Mathias thought little of their discussion at the time. He was more interested in trying to understand what had happened to Ripley at the hands of the IDA and why. His June 25, 1990, story — "The Three-Year Ordeal of Donald Ripley" — offered a sympathetic portrait of "an admired Nova Scotia financier [who] raised funds for hospitals and native groups [and] helped impoverished municipalities." And it raised serious questions about the fairness of the process by which Ripley was convicted.

None of it directly helped Ripley's employment situation, however. He'd been fined $115,000 by the IDA and suspended from working as a stockbroker for two years. Since he couldn't — "nor would I if I could" — pay the fine, Ripley concluded he'd effectively been barred from practising his chosen profession, so he began casting about for a new way to make a living.

He decided to become a writer. Over the next few years, he churned out a number of books, including a self-published one, *The Roos of Bay Street*, which chronicled his battles with the IDA, and *Bagman*, his memoir of his days as a political fundraiser, which was eventually published by Key Porter. He also began writing a column for *The Metro Weekly*, an eccentric Nova Scotia supermarket tabloid that combined local TV listings with political gossip and right-wing opinion.*

While casting about for ideas for his column, Ripley remembered Mathias's John Doe file from their earlier conversations and decided in late May 1993 to give Mathias a call.

At first, Mathias says now, he was reluctant to give Ripley a copy of the file, in part because he thought Ripley was "a very impulsive sort of fellow" who was always in the middle of some controversy or other, and in part because he'd once again begun discussing with some editors at *The Toronto Sun* — which was owned by the same

---

* The publication's editor, Jeremy Akerman, is one of those colourful, larger-than-life political chameleons Nova Scotia politics is famous for. A fire-and-brimstone speaker, Akerman was the popular young leader of the NDP during the Regan era, but then quit the party in a huff over what he took to be interference by its Halifax establishment. He resurfaced as a Tory, then became a Liberal, and finally ended up editing the *Weekly*, which he turned into an aggressive but entertaining soapbox for his own increasingly right-wing political views. Ripley fit in well.

company as *The Financial Post* — the possibility of reopening his Regan investigation. He decided to stall Ripley by telling him he'd think about his request and get back to him. But Ripley, who is nothing if not persistent, persisted. When Mathias hadn't responded by June 3, 1993, Ripley faxed him: "John Doe is two weeks old today." Finally, Mathias gave in, agreeing to send Ripley an edited version of the file. He attempted to excise those parts of the already self-censored document he thought might make it possible for outsiders to identify Regan as the politician or the CBC as the media outlet in question,* and then sent it to Ripley.

On June 18, 1993, *The Metro Weekly* published Ripley's "John Doe" column under the headline: "The News Business: Sexual Harassment or Sexual Crimes." In it, Ripley never named Regan. In fact, he claimed to have "just learned the facts" of a "shocking story [involving] multiple unwelcomed advances against women by a prominent and powerful man: 'John Doe' . . . while I was doing some research on a university project I am writing on systemic injustice." But Ripley did identify Mathias as the journalist who had prepared the original story, describing him as "a talented, nationally known, ethical journalist," who had uncovered this scandal years earlier but had been prevented from pursuing it by his media bosses. After outlining a number of the incidents in Mathias's John Doe file, Ripley finished with a flourish. He wrote:

> The questions are obvious. Is an important person more likely to escape justice than a socially disadvantaged person? Did the police receive reports? Will modern women's organizations ignore that behavior? Fear has many tools. Silence is the handle which fits them all. It is my guess that the RCMP will talk to Philip Mathias and he does not sound shy or afraid to me.

Philip Mathias wasn't shy or afraid, but he was wary when a mountie from New Minas eventually telephoned — following up on Ripley's official complaint — to ask if he would agree to meet with

---

* Mathias's editing decisions were sometimes hard to fathom, even for Mathias. As he admitted in his later court testimony, some of his cuts, in retrospect, seemed "ridiculous," even to him. While he removed references to "film," "filming," and "filmed," for example, he left in a reference to "documentary." Why?, asked Regan's lawyer, Eddie Greenspan. "I can't reconstruct my thought process," he said.

two officers from the Milton, Ont., detachment to discuss the contents of his Regan file.

The call created an ethical dilemma for Mathias, a reporter who had long prided himself on his own principled and well-developed sense of journalistic right and wrong. The problem was that, in this case, he couldn't figure out in which direction his moral compass should be pointing.

What role should a journalist play in a police investigation?

If you ask that simple question to most reporters, including (most of the time) Philip Mathias, the answer will come without hesitation and almost by rote: None. The journalist's job is to ferret out facts, figure out their significance, and present them to the public. The police officer's role is to investigate allegations of wrongdoing to determine if a criminal offence has been committed.

While the publication of a journalist's story may trigger a police investigation, that's only incidental as far as most investigative reporters are concerned. There's a sound ethical — and practical — reason for journalists to erect impenetrable walls between themselves and police officers. Reporters often have to talk in confidence to all sorts of people while developing and confirming stories. Those sources must have faith that what they say to reporters, especially on an off-the-record, or not-for-attribution, basis, won't suddenly show up, without their permission, in a police file. If that happens, journalists, who depend on the trust of confidential sources for their livelihoods, will be less able to do their jobs.

Philip Mathias knew all that. During a nearly thirty-year career as an investigative journalist, primarily for CBC and *The Financial Post*, he had reported on the political wheeling and dealing around Manitoba's infamous Churchill Forest Industries project. He'd exposed frauds against governments and followed money trails that led to secret Swiss bank accounts. In all those years, he'd never once approached the police to ask them to investigate anything, nor offered them even a peek at his own files. In ordinary circumstances, he couldn't imagine ever doing so.

But this was no ordinary circumstance. For one thing, his Regan file was thirteen years old. His story had never been broadcast or published. And it probably never would be. If he couldn't do what a journalist is supposed to do with information — publish it —

shouldn't he at least turn it over to the police so they could investigate for themselves? The women who had talked to him back in 1980 had told him their stories because they wanted the information to come out, didn't they? Since Mathias hadn't been able to accomplish that while acting as a journalist, perhaps, he told himself, he could do so now as a private citizen. On the other hand, wouldn't giving his information to the mounties violate the faith those women had placed in him to protect their privacy? Mathias couldn't decide. He put these dilemmas to colleagues at *The Financial Post*. After work, he tried them out on friends, acquaintances, anyone who would listen. He agonized. "I was like a drunk walking a straight line," Mathias says, "staggering from side to side, trying to balance all these ethical issues."

In the end, Mathias decided his duty as a citizen outweighed his professional interest as a journalist. He agreed to come to the Milton detachment on August 10, 1993, to talk with the officers about what he knew. But he did lay down certain conditions on his cooperation. He'd let the officers read his unedited John Doe memo and a 1980 legal opinion the CBC had prepared about his investigation, he said, but he wouldn't provide them with the documents themselves. And, while he would discuss his investigation, he wouldn't turn over the actual field notes he'd collected. He also promised himself he would be cautious about just how much information he volunteered.

It didn't matter.

By sitting down with the two RCMP corporals that afternoon and tentatively laying out the expansive table setting of all the facts and tips and gossip and rumours he had gathered during his abortive CBC investigation thirteen years before, Philip Mathias gave the mounties all the pieces they needed to begin their investigation. He had crossed the invisible line from journalist to police informant, and he'd brought with him across that divide a box full of political and legal dynamite. Before he agreed to talk to them, the mounties had nothing worth investigating. Now suddenly they had a task force's worth of work to do.

Operation Harpy,* as the investigation of Gerald Regan would

---

* In classical mythology, a harpy is "a rapacious, filthy-winged monster . . . a plunderer, an extortioner." RCMP officials would later insist that they chose the name for the Regan task force randomly and that the choice of name was insignificant.

soon come to be known, was about to begin.

The police investigation was intended only to answer one simple question: Were there reasonable and probable grounds to believe Gerald Regan had done even one of the awful things Phil Mathias and Donald Ripley suggested he had done?

But attempting to answer that question only raised more — and more interesting — questions.

Was it fair for the mounties to launch an investigation when, in fact, no victims had complained? Was the RCMP allowing itself to be inadvertently drawn into someone else's politically motivated witch-hunt? Or had the mounties themselves, for reasons of their own, singled out Gerald Regan for prosecution because he had once been a prominent public figure? Or — on the contrary — were the mounties finally doing the investigation other police officers should have undertaken years before but hadn't because Regan was such a powerful public figure?

Even if this last explanation was true, was it really fair for the police now to look into forty-year-old allegations Gerald Regan had kissed some young women who didn't want to be kissed? Could anyone fairly judge sexual conduct from the fifties and sixties by the very different standards of the nineties?

But all of that, of course, still begged the even bigger, more puzzling question. If Gerald Regan had actually done any of the things Mathias and Ripley suggested, why?

Why would a man whose good public reputation was the underpinning of his career and his life risk everything for a fleeting sexual conquest?

Or would he really have been risking anything at all?

Was Gerald Regan such a powerful figure in Nova Scotia politics he believed he could do whatever he pleased and get away with it? And what would that say about politics in Nova Scotia? about Nova Scotia?

Or was it perhaps all more complex even than that? Was Gerald Regan's quest for conquest — sexual, political — some kind of aphrodisiac: political passion feeding sexual desire pushing political ambition driving sexual obsession? And if that was true, where had it all come from?

Who was Gerald Regan anyway?

2

"A Lot of Crust..."

Gerald Regan was only four years old when he made his first solo entrance at a sporting event, a local baseball game being played at a field about a block from his home on Stannus Street. His parents were at the game too, along with his older sister Maureen and brother Walter. But they weren't sitting with Gerry. They didn't even know he was at the game until one of them noticed that everyone else in the bleachers was smiling at a little boy in pyjamas who was cheering wildly from the baseline. His parents had assumed little Gerry was where they'd left him an hour before: at home in his bed asleep.

By the time Gerry was seven, he was a well-known neighbourhood salesman, peddling greens "liberally spiced with not-too-edible dandelions" door to door. By the time he was fourteen, he had expanded his market to include the larger Windsor community, teaming up with a neighbourhood friend to launch a pirate radio station featuring Regan's play-by-play broadcasts of local baseball and hockey games. By the time he was in his early twenties, he was cockily telephoning the owners of National Hockey League teams to smooth-talk them into allowing players on teams that had finished out of that year's Stanley Cup play-offs to barnstorm the Maritimes playing against the hometown favourites. As his older brother,

Walter, Jr., once put it, young Gerry had that mix of confidence and persistence Maritimers often call "a lot of crust."

The problem for Regan was that some of his most obsessive ambitions — like playing competitive hockey himself, or attracting the interest of girls his own age, or actually getting elected to political office — required something more than just a lot of crust.

GERALD AUGUSTINE REGAN was born on February 13, 1928,* the third of the seven children of Walter and Rose Regan.

Though Regan would later joke about Windsor's puffed-up self-image — in speeches outside Nova Scotia, he was fond of applying to Windsor Mark Twain's derivation for the word "unique": from the Latin *unus* meaning one, and *equus* meaning horse — the Windsor in which he grew up was, like Regan himself, a proud, self-confident place.

Residents there are quick to brag about everything from the fact that, as one local writer put it, "Windsor and Hants County are blessed with a greater prevalence of sunshine than any other town or county in Nova Scotia," to their rather dubious claim that their town's tides are "world famous."

Windsor's most impressive claim to fame, however, may be its idyllic beauty. "It is a striking characteristic of Windsor," the young Joseph Howe wrote in *The Novascotian* in 1828, "that you can examine it from twenty various points and find each view materially different from the others; every one beautiful, but every one having some leading feature, or agreeable combination, peculiarly its own."

Members of the British colony's eighteenth-century governing council in Halifax must have thought so, too. They were so enamoured by Windsor's lush beauty, by the richness of its soil, and by its convenient, well-fortified location just forty miles from Halifax that — after kicking the Acadians off their farms in 1755 — these worthies awarded themselves choice lots of land in what is now called Windsor.

Most of the early landowners — who also included some of

---

* Intriguingly, Regan lost a full year of his life between the 1968 and 1969 editions of the *Parliamentary Guide*, the official source for the biographies of Canada's elected officials. During his first stint in the House of Commons (1963–65), Regan's birth date is listed correctly as February 13, 1928. It's the same in the 1968 listing, the year after he was elected as Nova Scotia's opposition leader. In the 1969 edition, however, Regan's birth date changes to February 13, 1929. It is listed that way in all subsequent editions of the *Guide*.

the colony's most powerful judges and merchants — didn't settle permanently in Windsor, but they did establish magnificent summer homes there and set up farms that were cultivated for them by tenant farmers. Windsor, as one local history explains it, "was not 'founded' but instead grew from an influential collection of politicians, merchants, and officers from Halifax, some New Englanders from Falmouth, and Ulster Irish and Acadian tenants." The Loyalists joined that mix after the American War of Independence.

Though a prediction that Windsor would someday become a "residential suburb for the business men of Halifax" never came to pass, the town, by 1825, had earned a reputation — in the words of the *Acadian Recorder* — as "the Athens of Nova Scotia, the abode of elegant hospitality and polished society."

That's not to suggest Windsor was without its lower classes. Besides the tenant farmers, there were factory workers lured by the promise of jobs in the many textile mills and furniture factories, quarrymen who mined the area's rich gypsum deposits, and, of course, blacks, many of them Loyalists from the American revolutionary war, who were forced to live on the outskirts of Windsor, out of sight of the "elegant hospitality and polished society."

Thanks to the area's abundance of natural resources, including gold, gypsum, and timber, and its proximity to the bountiful apple orchards of the Annapolis Valley, Windsor was a centre for shipbuilding and shipping, and a major exporter. By 1840, in fact, Windsor was the third busiest seaport in Canada.

That was ironic because Windsor's harbour was only really a harbour for a few hours each day. As one visitor from the southern United States acidly put it: "When the tide is not in, the mud is in." The ocean tides of the North Atlantic enter the broad mouth of the Bay of Fundy between Digby and Saint John, building up water pressure as the passage narrows through the Minas Channel and into Minas Basin, finally whooshing up the Avon River and into Windsor harbour in a rush that raises the water level by thirty to forty feet. But almost as soon as it arrives, the water begins to recede, leaving an "ugly gash" of mud flats from one bank of the river to the other. Shipping success, therefore, depended not only on superb navigational skills and a thorough knowledge of the tides but also on more than a little good luck.

Perhaps not surprisingly, Windsor's pre-eminence as a shipbuilding and shipping port did not survive much beyond the Golden Age
of Sail. The end of Windsor's own golden age, in fact, was sealed in
1897 when a fire,* whipped along by gale force winds, swept
through the town, reducing much of it to cinders.

As Windsor was rebuilding after the fire, a young man named
Walter Regan arrived in town to take a job as a bookkeeper at the
Wentworth Stores, the company store for the Wentworth Gypsum
Company, the leading gypsum exporter in mainland Nova Scotia.

Walter Regan, who'd been born and raised in Dartmouth of hardy
Irish working-class stock,† was an ambitious young man who wasn't
quite a patrician but not an ordinary worker either. He climbed the
Wentworth corporate ladder from bookkeeper to store manager
before eventually saving enough to buy his own general store in
nearby Falmouth in the early thirties. His success with the store
allowed him to buy several rental properties around town, which
he rented out, mostly to poor families. Although some in Windsor
considered him a slumlord, others say he treated his tenants well.

Like his brother John who served for a time as Halifax's deputy
mayor and was a Conservative power-broker during the Borden era,
Walter Regan soon became an important figure in Windsor politics,
joining the local Conservative association and becoming its president. In 1913, he won a seat on town council. He was a town
councillor for twenty-seven years.

"He was a good councillor," says the Windsor historian L. S.
Loomer. "He was very community conscious and seemed to be especially interested in the welfare of those who had little or nothing."
During the Depression, Regan looked the other way as many of his
customers ran up bills he knew they might never be able to repay.
"He kept people eating as well as he could," says Loomer, who adds
he once interviewed the owner of another general store in Windsor

---

* Fire is a continuing theme in Windsor's history. In *Windsor, Nova Scotia: A Journey in History*, L. S. Loomer lists fifty-one other "major fires" in and around Windsor from 1710 to 1992. One more recent major fire in 1920 led to the relocation of King's College to Halifax in the 1920s.

† The Nova Scotia genealogist Terry Punch says Walter Regan's grandparents, James Regan and Ann Barry, likely arrived in Nova Scotia from County Cork, Ireland, in the 1830s. John Regan, the third of their six children who was baptized at Saint Mary's Basilica in Halifax on August 18, 1840, was a shipwright who married Joanna Skerry, the grand niece of a locally famous Irish family. Walter Regan was born in 1888.

who had had to write off over $50,000 in uncollectable Depression-era bills. "I'm sure Walter had to do the same. He seemed to have a good understanding and sympathy for people," Loomer says. "I give him a lot of credit."

Walter Regan was already well-established in Windsor when he married Rose Marie Green, a pious Newfoundlander, in a ceremony at Saint Mary's Cathedral in Halifax on a July morning in 1921. Rose, who'd been living in Halifax at the time of her wedding,* was given in marriage by the groom's brother John. She was described as looking "very lovely" in a gown of white satin worn with lace overdress and a "piquant" white tulle hat. After a New Brunswick honeymoon, the couple settled in Windsor and began raising their family.

They would eventually have seven children, two of whom, a son and a daughter, died in infancy. Maureen, the oldest of the surviving children, was born in 1923 and eventually became a nun. Walter, Jr., the eldest son, was born in 1924, served overseas as an intelligence officer in the army during World War II, and later became a lawyer in Ottawa. Gerry's younger brother, Jim, who shared Gerry's passion for sports and broadcasting, began his career as a broadcaster, served for a time as an aide to Prime Minister Lester Pearson, and eventually ended up as a consultant for Liberal-connected Maritime companies trying to win cable television licences.

Greta, the youngest child, died in August 1942 during what should have been a routine operation to remove her tonsils. No one knew she was a hemophiliac. She was only eight years old at the time. Gerry was fourteen. Greta's death affected the entire family, of course, but according to those who knew them, Rose was most deeply and permanently scarred by the death. Always religious, she retreated even more into the comforts of her church.

Rose became such an important — and well-loved — member of her local Roman Catholic congregation that when she died in 1963, the parish priest, Father A. J. Laba, felt moved to depart from his usual practice and make a speech about her during the funeral. "It is not the custom of a Catholic funeral to give a eulogy of the deceased," he said. "My few remarks today are in the nature of a

---

* Among her previous suitors was Angus L. Macdonald, who would later become Liberal premier of Nova Scotia.

personal tribute to an outstanding citizen of this community, a staunch member of this parish and fine Christian and Catholic lady. Mrs. Regan was gifted with a keen and capable mind. In the obituary notice we read that she was a poetess. I do not know of the extent of her poetic work, but I do know that her observant and beautiful soul could well express in poetic language the beauty of God's creation as she observed it around her. She had a delightful sense of humour, which she retained in spite of the cross of ill health which she carried for years. She had a charming simplicity which enabled her to walk and talk easily with the great as well as the lowly. May I say here that if her children have distinguished themselves somewhat in civilian and religious life it is due in no small measure to the training she gave them and the talents they inherited from her."

Gerald Regan may indeed have inherited from his mother his talent for mixing with the rich and powerful as comfortably as with the poor and downtrodden. And she may have also been the one most responsible for inculcating in him his relentless, restless ambition. But others who knew her, especially after Greta's death, say Rose Regan may also have helped bring to the fore some of Gerry's less admirable traits, including his need to control other people. "She was very domineering herself, the boss of that family, make no mistake," says one. "I think Gerry got that from her."

Despite a lack of formal education, Rose was a "self-educated intellectual" whose favourite book was a collection of great speeches and writings through the ages that she'd memorized and taught Gerry to memorize. "Ask him to recite Socrates today and I'd bet he could still do it," says Phil Woolaver, a retired lawyer who got to know the Regan family when he and Gerry attended law school together.

Young Gerry's development was influenced by his father too, of course. Walter Regan was an institution around town. A tall, distinguished-looking man, he walked three miles each morning from the rambling Georgian family home the Regans bought in the early 1930s on Chestnut Street,* down Ferry Hill, across the covered

---

* The Regan house, which was built in the 1840s by the first mayor of Windsor, features one of the few remaining examples of Victorian hand-painted ceilings in Nova Scotia in one of its downstairs parlours. The house is also notable because it was one of only three houses on Ferry Hill that survived the fire of 1897. Bucket brigades stationed themselves on the roof to prevent flames from spreading to the structure.

bridge over the Avon River, and along Highway 1 to his Falmouth general store. He made the same trek in reverse each evening, rain or shine or snow.

Falmouth was a farming community and Regan's store was the main farm supply centre, carrying everything from cattle feed to clothing, from candy to puncheons of vinegar and molasses. "When a new carload of a cattle feed would arrive, Mr. Regan would send out postcards to farmers in the area to let them know it was in," says Howard Dill, a Windsor farmer whose family regularly shopped at the store and who remembers Regan, Sr., as a "very dedicated gentleman."

Though many indeed do describe him as kind and gentle, others have less fond memories. "He was known as 'Snuff' Regan because he had this habit of snuffing as he talked," says one woman whose family shopped there. "My parents used to say his thumb weighed three pounds; he always kept his thumb on the scale while he weighed things." Some children, she says, preferred going to Burgess's Store, Regan's main competitor in Falmouth, "because Old Man Regan didn't seem to like kids all that much," and the store itself was dark and forbidding, almost dangerous.

Rumours of the senior Regan's fondness for women other than his wife grew and expanded after Greta died and Rose retreated more and more into the comfort of her religion. He is alleged to have had a long-time mistress and was rumoured to have bedded a number of tenants in his apartment buildings.

A family tale from that same era may or may not be connected to the elder Regan's philandering. According to the story, Rose was going up to the attic in the family home one morning after Walter, Jr., had gone off to war and after Greta had died. She saw a strange man standing at the top of the stairs. She screamed. The man is supposed to have been the ghost of the house's original owner. He'd hanged himself in the attic when his wife ran off with the architect who designed the house. At the time, the Regans were using the unfinished bare attic where he'd hanged himself, as a maid's room.* That's one

---

*   Though the Regans certainly wouldn't be considered well-to-do, they weren't unusual in having maids. According to L. S. Loomer's *Windsor, Nova Scotia: A Journey into History*, "domestic servants were plentiful, and paid almost nothing beyond room and board. On into the 1930s middle class families, who could not do much more than afford clothes and groceries on tick, managed to have some young girl from the country to do all the cleaning up

reason, or so the story goes, why the Regans had so much trouble keeping maids. At one point, four of them quit in the space of a month. One finally confessed to Rose she was leaving because of the ghost in the attic.

But others, including a local woman who collects folktales, say they've never heard of any ghost haunting the Regan house. "The only ghost in the house," suggests another Windsorite, "was Walter, Sr. The maids kept on leaving because of Walter's frisky hands."*

GERALD A. REGAN, Walter and Rose's third child and second son, was a middle child. His brother, Walter, Jr., who was four years older than Gerry and who served overseas during World War II, was a better athlete, a thoughtful, respectful young man everyone seems to have admired. Though Walter, Jr., was occasionally impatient when his mother forced him to drag young Gerry along whenever he and his friends wanted to play a game of baseball or hockey, friends say Gerry looked up to Hez, as he was known, and would often consult him about important decisions in his life. Jim, his younger brother, was the fashionable, good-looking one, the boy the girls wanted to be seen with.

Gerry, on the other hand, the boy with a ski-slope nose and large ears and an ungainly physical manner, was one of those children adolescence did not treat kindly.

What set Gerry apart from his siblings was the fact that he was so ambitious townsfolk used to joke that his middle initial must stand for Ambition. Ambition, Regan himself remembers, was something his parents, Rose especially, encouraged. "[It was] the classic North American phenomenon of parents who hadn't been to university, pushing for upward mobility for their kids," he says. "There was an

---

and looking after the offspring. It may have been her alternative to domestic starvation and brutality, or urban prostitution. The subject is touchy, but the facts were well enough known. . . . Windsor has its own horror stories of servant girls and others. On rare occasions they turned up in court. On most occasions, hypocrisy prevailed, and there was great discretion, some of it still hidden away in provincial birth registers and church baptismal records."

* Mike Doyle, the house's current owner, says he not only heard a story about a ghost haunting the house but his family has also experienced what he calls a "presence" there. In the version of the story he heard, however, the ghost was supposed to be a young woman. She too hanged herself in the attic, but for reasons unknown. She is supposed to be a friendly ghost. Although he says he hasn't personally seen or felt the ghost, Doyle says others, including his wife and guests at dinner parties, have "experienced someone walking through the house. And every once in a while, the dog will bark for no reason at all, as if it senses a presence."

attitude, particularly from my mother, of encouraging ambition and I think that, out of that, you learn to look at things in a certain way."

The way Gerry Regan looked at it, there was nothing he couldn't do. And almost nothing he didn't want to do.

He was bright, precocious, and a good student, remembers Garth Vaughan, who was born within days of Regan and grew up in the same neighbourhood. "He and I sparred for the top spot among the boys in marks all the way through school," he says. "He was inquisitive and very opinionated about everything." Adds Conrad Taylor, another classmate at the Windsor Academy during the early forties: "I remember he had a particular interest in tracking battles from World War II and then discussing what was happening in class. He'd go on at great lengths in class about the various campaigns."

At home, his older sister Maureen told one interviewer later, Gerry was teasingly referred to as "the philosopher" because he was so well-read in politics and philosophy, and because he was eager to offer his opinion on whatever subject was under discussion. But despite his obvious academic ability, Vaughan says Regan was "no bookworm." "He had too many outside interests to be a top student," agreed Maureen.

During high school, he was the president of his Grade Eleven class — when he wasn't being called "Gabby," he was known to fellow students as "The Mayor" — the editor of *The Announcer*, the Windsor Academy yearbook, a sergeant in the Windsor Air Cadets, a member of the football team, a sports announcer at CFAB, and a member of the drama club. In Grade Eleven, Regan led a student campaign in support of construction of an assembly hall and gymnasium for the school. Though the campaign fizzled, he was impressive, making speeches and lobbying adults in various local organizations, including the powerful Orangeman's Lodge. In Grade Twelve, Regan was one of the featured performers in *The Perfect Gentleman*, a one-act romantic comedy by Anna Best Joder, which was staged at the Windsor Opera House. Regan played Mr. Crawford, a high school chemistry teacher who was smitten with the older sister of the play's young hero, a boy of eleven named Roger Ames who was desperately trying to be the perfect gentleman but somehow seemed doomed to always be doing clumsy things. Conrad Taylor played young Roger. "Gerry," he remembers, "was a great talker, but he wasn't what you'd call a great thespian."

Nor would anyone mistake Regan for a great hockey player, even though hockey remains one of his passions to this day. "Windsor has produced a lot of fine hockey players," Garth Vaughan offers dryly. "Gerry just wasn't one of them." Still, he was game. Though never good enough to make the fine varsity high school teams Windsor Academy produced during the forties, Regan did play intramurals and pond hockey,* and he was a regular at the pickup games Vaughan organized whenever he and the other boys could scrape together the $1.20 it cost to rent the Windsor arena for an hour.

"We were always on skates," Vaughan recalls. "The big Christmas gifts in those days were season's tickets for skating at the old rink, and everyone got one. The rink was only open from around Christmas to March 24 because it was natural ice, you see, and you'd have to check in the morning to see if the flag was flying on the cupola. If it was, then the ice was all right for skating and we'd all go skating after school."

Skating, says Vaughan, was Gerry's weakness as a hockey player. "He was always an awkward skater. But he knew where to pass the puck. And he understood the game better than most anyone else."

Partly because of his encyclopedic knowledge of the game and how it was played and partly because of his gift of gab, Regan found his athletic outlet as a sports broadcaster. Avard Bishop and his son Willard, who lived up the street from the Regans, had built their own amateur radio station in the early forties. Willard, who chummed around with Gerry's younger brother Jim, knew Gerry was interested in sports and was "a devil of a talker," so he invited him to be the station's sportscaster.

At the time, CFAB wasn't a licensed radio station. The Bishops had decided they didn't need a broadcasting licence because their station used existing power lines to carry its signal directly to homes in the community. Although reception was often spotty — "One woman told me she could only hear us when she was using her flatiron," Willard jokes today — it was good enough to get them into trouble with the authorities.

---

* Regan and his friends often played hockey at Long Pond in the woods near King's College School. According to Garth Vaughan's book *The Puck Stops Here*, Long Pond was the site of the first-ever hockey game in 1800.

During the war years, Windsor served as a transit camp for soldiers on their way to Europe. Though the soldiers usually spent only a few weeks or months in Windsor, they were, says Bishop, "well integrated with the townspeople." To show the army's appreciation for the town's hospitality, the local commandant one day decided to stage a talent show at a church hall featuring his soldiers and broadcast it over CFAB. "It was a great event," remembers Bishop. "The commandant even made a speech. But then some ding-bat mountie picked it up on his radio and decided we were violating the Defence of Canada regulations or something." Officials concluded the wired radio station was really a broadcasting facility, and therefore illegal without a licence. "So they dragged my father into court. He ended up pleading guilty and he was fined ten dollars and costs. After that, he decided to apply for a licence."

Whether broadcasting over the power lines or over the airwaves, CFAB was a true community radio station with news, regular live performances featuring local talent, quiz shows, and, of course, sports.

Windsor was a sports-mad community in those days. During the spring, playoff games featuring the town's senior hockey league team, the Windsor Maple Leafs, often drew crowds of 2,500 or more. They'd have to drive fifteen miles down the highway to Wolfville, which had the closest arena with artificial ice, to see the team play.

"Lots of time it would be standing room only," recalls Howard Dill, a local hockey buff. "The fire department chief would come out to the rink and they'd have to stop sales (because of building occupancy limits) with a line up still waiting to buy tickets. After a while, the chief would leave and they'd start selling tickets again."

Gerry Regan was at least as sports-crazed as other townsfolk. While still in high school, he gave fans their sports fill with a four-hour show on CFAB every Saturday afternoon. He also did play-by-play broadcasts of the Maple Leaf hockey and baseball games as well as, occasionally, a staged boxing match. "We'd set up these boxing matches in the backyard," Willard Bishop remembers. "Nothing much would really be happening but Regan would be giving the blow-by-blow of the fight." He pauses, laughs. "He embellished a little."

Regan learned on the job. Bishop remembers their first-ever broadcast from the Windsor Arena. "They gave us three feet of space along the boards to set up our equipment so there wasn't much room to move and Gerry wasn't too experienced with how to hold his microphone then. He'd hold it in front of his mouth but he'd forget to move it when he turned to follow the play up and down the ice. I remember I'd have to crank up the volume so he could be heard when the play was down at the end of the rink and then, when the puck came back the other way, Gerry's head would turn and suddenly he'd be screaming into the mike again."

It didn't take Regan long to get the hang of it. Even after he went to Halifax to attend university, Willard Bishop says, he would often call Regan to come home to broadcast a game. "I remember one game we were playing in Wolfville and I went to the gondola and got everything set up. It was three minutes to eight and the game started at eight and there was still no sign of Gerry. Finally, with about two minutes to go, he sauntered in, glad-handed with people down by the ice for another minute or so and then ambled up to the gondola with thirty seconds to spare. We did a quick mike check and then we were on the air." He pauses. "And you know, he didn't even have a piece of paper in his hands. He never did. But he knew all the players, and where they were from, and their records. He was good."

One of the players he would certainly have known was Donald Ripley, an aggressive young defenceman for the rival Kentville Wildcats. "Don wasn't a bad defenceman," recalls Howard Dill. "He was blocky and he carried himself well. But he had an awful yap on him. His nickname was 'Bucket Mouth.'"

By this point, Gerald Regan was spending as much time on the road broadcasting hockey games for stations in Windsor and Bridgewater as he was going to university.

He lived what his friend and fellow law school student Phillip Woolaver would recall as a "catch-as-catch-can life. I'm not sure he ever ate a regular meal. He lived on sugar, lots of chocolate bars. I remember one time when he was broadcasting a game and he had a sore throat, he gargled with Coca-Cola."

"It would be nothing for Gerry to hitchhike to Summerside [in Prince Edward Island] to broadcast a game and then come back for class the next day," remembers Pat Connolly, a fellow sportscaster at the time. Later, after he'd scraped together enough money for a "rickety old car, he practically lived in it. That car was like Columbo's car. You never knew what you were going to find in there."

At that time, Regan, Connolly, now the dean of Nova Scotia sports journalists, and Al Graham, later president of the federal Liberals and a senator, were Nova Scotia's up-and-coming young sportscasters. "We were all going to make it to the NHL as great broadcasters," says Connolly with a smile. Or, if not the NHL, at least to CJCH Radio in Halifax where the soon-to-be legendary Danny Gallivan was the reigning king of local play-by-play broadcasters.

"I was at CJCB in Sydney," Connolly says, "Al was with CJCB in Antigonish and Gerry was living in Windsor, going to Saint Mary's [University in Halifax], and travelling here, there, and everywhere to do games. Our paths crossed a lot."

But Regan wanted to be more than just a play-by-play man. "Gerry was also instrumental in the development of the Windsor Maple Leafs of the late fifties," Connolly notes. "He worked the telephones to get some very good imports from Quebec to come down and play for Windsor. There were a bunch of them, including Simon Nolet, who eventually ended up playing in the NHL for Philadelphia, and Jacques Allard,* who became one of the stars of the senior league." That year, the Windsor Maple Leafs came within a game of winning the Allan Cup, the national senior hockey championship.

Regan saw himself as a sports impresario too.† "I remember when he got this idea, which I thought was a little wacky, of bringing a couple of NHL teams that were out of the play-offs and have them play a series of exhibition games in the Maritimes," says older brother Walter, who was then a lawyer in Windsor. "I told him it was impossible; nobody was going to listen to a kid from Windsor. He said, 'Just watch me,' and he picked up the phone and called the president of the Chicago Blackhawks. Just like that. And got him."

---

* The team management had asked Regan to help recruit the Quebec players but his French may not have been quite as good as they'd hoped. They were actually looking for a goaltender when Regan lured Allard down east. "It wasn't until he arrived on the train that they discovered he was a goal scorer, not a goal tender," recalls Frank Gallagher of Windsor's Hockey Heritage Centre. Allard most certainly was a goalscorer. In 1963–64, he set a league record with 183 points in a single season.

† Regan's promotional ventures weren't just limited to sports. Al Hollingsworth, a journalist who grew up with Regan, remembers him arranging country music tours as well. "He brought Orville Prophet to Nova Scotia for his first tour," Hollingsworth says.

It was, in fact, a brilliant idea. In the days before satellite dishes and 24-hour sports networks brought saturation coverage of professional hockey into every town and village in the country, most fans in the Maritimes had never been closer to a real NHL hockey game than their weekly *Hockey Night in Canada* radio-inspired imaginings. "They were ready," says Connolly, "to storm the box offices, money in hand."

The players had good reason to like the concept too. In the days before agents and multi-million-dollar contracts, most players were paid so little they needed an off-season job to make ends meet. Regan's barnstorming tours meant they could continue to make money playing hockey even after their season ended. "The players loved it," says Connolly. "They'd start in Rimouski and then work their way through the towns — Campbellton, Dalhousie, Saint John, Halifax, and Sydney — and then on to Newfoundland. They'd sometimes play three games in a day and make more money during the post-season than they would if they'd gotten to the Stanley Cup final."

How did Regan finance the venture? Connolly laughs. "Gerry probably didn't have ten cents to his name until he got the first gate. But he could talk anybody into anything. And he came through."

Regan not only travelled with the team, Connolly says, but he'd also occasionally even play with them. "They'd sometimes have to fill out the roster with Maritime players and, of course, the whole thing was Regan's idea, so why not?"

In *Bagman*, Donald Ripley less charitably recalled one game involving NHL players and a team of "Nova Scotia Senior All-Stars." "Typically, [Gerry] waited until the last minute to work out the details. . . . The promise [to the players] of ten dollars and a borrowed hockey sweater was little enough . . . but the discovery that all ten hockey players and all their gear would have to travel to Digby [from Windsor] in only two cars was worse. Sadder yet, the so-called All-Stars, all boyhood pals of Regan's from Windsor, found out only at departure time that both cars had been borrowed from the two local used-car dealers on the pretext of being tryouts. . . . The cramped drive to Digby was done on a strict conservation basis, as the two cars had to save gas by coasting down all the hills."

Regan's hockey promotion venture ended abruptly in the mid-fifties, when NHL owners belatedly began to realize how lucrative he was making it for players not to make the play-offs. "Regan was in New York working on [plans for] the next year when Muzz Patrick [the owner of the New York Rangers] spotted him in the lobby of Madison Square Garden," Connolly says. "He said to him, 'There's not gonna be any more of your post-season tours. I don't care whether we make the play-offs or not. No more tours.' And that was the end of Gerry's little promotion."

But it was lucrative while it lasted. There are those who will tell you Regan — who had a personal reputation for frugality* — made more money promoting hockey games while attending university than he did in his first year as a lawyer. He was so busy with all those outside interests, in fact, he didn't make much of an impression at Dalhousie Law School where the saying attributed to him in the yearbook† is "work and worry have killed many a man, so why should I take a chance?" The write-up noted that Regan had found time during law school for "extensive work in the radio and sports promotional field outside of college," and that his "future plans include politics." There was nothing about his legal plans. Perhaps that was because he didn't have any. Few remember Regan being enthusiastic about law school or the life of a country lawyer.

Politics, and the life of a politician, did enthuse him. In fact, it obsessed him. Apart from sports, politics appeared to be his only consuming passion. His first political memory is of standing, enthralled, outside the *Hants Journal* office on the night of June 29, 1937, watching as the results of the provincial election were posted for the adults to ponder and discuss.

Regan was just nine years old at the time, but it could not have been lost on him that the Liberals won that election. The Liberals, it must

---

* Donald Ripley quotes Donald Reid, a boyhood friend of Regan's, suggesting that Regan was the only person he knew who could start the week with a dollar and end up with a $1.10 "just by osmosis. Reid borrowed the old cliché and said to Gerry, 'If you went to a funeral you'd have to be the corpse to get all the attention.' Gerry topped his line and said, 'No, I'd sooner be the undertaker and get all the money.'"

† Dalhousie Law School, which has turned out more than its share of successful politicians, jurists, and businesspeople, usually likes to brag about the quality of its classes. But perhaps not the Class of '52. Regan's classmates included Leonard Jones, who earned national notoriety for his anti-bilingualism campaign as the mayor of Moncton in the sixties and early seventies; Gordon Coles, a Regan appointee as Nova Scotia's deputy attorney general who came under heavy fire during the Marshall Inquiry for political favouritism; and G. H. "Paddy" Fitzgerald, a Tory who became Speaker of the Nova Scotia legislature but was later convicted of income tax evasion and, after he left politics, of raping a woman who'd come to see him about a legal matter.

have seemed to the young Gerry Regan, were Canada's natural governing party. The provincial party, under Angus L. Macdonald, had come to power in Nova Scotia in 1933 when Regan was just five years old. With the exception of five war years when Macdonald turned the reins of power over to another Liberal caretaker, Angus L., as he was familiarly known in Nova Scotia, would serve as premier for eighteen years until his sudden, unexpected death in 1954. In Ottawa meanwhile, the federal Liberals under Mackenzie King and his successor, Louis St. Laurent, held continuous power from 1935 until 1957 — for all but the first seven years of Gerry Regan's growing up.

That may be the reason Gerald Regan became a Liberal instead of a Conservative like his father. His father, Gerry confided to friends at the time, was "furious" at his decision. Though Walter, a fiercely partisan Tory, had taken his son to Tory headquarters during election campaigns to try to win him to the cause, Gerry had his gaze firmly fixed on the political prize from the day in 1940 when he first saw Angus L. Macdonald face to face and realized that Liberals were the ones who usually won the prize in Nova Scotia. Regan was then an apple-cheeked twelve-year-old, a member of the air cadet honour guard that greeted Macdonald when he came to Windsor to officially open Clifton House, an historic site that had been the local estate of the nineteenth-century author and politician Thomas Chandler Haliburton. Regan was so impressed by Macdonald, who stopped to shake his hand, that he decided that someday he too would be the premier of Nova Scotia, the *Liberal* premier of Nova Scotia.*

In 1947, Regan — then a university student working at the radio station in Bridgewater — was introduced to an up-and-coming Nova Scotia federal Liberal politician named Robert Winters. By 1949, they were teaming up to compete in the doubles competition in

---

* When I interviewed him for a magazine article in 1977, Regan claimed fellow Grade Eleven students at the Windsor Academy had predicted in the school's yearbook that he would be premier some day. The reality is slightly different. In the 1944–45 Grade XIA Class Prophecy, the entry for Gerry Regan reads: "On the first casual glance at the evening paper, my eyes were arrested by a bright red headline which screamed the words 'Regan Runs.' Remembering Gerry's orating powers I eagerly scanned the lines below his picture. What was he running for — Mayor, or Prime Minister? But alas! my high hopes were sent crashing to the ground; Regan was running all right, but, from the country on a charge of smuggling!" The Class Prophecy in Grade Twelve said that he would become a movie mogul. "Gerald Regan, super wonder-man of Hollywood . . . announced plans for the production of his new movie, which will be directed, written, acted, and even 'shot' by him — and it's called 'Alone.'"

the Canadian tennis championships.* They almost won. During the 1953 federal election campaign, Regan made his first political speech, at Winters's request, in a small community called Baker's Settlement in Winters's Lunenburg County constituency. The speech was a success. Winters, by then a federal cabinet minister, won and was promoted to minister of public works.

Gerald Regan, a fully committed Liberal, carefully cultivated the ground back in Hants County for his own planned run for office. Unfortunately for him, the once seemingly endless Liberal tide was about to go out faster than a receding tidal bore. Within a year of his hustings debut, Angus L. Macdonald was dead and the provincial Liberals were busily self-destructing in religious infighting. By 1956, they were ripe to be shunted aside by Robert Stanfield's Tories. Federally as well, a prairie tornado named John Diefenbaker was gearing up to blow away another tired Liberal government that had been in power for far too long.

If he'd had the ability to see into the near future at that stage, Gerald Regan might very well have reconsidered his pragmatic choice of party affiliation.

Regan would later tell a newspaper reporter he became a Liberal because he was attracted to the philosophy of Dr. Thomas MacCulloch, a pioneer educator who helped found Dalhousie University "and was effectively the founder of the Liberal Party of Nova Scotia." In that 1977 interview, Regan described his interpretation of MacCulloch's philosophy as "non-socialist reform. . . . I think I have more or less stood for those traditions as against the historical affiliation of the Tories with the Establishment." But when he explained his choice of political party to a girlfriend in the early fifties, he did not speak in such lofty terms. "The Liberals and the Tories are just the same," he told Mary Graham.† "The difference is that it's easier to get elected as a Liberal."

When they first met in the fall of 1953, Mary Graham was a seventeen-year-old senior at the Windsor Academy; Gerry Regan, at twenty-five, was eight years her senior.

Regan and his younger brother Jim already had reputations in

---

* Tennis was one sport that Regan excelled at.
† Mary Graham is a pseudonym. Unless otherwise noted in the text, women who allege Gerald Regan behaved with them in a sexually inappropriate way will be referred to by pseudonyms.

Windsor as "cradle-robbers. They liked young girls." During his own high school and university years, few remember Gerry with girls his own age, or indeed, being much interested in girls at all. "Really," says Howard Dill, "I never knew Gerry to date any girls, let alone many. He was never what you'd call a ladies' man. I always thought of him as being more interested in education, politics, and sports than in girls." "He tried," says Conrad Taylor, "but I don't think he was ever all that successful." "None of us were," laughs Garth Vaughan. "The boys would hang around together and play sports and talk about girls. But, as for Gerry and girlfriends, I don't remember any." The few girls his own age he tried to date remember him as awkward. "He wasn't what you'd call romantic," says one. "None of the boys our age were, of course, but Gerry was always very aggressive. He never seemed to know where to draw the line. He was always pawing and pinching. I don't think he knew what to do around a girl."

There is no question that the sexual climate has changed since Regan was growing up. As John D'Emillio and Estelle B. Freedman put it in *Intimate Matters*, their history of sexuality in America: "Study after study of high school and college youth from the 1930s through the 1950s confirmed the existence of a double standard. . . . Boys pushed while girls set the limit. Sometimes, boys acquiesced, but in many cases the line between subtle pressure and outright aggression was crossed, as girls found themselves forced to submit to petting or intercourse." In *How to Win and Hold a Husband*, a book published when Gerald Regan was seventeen, the author advised young women: "Remember that the average man will go as far as you let him go."

For teenagers like Regan who came of age in the years following World War II, the situation was complicated because the lines were shifting so quickly; the double standard was a moving target. Girls, wrote Ira Reiss, a U.S. sociologist who surveyed sexual attitudes among post-war adolescents, were often "half-willing," so it was sometimes hard for boys to know for certain if no really meant no.

It was also increasingly difficult, based on what they read and heard, for boys not to believe some form of sexual experiences had become their right as well as a rite of passage. In 1953, Alfred Kinsey released his landmark study of *Sexual Behavior in the Human*

Female, which claimed 90 percent of American females had participated in petting and fully half had had sex before they were married.
That fit in neatly with Kinsey's earlier findings that virtually all males
had engaged in some form of petting and that almost 90 percent of
them had had premarital sex. In 1953, the same year Kinsey published
his findings on female sexuality, Hugh Hefner published the first issue
of *Playboy*, a glossy magazine featuring pictures of naked women,
whose proudly proclaimed philosophy was to "enjoy the pleasures the
female has to offer without becoming emotionally involved."

If you were a young man in the mid-fifties and you weren't getting
your fair share of sex, you had to ask yourself, Why not?

If Gerry Regan was confused about how to act around females, or
how to expect them to behave in response, he certainly wasn't unique
among young of his time. During the course of researching this book,
I spoke with a number of Windsor area women who remember him
as perhaps a trifle more aggressive but not all that different from
other young men. "He'd do whatever you'd let him get away with,"
one told me. "I had to fight with a lot of the boys back then. That
was the way things were when I was growing up."

Mary Graham wasn't thinking about all that when she first met
Gerry Regan in the fall of 1953. He was the sophisticated older man
of her fifties romantic fantasies, one of the college men who were "so
much more 'romantic' in our minds than the 'boys' we went to
school with." Besides, he was ambitious. He was, as he told her over
and over again, going to be a politician — and sooner rather than
later.

There had to be a few stops along the way, of course, including a
stint in the early fifties helping out part-time — along with Jim — in
the family store after his father became ill. That, in fact, is how he
and Mary met in the first place. Mary and a group of her friends,
usually all girls, would regularly stop in at the Regans' store for a
bottle of pop on their way home from school.

Unlike his father, Gerry welcomed the girls. "Gerry would yak
with all of us," she remembers. "He was mildly flirtatious, but
mostly, he just seemed very interested in all of us." Especially Mary.
"He kind of singled me out. I was flattered to have this college-
educated man show an interest in me, a high school girl. I liked
talking with him."

One chilly afternoon in late November, Regan offered to drive Mary and several of the other girls home. They eagerly agreed. Regan dropped off the other girls first, but then, instead of taking Mary to her house, he detoured down a secluded back road and stopped the car. Without a word, she claims, he "lunged" at her and began to kiss her. She was stunned. And conflicted. As much as his sudden attentions frightened her, she was flattered too "that he would choose me as the object of his attentions." He told her he liked her because she was smarter than the other girls. "He made the wise move of not telling me I was beautiful. I knew better. But I was smart and he said he liked me because of it." He even confessed he was falling in love with her. "I wasn't that smart, I guess. I believed him."

After that, he would be there when she got out of school in the afternoons, sitting in his car waiting to drive her home. Or show up at noon hour at a soda shop uptown where the girls all went to buy Cokes during the school lunch break. Or come and sit beside her at a hockey game and then drive her home afterwards. Or discover that she and her girlfriends were going to the movies, and serendipitously show up to join her and drive her home. There was almost always, of course, a side trip down a secluded back road to park, and neck, and talk. "We would talk a lot, neck a little," she recalls. "I was able to keep, through much protestation, pretty well within my personal code of 'necking-only' limitations." Besides, she adds, they talked more than they necked.

"Gerry was fun to talk with," she remembers. "His favourite subjects were religion and politics, and he seemed to appreciate whatever I had to say." His views on those subjects were certainly not hers. She was, she says, from a "surprisingly liberal Baptist background where it was OK to question religious teachings. . . . Gerry seemed to accept his Catholic faith without question, although I didn't think he was seriously 'religious,' more Roman Catholic because it pleased his mother than for any strong sense of conviction." He believed, she remembers, in the divinity of Christ, the infallibility of the pope, the use of Latin in the mass, original sin, and the celibacy of the priesthood. On politics they argued principle over pragmatism, with Mary pushing her father's CCF agenda of socialized medicine, public ownership of utilities, cooperatives, and so on. "Gerry conceded these were 'good things' but political suicide to try to push such measures because powerful — wealthy — people just wouldn't support that kind of program."

Regan seemed to enjoy the discussions as much as Mary did. "That was the nice Gerry," she muses. "Then there was the not-nice Gerry who would suddenly start to lunge and grope."

It was the not-nice Gerry who showed up for their first real date to see a movie, *The Story of Three Loves.*

"I was expecting a bit of hugging and kissing before he took me home," Mary told me in a letter she wrote more than forty years later. "He parked his car on College Road near the tennis courts. And reached for me. I had no idea I was about to be forced to have sexual intercourse in the front seat of his car. Afterward, I was numb. Terribly ashamed. As though somehow, even though I had protested vigorously and tried to push him away, it had all been my fault."

Many years later, the RCMP interviewed Graham about what she says happened on this date but decided not to file charges, largely because she had continued to date Regan for several months after the alleged attack and the police felt that, coupled with the age of the charges, might make it difficult to win a conviction. The Crown also considered calling her to provide similar fact testimony during Regan's 1998 trial. In the end, chief prosecutor Adrian Reid says the Crown decided her evidence would not be "helpful" to its case, in part because hers was the only allegation against Regan that involved what would today be described as "date rape."

Regan, for his part, couldn't understand why she was crying, she says. He knew, he said with the complete confidence of someone who didn't know nearly as much as he thought he did, that she couldn't have been a virgin because he'd been able to enter her so easily. "That added even more to my confusion," she says now. Besides, he told her, it was all right because he loved her. But he added ominously she couldn't tell a soul about what had happened. "If your father hears about this, I could be charged with statutory rape because you're under the age of consent," she claims he said, adding that his future law career and political ambitions "could be ruined if I was stupid enough to tell." He promised her he wouldn't do it again.

She says he did. On several occasions. "He was very strong, and my objections carried no weight." Once, however, she recalls, she did manage to get his attention. "We had been to a hockey game. On the way home, he parked his car on a side road. He began kissing me and suddenly forced his very long tongue into my mouth. I'd never been kissed that way before and I didn't like what he was doing. I managed to pull away and voice my strong objections and revulsion. He then grabbed me, forcing me into another deep tongue-thrust kiss. At which point I bit. As hard as I could. Gerry straightened up behind the wheel, clutched his tongue in surprised agony. Through his tongue in fist, he managed to mutter and sputter, 'What did you do that for?' I repeated my earlier objections but I didn't apologize. Angrily, he revved up his car and delivered me to my door — in silence."

But Regan was not often or easily dissuaded. At one time, Mary even thought she was pregnant. "He told me he'd marry me," she says, "but he said we'd have to move to Manitoba so he could start his political career where no one would know what had happened." Luckily for both of them, the pregnancy turned out to be a false alarm.

Mary says she did try to talk Regan out of having sex with her. "I told him how terribly ashamed and guilty I felt. He merely laughed and said it wasn't a problem for him. As a Roman Catholic he could just go to Confession and be absolved of guilt." That frightened her even more. "I feared he would be naming me in his confessions."

He didn't have to. Many of her friends, who she says, knew of Gerry's reputation around young girls, tried to convince her to stop seeing him. Her older brother obliquely warned her that "Gerry wasn't nice to girls," and said she shouldn't go out with him. Some of her girlfriends told her Regan was too old for her, and "too fast," too. "I told them he wasn't like that with me," she says now. "I was in a state of denial."

Still, she couldn't help but hear the stories. There were already plenty of them in Windsor, she remembers. He'd driven home two of her friends once, they confided to her, and he'd made a lunge for one of them when she tried to get out of the car. "There was a real tug-of-war before she got away."[*]

---

[*] Although one of these two friends doesn't deny it happened, she believes such incidents involving Regan have been blown out of proportion. "Gerry wasn't any different than lots of other guys I knew in the fifties," she says.

Regan himself didn't do much to bolster her confidence in the genuineness of his affections. He even bragged to her he had a girl-friend in Halifax he was seeing at the same time he was dating her. "She was older than me, about twenty-five, and her name was Carmelita, he said. He told me Carmelita suspected he was also seeing girls back in Windsor. She told him: 'I'll bet you're *making merry* whenever you're home.' Gerry thought her choice of words was very funny."

Their age difference began to bother Mary after a while, but Regan was dismissive, saying that "I benefited because of his experi-ence, that his being older was good for me."

But Regan, for his part, was careful too to keep the character of their relationship a secret from their families. He never picked her up at her house — "We'd meet at hockey games; he'd just come up and sit down with me and then we'd go off together afterward" — and he never introduced her to his family. "I remember one day we had to stop at his place to pick up something and I asked if I could come in with him. He said, 'No.' His mother was there — I think there was a real restrictiveness in his dealings with his mother — and he didn't want to have to explain that I was a Protestant. And worse, that my parents were CCF."

That's not to suggest Mary's parents were any more enamoured of Gerry. They didn't like his religion, his politics, or — most of all — the fact he was eight years older than their daughter.

By the spring of 1954, Mary had had enough too. She broke up with him. "That made Gerald Regan very angry with me," she recalls. Shortly after their split, she says, a rumour circulated in her school that she was pregnant by a school friend from Hantsport. The story eventually reached the boy's father who confronted his son about his supposed indiscretion with Mary. The friend then told Mary, and the two of them set out to trace the source of the rumour. She claims she discovered Regan had been the one spreading stories. "When I confronted Gerry about starting the rumour, his response was to the effect, 'Well, so what? You don't think I was going to let you get away with dumping me, do you?'"

A short time later, while she was writing her Grade Twelve exams, Regan showed up at school in his car. "I really need to talk to you," he said. Against her better judgment, she agreed and Regan drove them out to an old quarry on the outskirts of town. This time, however, he didn't come on to her at all. He just wanted to get a few things straight, he said. He'd only gone out with her in the first place, he told her, because he knew that sooner or later he'd get what he wanted. And he repeated his contention that she wasn't a virgin when they met. "I was crying so hard and he just sat there," she recalls. "Then, I guess he suddenly realized, 'My God, I've done something to hurt this person,' and then he began to cry too."

She didn't speak to him again for several years until they met by accident one afternoon at Windsor's annual country fair, the Hants County Exhibition. Regan, in an expansive mood, seemed to have long since forgotten what had passed between them. "I've met the girl I'm going to marry," he fairly bubbled with enthusiasm. She was a young woman named Carole who was working for the summer at the Digby Pines Resort Hotel, he explained, and then proceeded to offer Mary a list of all the reasons they were meant to be together. "She's crazy about me," he said, "and she's very pretty. She's Anglican but she'll convert. Her father is a Liberal MP. And she'd make a super hostess."

Mary waited to be sure he had finished. "Did you forget anything, Gerry?" she asked.

He looked at her blankly.

"Do you love this girl?"

Regan didn't answer. Perhaps irritated by the question or by the questioner, he simply turned on his heel and walked away.

OTHERS WOULD HAVE BEEN quick to argue that Gerald Regan was very much in love with Carole Harrison. The daughter of a Saskatchewan Liberal member of Parliament, they'd met in May 1954 at a National Young Liberal Convention in Ottawa. Carole was a "rather reluctant" eighteen-year-old Saskatchewan delegate to the convention. "My father was worried there weren't enough delegates from Saskatchewan," she explains. While handing out small packets containing Saskatchewan wheat on the steps of Parliament Hill — "Eat Bread With Every Meal," the label urged — she met a young Nova Scotia lawyer named Gerry Regan.

They quickly became an item, corresponding regularly that winter. The following summer, Carole, who'd completed her first year at

Carleton University, took a summer job as a relief clerk at the Digby Pines, an hour down the highway from Windsor.

Regan suddenly became a frequent visitor at the home of Phillip Woolaver, a friend from law school who'd moved back home to Digby to start his law practice and raise his family. Regan's "world revolved around Carole," Woolaver recalls. "They kind of envied [my wife and me]," he adds. "Oftentimes they'd take our daughter Pearl out with them when they went out together. I think they were already thinking very seriously about getting married."

They were. In fact, Carole decided not to return to university at the end of the summer. In part, she admits, the decision had to do with the fact that her parents had recently separated and money was tight. But there was also, she adds, the reality that she and Gerry Regan were getting "serious" about one another. By April 1956, she'd managed to land a job in Halifax not only so she could earn money to get married but also so that she and Gerry could finally pursue their courtship in the same city.

On July 18, 1956, the day her sister was married, Gerry Regan proposed to her. By then, she was already studying to prepare for her conversion to Catholicism. While she may not have known anything about what Mary Graham would later claim Gerry Regan did to her, Carole — like Mary — couldn't help but know of Gerry's political ambitions. While she went home to Ottawa to prepare for their wedding on November 17, 1956, Regan kept himself busy running, unsuccessfully as it turned out, for the Liberals in the October 30, 1956, provincial election.

ELIZABETH SINCLAIR didn't know anything about Gerry Regan's political aspirations. In fact, she told police investigators decades later, all she knew of Regan at that time was that he lived a few blocks away, that he was a lawyer and a sportscaster, and that he must have known a friend of her mother's, Bertha Rhodenizer.

Rhodenizer was living part of the time in the Sinclairs' house in Windsor while she navigated her way through the traumas of a messy divorce. Sometime in the summer of 1956, Rhodenizer had to go to Halifax to deal with some business, and Elizabeth went with her to visit her cousin Jean and Jean's husband, Jim Rose, in the city. They were a childless couple in their forties who liked Elizabeth to visit them.

During Gerald Regan's 1998 trial, Sinclair would testify that Regan drove them to Halifax and then, a few days later, drove Elizabeth back home by herself. What Sinclair claims happened on that drive home to Windsor led to criminal charges against Regan: three counts, including rape, forcible confinement, and unlawfully having sexual intercourse with "a female person who was not his wife and was of previous chaste character and was fourteen years of age or more and was under the age of sixteen." On December 18, 1998, a jury found him not guilty of all of the charges involving Sinclair.

At the time of the alleged attack, Sinclair testified, she was barely fourteen, a tall, thin, late-blooming teenager who had never been out with a boy and could conjure up only the haziest notions about sex and sexuality. Gerald Regan was twenty-eight years old, dividing his time between his fledgling Windsor law practice and a new job as a part-time sportscaster for CJCH Radio in Halifax. Regan had applied for the job when Danny Gallivan moved to Montreal to become the voice of the Canadiens in 1953, but the position had gone to Pat Connolly instead. But then, two years later, Connolly had been lured away to become the sports voice for the new CBC-TV station in town, and Regan was his obvious successor.

Perhaps not surprisingly, Regan and Bertha, who was well-known in Nova Scotia as a competitive tennis player, talked sports on the drive to Halifax that day. According to Elizabeth, Regan told Bertha he was heading on to Liverpool from Halifax so he could do a play-by-play broadcast of a baseball game the next night. But he would be coming through Halifax again in a few days, and he would be happy to pick them both up for the return drive to Windsor.

While the two grown-ups chatted in the front seat, Elizabeth sat quietly in the back, imagining the fun she would have with her cousins in the city. Regan dropped Elizabeth off at their apartment on Prince Street and the two adults then drove away.

A few days later, Regan telephoned her at her cousins' to say he would be by shortly to pick her up. She waited for him on the sidewalk, her overnight bag by her side. She was wearing her mother's all-weather coat because it had been raining that day. When Regan arrived, Bertha wasn't with him. There'd been a change of plans, he said; Betha would be staying in Halifax a while longer so it would be just the two of them on the return journey. This time, Elizabeth sat in the passenger seat beside Regan.

At first, according to her testimony, Regan headed along the familiar Route 1 they had travelled on the journey to Halifax. But when they reached Mount Uniacke, about halfway between Halifax and Windsor, Sinclair testified, Regan suddenly turned down a dirt road on the right. The narrow road led down past islands of stacked pulpwood alongside the road and then turned slightly to the left, opening into a large gravel pit. Though it wasn't far from the main road, the highway was no longer visible. There were no other cars in the gravel pit. Regan stopped the car, turned off the engine.

Eizabeth Sinclair's allegations about what happened next would become the basis, thirty-nine years later, for the most serious of the criminal charges filed against Gerald Regan: an allegation that he raped a minor.

"I want to talk to you," Sinclair claimed Regan began. She wasn't frightened. He was an adult, after all, a friend of Bertha's. "I've been watching you," he continued, reaching over, putting his arms around her, one hand flicking down the lock on the passenger door. "I like you." He kissed her suddenly. His tongue was in her mouth, choking her. "I was very frightened," she said. "But I couldn't say anything because he was still kissing me. I'd never been kissed before."

"Don't be afraid," he said when he finally pulled his mouth away from hers. "I'm not going to hurt you." She testified during Regan's 1998 trial that he then pushed her down on the seat. Her head was jammed up against the passenger door. She felt one hand pushing up her coat, then her skirt, while his other hand held her arms in position behind her head. She could feel him pushing aside her underpants. "He was all over me, he was hurting me," she would tell a hushed courtroom forty-two years later. He was inside her.

And then, as suddenly and violently as it had begun, it was over. Regan, she said, had withdrawn his penis, ejaculating on her leg. She saw his penis. It was the first time she'd ever seen a man's genitals.

There was blood too, her blood. And she was crying. "I didn't mean to hurt you," she said he told her. "It won't always be like this. You'll see, you'll enjoy it." She couldn't imagine it.

Regan used his handkerchief to clean her up, then rearranged his own clothes. For the rest of the ride home to Windsor, she sat huddled beside the passenger door, as far away from him as she could get. He was not unfriendly, but he did warn her not to tell anyone what had happened. "No one would believe you anyway," he said.

When Regan finally let her off outside her parents' house, she testified, she quickly ran in, through the large entrance hallway and up the stairs to the bathroom, hoping to avoid her parents. Once inside, she took off her underpants and hid them in a drawer in the large dresser her mother kept in the bathroom. Then she noticed blood on the coat she'd been wearing. Desperately, she tried to wipe it away with a facecloth. Afterward, she took it downstairs, hung it in the closet, and tried to pretend nothing had happened.

She didn't say a word to her parents. That was partly because of Regan's warning, but also, she explained years later, partly because she knew very little about sexual matters at the time and she couldn't figure out how to tell her parents what had happened to her.

According to her evidence, she eventually confided her story to a school friend. Janice Corkum was babysitting one day next door to where Elizabeth lived, so she came over to keep Janice company. They had talked and the talk, as it often does with teenaged girls, turned to boys, and to sex, and one thing led to another, and Elizabeth, without even meaning to, let her secret slip. Janice was less shocked than Elizabeth had expected. Gerry Regan, Janice confided to Elizabeth, had tried to rape her too.

In March 1995, Regan was charged with the indecent assault, attempted rape, and forcible confinement of Janice Corkum, too. On December 18, 1998, he was found not guilty on all counts.

By the time of this alleged assault sometime during the late fall or winter of 1956–57, Regan had already begun to assemble the pieces of what would become his adult life. He'd run in his first election, the October 1956 provincial campaign that ended twenty-three years of unbroken Liberal rule and brought Robert Stanfield to power in Nova Scotia. Running in Hants West, Regan, still only twenty-eight, had put in a respectable showing, losing by a slim enough margin that he was already making plans for his next run at elective office. And, on November 17, 1956, he married twenty-year-old Anita Carole Harrison in St. Theresa's Roman Catholic Church in Ottawa. Photographs from that event show a smiling young couple.

Janice Corkum didn't see those pictures. But she told police investigators in the fall of 1993, that she did see a package containing proofs of the wedding photos lying on the front seat of Gerald Regan's car on the night he drove Janice and some friends home from skating.

She was fourteen at the time, tall and thin. Like lots of teens in Windsor, she was a regular at the evening skating sessions at the Windsor Arena. So was Gerry Regan. On this particular evening, she later testified, Regan came up to her and a few of her friends as they were sitting on the sidelines taking off their skates at the end of the session. Would they like a drive home?

Sure, why not? They all knew Gerry Regan. He was a neighbour. He knew Janice's parents. They went to church together. He'd even visited their home from time to time. Sure. Why not?

"Just be careful of the pictures," he said as they piled into his beat-up old Chev. "They're my wedding photos."

She'd expected to be dropped off first — she lived closest — but, according to her evidence, Regan passed up the most logical routes to her house and opted instead to drive the others home. But that was all right too, she thought. It gave her the chance to move up in the pecking order. By the time the last other young person was let out, Janice had made it to the front seat.

But Regan didn't drive toward her house then either. He went up Hospital Hill instead. "I thought of saying that it would be easier to drive the other way," she said in court, "but I didn't want to seem disrespectful and I figured he must know where he was going." Then, he turned down the road that led behind the hospital. She suddenly realized where he was going. To Lovers' Lane, the wooded area near King's College (where Regan had allegedly taken Mary Graham). Lovers' Lane, Janice knew, was what the other kids called the area where teenagers came to kiss and nuzzle after movies or dances or skating. Her parents had warned her to stay away from "the woods. I was taught that the woods were not a good place to be." Not only was she "in the wrong place," but she was also — and more importantly, as she put it years later — "with the wrong person."

Gerry Regan stopped the car, she testified, and turned off the engine. She began to cry. He tried to reassure her — he was going to make her "a big girl," she testified he said — but she wanted no part of any of it. Janice knew, without really understanding the details, that she would not — in what she says were his words — "like what I'm going to do." She tried threatening. She would tell her parents, she said, she would tell his wife, she would tell their priest. She noticed the package of wedding photos on the seat. "I'll use my skates to cut them up," she warned him. Finally, she claimed in her testimony at Regan's 1998 trial, Gerry stopped listening. He lunged at her, started to kiss her, began to undo her clothing. Then he was on top of her, his chest on her face suffocating her. She screamed. Her legs kicked frantically at the steering wheel. She was becoming hysterical. Taken aback momentarily, Regan backed away from her, just for a second, but it was enough. She grabbed for the car door, discovered it was locked, and then jumped over the front seat and into the back. He followed her. "I discovered I was now in a worse situation," she explained later. "There was no steering wheel to impede him."

Forty-two years later she would tell a Halifax courtroom full of strangers that he pushed her down on her back on the back seat, pushed up her sweater around her armpits, took off her bra, and then pushed down her black slacks and the long blue underwear she'd worn skating. Her panties followed. He was kissing her — "It was more like slobbering," she said — as he undid his own pants and pulled down his underpants. "I could feel his penis, and his hair, on my stomach."

Suddenly, she said, it was over. Regan calmly got off her and rearranged his clothing. He climbed back into the front seat, invited her to join him there. "I'll drive you home," he said. She tried to pull up her pants, then noticed a strange odour. He had ejaculated on the slacks.

"I don't know why you're crying," she claimed he said as he drove toward her house. "We didn't do anything wrong." He told her she was pretty and he was happy he could give her a ride home. "He continued to talk as if nothing had happened," she testified. "I thought there must be something wrong in his head."

He stopped the car a few houses away from hers. "If you tell your parents," he said, "you'll be in very serious trouble."

And then he let her out. She ran in the door. Her mother called out to her from the living room. Luckily, her parents had friends over to play cards that night. Rather than hanging up her skates in the closet near the living room and being forced to talk with them, Janice decided to take the skates to her room instead.

Then she went to the washroom, she told the court. She tried to wash the stain from her slacks but soon gave up. Instead she took a pair of scissors and cut up all her clothing — her slacks, sweater, and underwear — and stuffed them into a laundry bag she hid under her bed. "I felt terrible," she remembered. "My mother had knitted that sweater."

Later, after her parents' friends had left, Janice's mother came into the bedroom to say good night. Janice was pretending to be going to sleep. "Don't turn on the light," she said. So her mother simply kissed her on the forehead and softly sang the children's rhyme she had used to get Janice to go to sleep when she was a little girl. "Mares eat oats and does eat oats and little lambs eat ivy . . ."

Janice didn't feel like a child anymore. "I felt that my childhood ended right there," she said in her evidence. She didn't go to school the next day, or for several days after that. She was sick, she told her mother.

Later, she took the bag with the cut-up clothes and dropped it in a garbage pail at a neighbour's house.

She'd see Gerry Regan from time to time after that — in church, with his wife on the street. He even came to the house once to see her father. She can't remember exactly how she reacted — "I hadn't expected to see him there" — but she said in court: "Mother reprimanded me for however I reacted." When they did speak, she said, Gerry Regan "just treated me like nothing ever happened."

3

Politics
Nova Scotia–Style

If you're going to begin to understand Gerald Regan, there are some things you'll need to know first about how politics has played itself out in rural Nova Scotia for most of this century, and certainly during the fifties when Regan was mastering the tools of his politician's trade in Windsor. While he didn't invent the system of politics Nova Scotia-style, he didn't object to it and he had no particular interest in reforming it. Gerry Regan understood how the game was played and knew enough to play it well to advance his larger interests.

The first of the things you need to understand is that politics in the towns and villages and countrysides of Nova Scotia was a very personal, intimate affair well into the 1970s. Everyone knew everyone. And, because politics was as much a part of everyday life as the weather and the tides, everyone also knew how almost everyone else voted. In many small towns in Nova Scotia in those days, as Geoffrey Stevens put it in his 1973 biography of Robert Stanfield, "a man would have had a better chance of taking a mistress and keeping it a secret than he would have in changing his political allegiance without his neighbours knowing."

Of course, people rarely changed their political allegiances in rural Nova Scotia where party preference passed down from generation to generation like the family farm or grandma's favourite rocking chair.

Because of that, the parties soon lost whatever philosophical under-
pinnings they might have once had and, by Confederation, "the most
suitable designations for the administration and its opposition had
become the Ins and Outs," according to the Nova Scotia political
historian J. Murray Beck. "The struggle between the two was for
place, power, and the spoils of office."

In many ridings, including those in Regan's Hants County, there
were about as many Liberals as there were Tories, so the outcome of
each election often turned on the choice of the few independent
voters in the constituency and — perhaps more importantly — on
the willingness of supposedly committed voters to actually go out
and cast their ballots.

Since most rural communities also tended to have quite a stable
population base, politically sophisticated party organizers would
know, before the votes were cast, the potential support available for
their candidates, almost down to the last vote. "You'd know your
hard-core supporters and you'd know their hard-core supporters,"
explains Walton Cook, a Liberal MLA during the first Regan administration, who honed his political skills in fiercely partisan Lunenburg
County during the forties and fifties. "After that, you go through
everyone in your poll, maybe 200, 300 people, and you'd study them
severely, analyze them one by one. If a fellow had been Liberal before
but had got a job with a Tory since the last election, you'd check to
see if there'd been any change in his attitude. Did his salary increase?
If so, chances are you'll see some sign of disloyalty." Newcomers were
scrutinized with care. Cook says he was once delegated to "wine and
dine" the new schoolteacher to determine where her sympathies
might lie. "With the doubtful ones, you'd look for any kind of sign:
Who do they chum around with? Who did they go to the [Fisheries]
Exhibition with? Who did they get drunk with? Whose wife did they
sleep with? You look at all the social, economic, religious, political
factors and then you figure out how to deal with them."

That's where the fine art of Nova Scotian politics entered the
equation.

Organizers for both parties freely dispensed election day "treats"
— a pint of rum here, a few crisp, new dollar bills there — in order
to grease the squeaky wheels of democracy. "The first thing I learned
about politics as a child in rural Nova Scotia," the late poet Alden

Nowlan wrote, "was that you got paid for your vote. Before I knew the name of the prime minister I knew that on election day a local ward heeler would drive into the yard with a two-dollar bill (in later years it was a five-dollar bill) for my grandmother and a bottle of rum for my father."

Walton Cook's first political job in Northfield, a rural Lunenburg County community where his grandfather, a Liberal road contractor known as Big Bill Wentzell, held sway, was to drive voters to the polls on election day. And, not incidentally, to deliver boxes of chocolates to all the Liberal and could-be Liberal ladies of Northfield. "Every poll had two or three hundred dollars from the constituency organization — they got it from headquarters in Halifax — specifically for the purposes of giving out rum and chocolates."

Buying voters didn't necessarily always involve convincing people to vote a particular way. Electors that organizers suspected might be tempted to vote the wrong way, in fact, would often be offered their pint of rum as an inducement not to vote, especially if they agreed to drink it all on the spot.

Sometimes, in larger communities where people were less likely to recognize others by sight, normally upright, law-abiding citizens would be born again as zealously partisan poll captains and would, with barely a moment's ethical pause, hire a few local ne'er-do-wells to act as "ringers," who would get to vote by claiming to be one — or many — of the community's recent dearly departed.

If circumstances demanded, entire, conveniently and appropriately stuffed ballot boxes could even be conjured as if by magic out of the whole cloth of electoral need. In one of the Hants County ridings where Regan did his electoral basic training, for example, a Liberal poll chairman just happened to "find" a ballot box in his shed immediately after the 1953 provincial election. The rest of the ballots had already been counted and the Tory candidate appeared to have won the riding by a single vote. But the newly discovered ballot box — the seal on which had inexplicably been broken — just happened to contain enough Liberal ballots to give that party the seat.[*]

Regan himself told Alden Nowlan about another incident that had happened in Maitland, Hants County, "in the old days [when] every

---

[*]   The result was eventually overturned in court and a new election ordered. In the by-election, the Liberal candidate won by one vote after the returning officer broke the tie by voting Liberal.

vote went Tory. Then one election the poll clerk found two Liberal ballots in the box. 'Throw them away,' said the deputy returning officer, 'the s.o.b. must have voted twice.'" Perhaps understandably, Geoff Stevens in *Stanfield* called Hants County "one of the weirdest political units in the country."

But Hants County politics was, in fact, very much politics as usual in much of rural Nova Scotia in the fifties. In fact, it was probably not all that different from trench politics anywhere; the difference in Nova Scotia was that it all happened in full public view and the participants weren't ashamed of the games they played.

Government MLAs and their local henchmen wielded enormous power, controlling the hiring of as many as 1,500 short-term workers in the course of a year. They decided who got to work on the roads, plowing and salting in winter, fixing potholes and paving roads in the spring and summer. And they even had a hand in the hiring of every local provincial government employee from game wardens to file clerks.

There was nothing subtle about it. "I done all in my little power for you, Mr. MacIsaac," one job seeker wrote to his MLA in the late 1800s. "I can prove that I got two more votes for you. . . . I am out of work with a family to support and if you see your way clear to help me, I will never forget you." In the late twenties, a Tory worker with "seven Tory votes in my family" put his case for a job to Premier Edgar Rhodes starkly, ending his letter with an unveiled threat: "It is pretty hard on a young fellow to be supporting a government that can't do anything for him."

Handing out a job to someone whose only real qualification was party loyalty could certainly lead to inefficiencies. Worse, the system was open to abuse that could — and sometimes did — lead to tragic consequences.

Consider the scandal in the late 1990s concerning Nova Scotia's youth detention centres. According to documents filed as part of civil lawsuits against the provincial government in connection with sexual and physical abuse at the centres during the fifties, sixties, seventies, and eighties, many of the alleged abusers were unqualified political appointees who were handed patronage positions as a reward for services to the party. In many cases, their political masters continued to protect them even after they'd been caught abusing children.

In 1961, for example, Jack Sands, the superintendent of the Shelburne facility, wrote a letter to his superior asking that someone do something about Burton Smith, one of his own counsellors. "A common practice of his is while lining up the boys, to go down the line hitting each one on the head with a piece of broomstick or radiator brush," Sands wrote. "To continue him in a counselling position is to jeopardize much of the positive attitude which we have developed among the staff and between the staff and the boys." Sands wanted Smith fired, or at least transferred. But the local Tory MLA, James Harding, came to the man's defence in a letter to W. S. Kennedy Jones, the Tory minister in charge of the school. "Mr. Smith is a longtime Conservative with a very large family of brothers and sisters," Harding wrote, "and I feel that anything possible should be done for him to ensure not only his employment at the school but promotions when they come along."

That same year, the superintendent at the Nova Scotia Training School for Girls in Truro, E. J. Dick, tried to deny an employment extension to David Collins, a sixty-five-year-old maintenance man who had unbuttoned the blouse of a seventeen-year-old inmate and "put his hands inside said blouse." Collins's local MLA was the powerful Tory highways minister G. I. Smith, a confidante of Premier Stanfield. Smith also wrote a letter on his constituent's behalf to the province's Minister of Welfare, explaining that the man's wife had recently died, that he was facing financial difficulties and should be granted a one-year extension.

But perhaps the most disturbing allegation of political interference in the operation of the youth centres involves an incident during the Regan administration. In 1975, a counsellor named Patrick MacDougall, who'd already been investigated for sexually abusing two boys at the Shelburne school in the sixties — authorities then said there wasn't enough evidence to substantiate those allegations — admitted to school officials he had sexually abused another boy. Instead of firing him and reporting the matter to the police, the province's Minister of Social Services, Harold Huskilson, who was also the MLA for Shelburne, allegedly arranged for MacDougall, a Liberal party supporter, to be quietly transferred to the Sydney Children's Training Centre, a facility for profoundly retarded youngsters. As night watchman there, MacDougall — who was later convicted of numerous sexual assaults on boys in Shelburne and sentenced to prison — would have had keys to the rooms where the children slept.

Although Huskilson denied playing any role in MacDougall's transfer, Fred MacKinnon, Huskilson's deputy minister at the time, insisted in a 1997 discovery hearing that the MacDougall case was "discussed with the minister in detail. He would have known about every aspect of it happening. . . . If the decision had been left up to me at the time, I would have gone for firing him."

All of this created a kind of master-slave relationship between those who wielded power — the politicians — and those — ordinary party supporters, bureaucrats — who were subject to the whims of their political masters. How big a psychic leap would it have been for a powerful politician — or someone who aspired to be one — to see sexual favours as a similar right of power?

DESPITE LOSING HIS OWN first try at elective politics in 1956, Gerald Regan's active involvement in the Liberal party did produce some professional dividends. At one party meeting in the early fifties, he met an equally ambitious young trade unionist named Tom Shiers. Many people, including Shiers, will tell you that Tom Shiers "made" Gerald Regan. While that may be an exaggeration, it is certainly true Shiers offered Regan entrée to the provincial labour movement and provided him with his first real province-wide public platform as a hero of the working classes.

Shiers was a Windsor boy too, but from the town's labouring class. His father and his grandfather before him had been quarrymen, working in Windsor's gypsum mines. After World War II, Shiers returned to join his father in the quarry.

Thanks to geology and geography, Windsor has been one of North America's prime producers of gypsum since Nova Scotia belonged to the French. Because gypsum could be found on or near the surface of the land, it was easy to mine. And because the mines were close to a suitable harbour, the raw gypsum could easily be transported by sea to market. After World War II, North America was embarking on a massive building boom, so gypsum — a key ingredient in plaster and cement as well as the increasingly popular drywall — was in great demand and Windsor's gypsum industry prospered.

Windsor's largest gypsum producer, the Wentworth mine, was

owned by the Canadian Gypsum Company, which was itself a wholly owned subsidiary of the United States Gypsum Company (USG), the largest gypsum company in the world.

USG was also, according to Shiers, "one of the most anti-union companies in the world," presided over by a caricature capitalist named Sewell Avery.

Even W. H. Jost, USG's Nova Scotia lawyer, was under no illusions about the man for whom he worked and his views of organized labour: "Any self-respecting labour leader would have regarded Mr. Avery as a troglodyte (no doubt expressed in saltier language)," Jost wrote in a mid-eighties memoir. "I fancy he would have regarded any labour leader as scum of the earth."

At the time, of the company's more than sixty units around the world Windsor was one of only eight with a union. It had originally been organized in 1912 by a large international union. But the international, "in cahoots with the company," according to Shiers, pushed the local membership to drop out and form their own independent — for which read company — union in 1928.

After Shiers returned from the war, he became president of the small union and led a successful campaign to bring it back into the organized labour fold. The purpose, he says, was to "give us some clout against the mighty U.S. Gypsum."

That didn't go over well with the company's owners who maintained a firm "never-give-the-union-an-inch" policy. So the company fought the union's decision to affiliate with the Canadian Labour Congress, forcing a vote among the employees, which the union won, but only narrowly. Emboldened by the reality that a significant number of workers had voted against affiliating with the CLC, the company stepped up a harassment campaign against the union in hopes it could eventually get rid of it altogether.

The union fought back by filing grievances and forcing the company to respond to them at arbitration hearings. To argue the union's position, Shiers needed a lawyer. Luckily, he happened to have met a bright young Windsor lawyer named Regan at a Liberal party meeting. Regan, it turned out, wasn't all that busy. In fact, he was happy for the work.

Although others have said that Regan had little interest in practising law, Shiers remembers him as an "excellent lawyer, extremely competent. You'd sit with him in court and you'd think of something and scribble him a note. He'd take one look and he was off like a dog with a bone in its teeth."

The gypsum workers' union became his primary client for most of the fifties. The company, in its efforts to get rid of the union, employed every legal weapon in its arsenal. During the spring and summer of 1957, as negotiations for a new contract stalled and sputtered, the company refused to budge on what the union considered the two key issues: union security and a wage increase of "a few pennies" an hour. Finally on October 31, 1957, the company's 125 quarrymen downed tools.

At first, the strike was a civilized affair — the union and company even made a deal to allow the company's annual Christmas party for the workers' children to take place in a hall paid for by the company but under the auspices of the union — but that changed after Christmas when the workers realized the company wasn't prepared to make any concessions and, indeed, appeared bent on destroying the union.

USG, in fact, had been able to replace almost one-third of its Windsor output by stepping up production at a quarry it purchased in Cape Breton. The Windsor workers fought back by refusing to allow supply trucks and supervisory personnel to cross their picket lines. The company countered with injunctions.

That finally brought Jost into the courtroom to face Regan for the first time. Jost, who'd been curious about the young Windsor lawyer he'd heard so much about, was impressed. "At every step of our struggle," Jost wrote later, "I found him to be a hard-fighting and honourable adversary whose word, when given, could be depended upon without any reservation."

On the picket line, however, there was no mutual respect and even less civility. After the company publicly invited the strikers to abandon their union and return to work, there were scuffles at the plant gate, fires in some of the mine outbuildings, and — most ominously — the theft of explosives from a company storage area.

While the trench battles raged, Shiers and Regan criss-crossed the province meeting with other trade unionists to try to drum up moral and financial support for the gypsum workers. Although local labour groups were generally supportive, Shiers says the Canadian Labour Congress, with which the Windsor union was directly affiliated, soon lost interest. "They just wouldn't give us enough support to keep going."

Finally, on November 20, 1958 — fourteen months after it began — the strike ended. The workers, who had lost more than 1.4 million dollars in pay during the dispute, received a small wage increase. But the company refused to move in its insistence it would not countenance a closed union shop, and it also refused to rehire thirty workers it claimed had been responsible for acts of violence and vandalism during the strike.

Despite the bitterness the strike engendered on both sides, W. H. Jost's initial good feelings about Regan only increased as the strike dragged on. "When it was all over, I entertained a conceit that, at certain junctures, had our principals seen fit to leave us to our own devices, Gerry Regan and I could have hammered out something which would have saved everybody a lot of trouble and possibly some grief," he said.

Good as that might have been for the gypsum workers, it would not have served Regan's larger political aspirations nearly as well as the status the strike conferred on him as a defender of the underdog in a very public confrontation between an all-powerful multinational company and a diehard band of powerless Nova Scotia workers.

At first, however, Regan must have doubted the strike could help his long-term political ambitions at all. The dispute, which had divided families and threatened businesses, couldn't help but leave a bitter aftertaste in a small town like Windsor. Although many local merchants had tried to be understanding — one insurance agent even paid the premiums for his striking clients during the strike, and an appliance and furniture store continued to repair customers' appliances "although sometimes there wasn't much chance of payment for a long time" — the strike hurt everyone in the community in some way or another. *The Financial Post* reported later that it took at least a year for Windsor "to get back on its business feet."

In truth, the strike probably didn't win many votes for Gerald Regan when he allowed his name to stand for election in Hants West again in 1960. This time, against the same opponent, he managed to exactly double the margin of his defeat to 210 votes.

"Will you run again?" Carole asked him after the ballots had been counted on election night.

"What, and try for 420?" Regan asked wryly.

For a while after that, he settled into what had become a success-ful labour law practice. Because Shiers considered Regan not only a good lawyer but a good fellow, he began recommending him to other labour leaders he knew who needed legal help. By the late fifties, Regan was one of only about three lawyers in the province regularly representing unions. "He was very good," says Shiers. Others, like Leo MacKay, secretary of the Pictou Labour Council at the time and later the secretary of the Nova Scotia Federation of Labour, took a more jaundiced view. "Everybody used Regan not because he was so great but because there weren't very many labour lawyers around Nova Scotia at that time," he says simply.

But Regan's personal charm won over others, including J. K. Bell, the secretary-treasurer of the Halifax-based Maritime Marine Workers' Union, who put Regan on a small annual retainer. "Because we had him on a retainer, the guys in the [ship]yard just assumed he was there for them," Bell recalled in his memoirs. Regan represented individual workers charged with everything from driving too fast to making moonshine. He especially enjoyed outsmarting the police in the court-room. "I remember one time one of the fellows in the yard got arrested for having mash in his house," Bell recalled. "A mountie arrested him on a Friday but it was a long weekend and he made the fatal mistake of not getting the mash tested in the lab until Tuesday morning." In court, Regan told the judge his client wasn't contesting the fact he owned the alcohol-making ingredients, simply whether the ingredients had come together to create illegal alcohol while his client had it in his possession. "It became illegal in the custody of the mounted police," Regan claimed. The judge gave the man the benefit of the doubt and dismissed the case. He, like most of Regan's other worker clients, didn't bother paying his bill. "The boys in the yard thought that any time they got in trouble, Regan was already being paid by the union, so they never paid him," Bell said. "Regan and I often laughed about it afterwards. We just gave him a few hundred dollars' retainer a year."

Regan often represented labour interests on provincially appointed conciliation boards. He turned out to be very good at resolving conflict and was sometimes even asked to chair the boards. In 1961, for example, he chaired a conciliation board that had been asked to settle a seemingly intractable dispute between a financially troubled Stellarton textile firm and its unionized workers. The union wanted higher pay, the company said it couldn't afford a penny more. "Both sides were adamant," the Halifax *Chronicle-Herald* reported, "but the youthful labour lawyer was able to bring both sides to an agreement." It did not provide any direct increases in wages but set up an incentive plan that tied additional wages to increased productivity.

Regan's work for the unions turned out to be lucrative. He was earning $25,000 a year by the early 1960s, far more than many of his fellow lawyers in Halifax at the time. He could very easily have settled comfortably into the role of a successful small town lawyer, but his heart never seemed to be in the law. As good as he could be in a courtroom, Regan always saw the law as a means to an end rather than an end in itself, which may explain why his legal practice seemed to be in a kind of perpetual limbo.

Regan had purchased an established Windsor practice. Along with an office above the *Hants Journal* on King Street, he inherited the practice's secretary, who'd worked for a succession of young lawyers over the years but none quite so frustrating as Gerry Regan. "She'd go into fits of apoplexy each day wondering why her boss was late for his appointments this time," recalls an acquaintance.

Often, it was because he was at the lunch counter in Foster Bateman's Rexall Pharmacy, a popular gathering spot near Regan's law office. "Gerry was a traveller," recalls Bateman. "He never liked to hang around in any one place too long. He'd go into his office about nine or 9:30, spend a few minutes there, and then come over to my shop for coffee and toast. He'd spend some time with the fellows — about a half a dozen regulars who used to come for coffee every morning. Everybody talked politics around here. Then Gerry would be off — to the courthouse, the registry of deeds, that sort of thing. In the afternoons, he'd be back for more coffee, more talk."

Even though Bateman was a Tory and the upstairs room above his pharmacy served as official headquarters for Tory candidates during campaigns, he remembers Regan as a "good fellow to have around. I liked him."

So did Barbara Hoyt, a sixteen-year-old Grade Eleven student at King's Edgehill School who worked part-time at Bateman's. "Gerry was in just about every day," she said at Regan's preliminary inquiry in 1996. "Foster was PC, Gerry was Liberal and they didn't see eye to eye. Sometimes, I'd see them talking together near the back of the store where the pharmacy was."

For some time, at any rate, Regan was just another customer, friendly enough but nothing out of the ordinary. But then, Hoyt testified, she was asked to babysit the Regans' children, in 1959. Her allegations of what happened that night were the basis of a sexual assault charge against Regan in 1995. After the preliminary hearing, this charge was dropped without an explanation from the Crown.

Gerry and Carole had just built a new bungalow for their growing brood on King Street, just across from Maplewood Cemetery and near the entrance to College Road. Barbara's family lived less than half a mile away on O'Brien Street near one of Walter Regan's apartment buildings. Although Barbara and her sister both babysat regularly for extra spending money, she says she only ever minded the Regan children once. Today, she doesn't remember how she got the job.

The two children — Gerry, Jr., three, and Geoff, one, were already in bed by the time she arrived at the house sometime between eight and nine in the evening. The night passed uneventfully. When the Regans returned home sometime after 2 a.m., Gerald Regan insisted on driving Barbara home, she testified. Barbara sat in the front seat on the passenger side, her school books beside her. "We were almost to my house, about three or four houses from mine, when he pulled off to the side and stopped the car," she told the preliminary hearing. "He put the car into park and turned off the lights. There were no streetlights around, no other lights. He moved over from behind the wheel to me. He grabbed me by the shoulders and he muckled on to me. He planted his mouth firmly on mine." His kiss, she said later, was "juicy . . . very open, drooling almost." She could smell liquor on his breath.

Although she was barely five-foot-three and a shade over 100 pounds — "He was much taller, masculine, much more powerful than me" — she managed to push him away. His sudden attack shocked her. "I'd never had anything like that happen to me before," she said. But when she resisted, she allows, Regan didn't pursue her. Instead, he simply moved back to his side of the car, turned on the lights, and drove her the rest of the way home in silence.

Frightened that she'd be blamed for what had happened, she didn't tell anyone except her boyfriend. But she says she did her best to avoid Regan after that. She kept her distance in the pharmacy. "I mainly remember meeting him on the street," she said in court. "I would cross so I wouldn't have to run into him. I remember I met him once at the courthouse."

"Anything wrong?" he asked.

"Nothing," she answered.

IN THESE YEARS, according to their later evidence, two other complainants were trying to come to terms with their experiences. Janice Corkum was having difficulties putting aside her own feelings of humiliation and shame from the night Regan drove her home from skating, she testified in 1998. But then, in the spring of 1961, she met a man and fell in love. After he proposed to her, she felt she had no choice but to tell him what had happened. She took her husband-to-be — a man who had still "never seen me undressed" — to King's College Woods and told him, as obliquely as possible, exactly what she claimed Gerald Regan had done to her. He was supportive, more understanding than she had expected, she told the court. Still, she testified she couldn't stand even being near where the incident had happened.

"I'm not comfortable here," she said that night. "I want to go home."

Four years later, Elizabeth Sinclair also told her husband-to-be about the encounter she claimed she'd had with Gerald Regan in 1956. She did so in order to explain to him why she hadn't been a virgin when they met, she said to the court.

What she didn't tell him at the time was that she'd later met and fallen in love with another young man in Windsor, a hockey player from the wrong side of the tracks named Clare Weir. In 1960, she'd had his baby and given it up for adoption, largely because her mother believed Weir wasn't good enough for her daughter.

She spent the next two years travelling in Europe, trying to put her anger about Gerald Regan and her sadness about the child she'd given up behind her, she said later.

After she returned to Canada determined to make a fresh start in life, she met the man who would become her husband. He would not learn about Clare Weir and their baby until thirty-two years later when Eddie Greenspan, Gerald Regan's defence lawyer, brought them up to try to discredit her allegation that Regan had raped her.

4

Prince Charming and the Babysitters' Club

By the early sixties, Gerald Regan was beginning to look beyond the seemingly barren ground of Windsor as he continued to chase the distant skirts of electoral success. When the sitting Tory member of the legislature from the neighbouring Hants East constituency died in 1962, Regan parachuted in to claim the Liberal nomination. That riled a local Liberal stalwart, Jack Hawkins, who would later become a cabinet minister in Regan's government. Hawkins felt he would have made a better candidate. Still, he says Regan impressed him as "a whirlwind campaigner. . . . He had visited every door, and could remember every important name and face in East Hants." He still lost, though by only seventy-seven votes this time. It was, noted Hawkins, "quite an accomplishment considering the difficulties of an outside candidate."

Regan was even more the outsider in the 1962 federal election where he filled the role of the designated Roman Catholic candidate* in the dual riding of Halifax on the same ticket with Jack Lloyd, a

---

* To telegraph his local connections and his Catholic heritage to voters who might not have noticed them otherwise, Regan's campaign literature described the Windsor-born candidate as the "son of Walter E. Regan, formerly of Dartmouth. Gerald has two brothers and one sister — Sister Rose Edward of the Sisters of Charity." It also described him as "a leading hockey player."

former Halifax mayor. "They called me late one night and offered me the Halifax candidacy," Regan would recall later. "I told them they were crazy and went back to sleep." After a night's sleep, he decided they weren't so crazy after all. Although the hard truth was that he'd only been offered the opportunity to run because party insiders considered the Halifax seat a lost cause and because no one else more important or better connected wanted to be the sacrificial lamb, that losing campaign turned out to be the springboard Regan needed.

As that year's national election results made clear, the federal Tory tide was ebbing almost as quickly as it had risen. Diefenbaker's huge 1958 majority government had been reduced to a woeful — and woefully inept — minority. Less than a year later, the Tories lost a confidence vote in the House of Commons and Diefenbaker was forced to call another election for April 8, 1963. Given the short time between the two elections, Regan retained first call on the Halifax nomination. He ran again but this time — in his fourth try at electoral politics in six years — he won. Regan polled fewer votes than Lloyd, but managed to defeat his nearest Tory rival, incumbent Robert McCleave, by a healthy margin of 2,625 votes.

Gerald A. Regan, thirty-five, member of Parliament. At last.

IT SHOULD HAVE BEEN an opportune time to be an ambitious young Liberal MP in Ottawa. And, for many of them, it was. The party, the city, and the country were all in a period of dramatic transition. As Peter Newman put it in *Distemper of Our Times*, his chronicle of the Lester Pearson era, the country was in a psychic struggle "between a New Canada quixotically seeking a midwife to be born and an old Canada stubbornly refusing to disappear."

Newman, then the Ottawa bureau chief for *The Toronto Star*, saw Regan as a member in good standing of this new Canada; in fact, he singled him out in a 1963 magazine article as one of a group of a dozen freshman politicians who were "the brightest MPs ever to appear simultaneously in a Canadian parliament."

Regan's backbench seatmate was an ambitious but awkward young lawyer from Shawinigan, Quebec, named Jean Chrétien. Chrétien liked to practise his halting English on Regan and some of the other "ambitious young mavericks," as Chrétien described them. After hours, they would gather in the Newfoundland MP Richard

Cashin's office to drink and talk. Cashin, says Chrétien, was known as "'Prime Minister' because he supplied the booze." Once, Chrétien recalled in *Straight from the Heart*, he was called upon to act as the judge at a party organized to settle "a big argument" between Cashin and Regan over whether Newfoundland or Nova Scotia produced the better lobsters. "There was a lot of white wine that night so no one cared who won," Chrétien wrote diplomatically.

Though Regan was one of the few new MPs who had brought his young family to live with him to Ottawa, he was still considered part of the parliamentary party crowd. "It was a bachelor's town then, and you could go to parties every night if you wanted to," remembers Ron MacDonald who was a political reporter for the Halifax *Chronicle-Herald* at the time. Regan was not considered unusual, and, besides, he worked at least as hard as he partied.

As an MP, Regan became a vocal regionalist who brought with him to Ottawa an historical, non-partisan — and not untypical — Maritime sense of grievance and outrage at Central Canada for having economically subjugated the region after Confederation. He once described his job as having to "keep reminding them [Central Canadians] what is happening to us as a result of their protective tariffs and favoured geographical position." A Maritime member of Parliament, he added almost unnecessarily, "must be very vocal, very parochial."

But Regan was more than just a loud Maritime-Firster. He also became active in the Commonwealth Parliamentary Association,[*] and earned a reputation for pushing for greater trade links between Canada — especially the Maritimes, of course — and the Caribbean. He gained international headlines for one speech in England in which he proposed that Canada should annex part of the Caribbean, including the Virgin Islands.

For a backbencher, Regan managed to attract more than his share of headlines and favourable press. "He ingratiated himself with reporters," MacDonald notes, "reading up on all the old [press] guys on the Hill. He treated them like heroes, which was a good way to get their attention."

Douglas Fisher, an NDP MP turned newspaper columnist, was

---

[*] From 1973 to 1976, Regan served as chairman of the executive committee of the Commonwealth Parliamentary Association, the first Canadian elected to the post.

among those who found himself attracted to the former labour lawyer, and in print praised Regan's "engaging Irishness and humour that flows out into his speech and committee work. . . . His shrewdness comes out in committee work where he seems to anticipate all the acute questions one should ask."

Regan didn't ignore younger reporters either. Linden MacIntyre, who went on to become an award-winning television journalist with CBC-TV's *the fifth estate*, was a rookie reporter in the Halifax *Chronicle-Herald*'s Ottawa bureau during Regan's term as an MP. "I remember him walking through the [press gallery] hot room one day," MacIntyre says. "He saw me and he came over and said, 'You're the young fellow from the *Herald*, aren't you?' 'Yes.' 'You're awfully young.' 'I am.' 'How young?' 'Twenty-one.' He looked surprised. He said to me: 'My God. If I was twenty-one, I wouldn't be here.'"

Like most of his fellow reporters, MacIntyre says Regan was "charming and fun to be around." In a 1965 newspaper profile of Regan, written shortly before the Halifax MP returned home to seek the leadership of the provincial party, MacIntyre wrote admiringly: "On first meeting him, one gets the 'hell of a nice guy' impression. And, in the Commons, his manner of speaking loudly and clearly, laughingly when the subject is light and bitterly when the subject is serious, has been known to bring thoughtful smiles to the faces of senior politicians on all sides of the House."

But not always. Jack Pickersgill, Pearson's minister of transportation and one of the most powerful members of the party's Atlantic caucus, was miffed at Regan on at least one occasion, when he voted for a Social Credit motion — and against government policy — because he believed the opposition motion was in his region's best interests.

Still, says Richard Cashin, Regan was never "an undue maverick. And he could get away with the odd act of independence because he worked so hard and he was generally well-regarded by everyone."

For all of that, Ottawa turned out not to be the prize Gerald Regan had been seeking. Even though he'd invested in real estate*

---

* Regan bought two eleven-unit apartment buildings in nearby Vanier in 1963 for $148,000. He paid $19,878 cash down and took out mortgages for the rest. This was not Regan's first real estate investment. He had already bought a 140-acre farm near Windsor for an undisclosed all-cash sum.

soon after he arrived in the city, Regan had no intention of actually hanging around the national capital any longer than necessary.

For starters, the issues that were beginning to dominate the political agenda in Ottawa — bilingualism, biculturalism, national unity — were not Gerry Regan's issues. The emerging French fact in federal politics, in fact, was almost certain to marginalize a unilingual anglophone from Nova Scotia who mangled the French language more than Jean Chrétien did English.

Perhaps of more immediate importance to him at the time, however, was the reality that Regan's own opportunities for advancement in Ottawa were limited.

While most of the dozen MPs Peter Newman had singled out in 1963 were moving up the pecking order by 1965 — one was a cabinet minister, six were parliamentary assistants to ministers, and another was the head of the parliamentary defence committee — Regan's upward path was blocked because of where he came from and who was in line ahead of him.

Nova Scotia could justify just one cabinet position and it was already occupied — by Allan MacEachen, the wily former St. Francis Xavier University economics professor who'd spent six years as an MP and had served as a special consultant and confidant to Lester Pearson during the Diefenbaker years before being sworn in as Pearson's minister of labour in April 1963. In the unlikely event MacEachen quit or lost at the next election, he would most likely have been replaced by another St. F. X. academic — the scholarly John Stewart, who'd written books on the wartime operations of Parliament and the moral and political thought of the Scottish philosopher David Hume, and had already served two stints as parliamentary secretary to the ministers of external affairs and secretary of state. To make his chances of promotion even more remote, there were rumours Regan's former mentor, Robert Winters, who had been out of politics since being defeated in 1957, was considering a comeback in the next federal election.

There were personal considerations as well. In March 1965, John David, the Regans' eight-month old son,* died after a fall at the

---

* By then, the Regans had three other children: Gerald, Jr., seven, Geoff, four, and Miriam, three.

family home in Ottawa. Friends say it made Gerry and Carole realize how much they missed the family and friendship support structure back in Nova Scotia.

And there was now a job opening closer to home and to Gerry Regan's heart that made moving back to Nova Scotia an attractive option.

Linden MacIntyre remembers flying to Halifax with Regan that spring. "It was a Saturday morning and we were the only two people on the plane to Halifax, so we ended up sitting together and talking the whole trip. He was very personable, very thoughtful, very open. He talked about his life on the Hill and his frustrations with that. He talked about how one of his children had died very tragically in an accident and how that had affected him* — I think he said that he and wife had really seemed to bond as a result — and then he talked about what he wanted to do with his career."

"It might be too early for you to report this just yet," Regan confided, "but in the next few days I'm going to make an announcement. I'm going to run for the leadership of the provincial party."

Ron MacDonald believes Regan had been preparing for his return to Nova Scotia almost from the moment he arrived in Ottawa. "He used his two years in Ottawa to build up his support back home. He spoke out about all sorts of Nova Scotia issues, not just ones that affected his constituency. And it didn't matter how small the meeting or how important the group, Regan would go and speak to it. He had a lot of IOUs he was able to call in in 1965."

By then, the Liberal Party of Nova Scotia desperately needed a new leader. In less than a decade, Angus L. Macdonald's once invincible political machine had collapsed in a heap. In the 1953 election, Macdonald's last as leader, the Liberals had dominated the province, winning twenty-two of the legislature's thirty-seven seats. Just ten years later, in the election of October 1963, the party was reduced to a mere rump of itself with four members in what had become a forty-three-seat House.

---

* Regan rarely talked about John David's death, even with close friends like Phillip Woolaver. "He wasn't the kind of person to share that sort of thing," Woolaver says, "and he had a hard time talking about things like that with other people. We lost a child too, and I remember a friend telling me that Gerry wanted to call me but he didn't know what to do. It was the same when my brother drowned. A friend said, 'Gerry doesn't know what to do about your brother.'"

When Earl Urquhart, a nondescript Cape Breton lawyer and veteran MLA, replaced Macdonald's successor, Henry Hicks, as party leader in 1962, the Tories couldn't believe their good fortune. Watching the televised Liberal leadership convention that selected Urquhart, "the smile on Bob Stanfield's face was from ear to ear," as the Tory strategist Flora MacDonald later described it. Party organizers were so anxious to take advantage of the Liberals' vulnerability under Urquhart, they persuaded Stanfield to call the next election two years early. The Tories nearly wiped the Liberals off the electoral map and defeated Urquhart in his own riding.*

To make the future even more ominous for the Liberals, the Tories' share of the popular vote in 1963 topped 56 percent, three points higher than Angus L. himself had ever achieved. And Conservative party strategists were quick to point out that if the Conservatives had gained a total of just 559 more votes in the four ridings they didn't win, the result would have been a clean sweep of all the seats.

The result of all of this was that Robert Stanfield developed not only a God-like personal aura — Nova Scotians "consider him the most wonderful man to come along in 2,000 years," Jim Atchison, the province's luckless NDP leader, lamented only partly facetiously — but also a critically important and self-fulfilling image of political invincibility.

There was certainly room for debate about the reasons for Stanfield's incredible personal and political popularity. Geoffrey Stevens, in *Stanfield*, suggests that his popularity — and his legacy — was largely the result of the fact that Stanfield had managed to convince Nova Scotians, after generations of having had their confidence worn away, "that they do not have to remain backward, retarded and depressed. He convinced them they had a future worth working for."

For his part, Dalton Camp, Stanfield's electoral *éminence grise*, argued that the dour son of the famous underwear makers had an uncannily acute perception of "what Nova Scotians really wanted from government," and an even more uncanny ability to articulate it in his own halting but sincere way.

---

* The Tories had done the same to Henry Hicks in 1960, defeating him in his own riding, which he lost by fourteen votes.

Allan MacEachen, Stanfield's federal Liberal counterweight, claimed — not without some justification — that the real explanation for Stanfield's success was simpler but perhaps even more difficult for the Liberals to overcome. The Dennis-owned Halifax *Chronicle-Herald* and *Mail-Star*, the two largest and most influential newspapers in the province, "gave [Stanfield] twenty years of unswerving devotion," MacEachen told Stevens. "They treated him as though he were a member of the Royal Family, though his talents are no greater than any of ours."

Whatever the merits of these conflicting claims, there was no disputing that Stanfield's ever-increasing electoral success — twenty-four seats in 1956, twenty-seven in 1960, thirty-nine in 1963 — was having a dramatic impact *inside* the provincial Liberal party. For nearly thirty years, a Halifax-based elite of lawyers and businessmen had run the organization as their own personal fiefdom, doling out patronage to the favoured few and handpicking their own choices from among the supplicants who aspired to higher party and elective office.

Within this rarefied circle, Gerald Regan, a former sportscaster and small-town lawyer, was still regarded as a gauche, over-eager outsider; certainly not someone *they* would have chosen as their party leader.

But by the mid-sixties the party's failures had marginalized this elite to the point where their blessing didn't carry nearly so much weight. In 1962, for example, Earl Urquhart narrowly defeated the establishment's candidate, the well-connected Halifax lawyer and MLA Gordon Cowan, for the party leadership. During the 1963 annual convention, a Cape Breton–centred "ginger group" of young lawyers had given the party establishment fits by challenging their officially approved slate of candidates for executive office. "We should not put up with the same list of the executive year after year," argued Allan Sullivan, a passionate, thirty-one-year-old Sydney lawyer who'd been an unsuccessful Liberal candidate in Cape Breton West that year and would eventually become one of the most powerful members of Gerald Regan's cabinet. Though the rebels were disorganized and lost that preliminary skirmish, they were back again the next year, and this time they managed to defeat the nominating committee's choice for party president. The times were certainly a-changing.

During that November 1964 convention, Earl Urquhart reluctantly announced he was stepping down as party leader. Though he had been personally close to Angus L. Macdonald — some described him as a kind of surrogate son — Urquhart was such a weak orator he was incapable of re-igniting the Liberal flame. "By Jeez, if you wanted to empty a hall, he'd be your man," joked the Digby Liberal Phillip Woolaver.* Though the party elite had the smarts to realize the reluctant Urquhart had to go and the clout to convince him to quit and await the certain reward of a Senate appointment,† they had no obvious candidate waiting in the wings to replace him in 1964. And they would have even less influence on the choice of the party's rank and file.

So this time, rather than running their own candidate as they had in 1962, the party establishment began scouting the prospective leadership candidates for someone its members could support — and who could, in turn, be persuaded to continue to let them run the party.

Gerald Regan, whose 1963 federal victory had blindsided the party establishment, was one of those candidates. And they clearly needed to get to know him better.

That may have been the backdrop for a surprising incident during the official opening of the Angus L. Macdonald library in Antigonish on July 17, 1965, just a week before provincial Liberals were slated to gather in Halifax to choose a new leader.

At the reception following the opening ceremony — at which Prime Minister Lester Pearson was awarded an honorary degree — Irvine Barrow, a former party president and longtime key backroom operative, awkwardly approached George Hawkins. Hawkins was the son of a Liberal senator and veteran political insider. While Barrow may have regarded the younger Hawkins as a member-in-

---

* Woolaver was among those who helped convince Regan — if he needed convincing — to return home to Nova Scotia to seek the party leadership. "I was in Ottawa during the Rivard scandal," Woolaver remembers, "and Pearson seemed to be bumbling and stumbling along while Dief was at his peak. I told Gerry what I thought was happening back in Nova Scotia and how I thought the whole thing was coming unstuck. I went through the list back to Murray and Harrington of opposition leaders who'd become premiers and I said if he came back he probably would too."

† During the Stanfield era, the quickest route to a Senate seat seemed to be through the provincial party leader's office. Harold Connolly, who replaced Macdonald, was appointed in 1955, Hicks in 1972, and Urquhart in 1966.

training of the party establishment, he also knew him as a bit of a rebel who just happened to have plenty of friends among the party's young Turks.

"George," Barrow began nervously, "I'd like you to do me a little favour. I'd like you to introduce me to Regan." Hawkins still marvels that, on the eve of the leadership convention, a power-broker like Barrow didn't know the party's Halifax MP and the leading candidate for the provincial party leadership well enough to introduce himself. "It was another sign of how out of touch the party's old guard had become," he says.

Hawkins helped make Gerry Regan's day that day not only by introducing him to Barrow* but also by confiding to him the details of a secret trust fund Hawkins's father had helped set up and which was now controlled by Barrow, a chartered accountant, and Frank Covert, a well-connected Halifax corporate lawyer and party insider.

The off-the-party-books fund, Hawkins explained to Regan, had been established years before by his father, Charles Hawkins, then the party's president, and E. L. Macdonald, the party's longtime treasurer. Macdonald distrusted Angus L. Macdonald (no relation), so he set out to create a little nest egg outside the premier's — or the party's — control. "When a candidate would come looking for money to run a campaign, Macdonald would say, 'I'll give you a size seven if you'll sign a note for a nine,'" Hawkins explains. "In those days, they talked about money as if it was a shoe size. They'd say, 'I need a size seven,' when they meant $7,000." When the candidate paid off the full amount of the note, Macdonald would put the difference into various bank accounts and safety deposit boxes. By the time Macdonald died, the value of the little nest egg totalled around $250,000.

As George Hawkins quietly explained to Regan that day, interest from the Hawco fund might be available to help support the next leader. The capital, which was mostly invested in blue chip stocks, produced an income of at least $14,000 a year, Hawkins told Regan.

"You don't know what that means to me," a surprised — and

---

* During Barrow's 1983 trial for influence-peddling in connection with party activities, Regan would testify that Barrow had been influential in convincing him to leave federal politics and run for the provincial leadership in 1965.

grateful — Regan told Hawkins. "I had no idea what I was going to do for money without a job, without a seat."*

The fund had already been used to supplement Henry Hicks's salary as Opposition leader, and there are rumours it was the threat of its withdrawal that finally helped convince Urquhart of the wisdom of resigning when he did.

For his own part, Hawkins says he still wasn't sure Regan had the right stuff to be leader. "Finlay MacDonald [the Conservative party president and owner of CJCH radio, who had lost to Regan in the 1963 federal election in Halifax] and I had driven down to Antigonish together that day [for the library opening]. We talked about Regan on the drive down. I remembered Gerry from his time as a student at Saint Mary's when he was just this loud sportscaster with a weak command of grammar. We talked about how people were laughing at him and at the idea he wanted to be the leader of the party. And I remember MacDonald, who knew him from the radio station, saying to me: 'Anyone who laughs at Gerry will underestimate him, and they will underestimate him at their great peril.'"

It turned out to be good advice that MacDonald's own party didn't heed. Ultimately at *their* great peril.

HEADING INTO THE JULY 1965 leadership convention — the party's third in just eleven years — Regan's chief opponents were a forty-three-year-old lawyer, Robert Matheson, a prominent Halifax politician with roots in industrial Cape Breton; and Colin Chisholm, a forty-six-year-old Antigonish businessman and former agriculture minister in Angus L. Macdonald's last government.†

Many attractive potential candidates, such as Allan MacEachen and the Nova Scotia Liberal house leader Peter Nicholson, had opted to pass on the race. MacEachen had an important cabinet post in Ottawa; he wasn't about to abandon that for the uncertainty of leading a Liberal opposition from the Speaker's Gallery in Halifax. Nicholson, one of the province's most respected and loved politicians, was said to be worried about what the pressures of the job

---

* According to later published estimates, Regan received between $6,000 and $13,200 a year from the fund during his fifteen years as party leader.
† Arthur Yates, a fringe candidate whose chief claim to fame seemed to be that he had served in the British and Canadian military for twenty-seven years, was also on the ballot.

might do to his family. His own health was precarious, and his wife had problems with alcohol.

As the only sitting Liberal politician in the race, Regan had the inside track for the job. He could also draw on his own rural roots, his years roving the province as a sportscaster, labour lawyer, would-be politician, and MP to woo delegates to his cause.

And woo them he did. Regan was certainly a better campaigner than any of his opponents. "In a hotel lobby or similar venue," Jack Hawkins wrote, "he was in his element. Never bashful, he was a master of the quick introduction, the total recall of names, past meetings, friends, and the health of relatives — all those things that make up the fabric of political small talk and that create the impression of interest and warmth. Even then, he was never a man for long conversations. . . . You must meet as many people as possible. Make a favorable impression and then get out fast."

Despite Regan's acknowledged campaigning abilities, his supporters weren't about to leave anything to chance in the days before the convention, including the possibility that religion might once again play a role in the outcome. Chisholm was a Catholic and might be expected to take some of the Catholic vote away from Regan. To prevent Matheson, an elder in the United Church, from having a free ride with Protestant voters, Regan's operatives spent the night before the convention trying to manufacture a floor nomination for Walter Purdy, the mayor of Amherst. They didn't believe he had any real chance of winning but they hoped Purdy, a Protestant, would draw votes away from Matheson.

That ruse turned out to be unnecessary — just hours before the balloting was scheduled to begin, Chisholm, suffering from exhaustion, abruptly abandoned his leadership bid on his doctor's advice — and Purdy himself ended up nominating Regan, whom he described as "a young man with great energy and a deep sense of public service."

Regan's speech to the faithful in the Halifax Forum on that hot, humid July day was surprisingly uninspired. "I expected a barn burner of a speech," Jack Hawkins would recall later. "The speech was flat and seemed to lie in the air without response, except polite applause."

Still, there was no doubt Regan would win. The only question was by how much. In the end, it was a convincing victory. Regan easily won on the first ballot, picking up nearly twice as many votes as Matheson.*

The party's establishment, sensing a winner, had followed the delegates and fallen into line, albeit uneasily, behind him. The only question for everyone now was whether Regan could actually defeat Stanfield or whether he would soon become just another footnote in party history, losing his own seat and then being dispatched to his Senate reward in order to make way for the next hapless leader.

NO ONE WOULD EVER ACCUSE Gerald Regan of not doing everything in his power — and then some — to bring down the Tories. He knew it wouldn't be easy. He had no seat in the legislature and, with the exception of Peter Nicholson, his loyal house leader, the rest of the party's tiny caucus of sitting MLAs tended to be more interested in tending to their own political pastures — and protecting their personal political futures — than in launching a full-frontal assault on the apparently unassailable Stanfield.

That quixotic mission was left almost entirely to Regan, who filled up almost every waking hour over the next five years relentlessly criss-crossing the province in his battered old station wagon,† sometimes addressing as many as four different meetings in a single night before returning to Halifax in the wee hours of the morning; and then showing up a few hours later, shaved and fresh-faced, at the legislative chamber to seek out any available reporter to pronounce himself shocked and appalled at whatever it was that the government had said or done in the house the day before. During those crusading years, says Jack Hawkins, "there was no legion hall, no schoolhouse meeting, no fire hall too small for Gerry Regan."

Though the strategy had its merits — Regan certainly did become better known to the general public and his constant attacks and scandal mongering earned him television exposure — the total focus on Regan and Regan's total focus on attacking the government also opened him up to mockery from the Tories, who eagerly resurrected his childhood nickname of Gabby.

The first major test for the party's new leader came less than two

---

* The final tally: Regan, 379; Matheson, 201; Yates, 8.
† Doug Harkness, a television reporter who covered provincial politics for CJCH-TV during the sixties, estimates Regan put 200,000 miles on his car in those years.

years later when Robert Stanfield announced plans for a provincial election to be held May 30, 1967.

"Everyone knew Stanfield was going to win but we were convinced we could make some big gains in '67," remembers Michael Kirby, now a Liberal senator but then a brilliant young Dalhousie University mathematician and political neophyte who was dragooned into serving as the chair of the party's hastily assembled 1967 election policy committee.

Freed from mundane concerns about what they would do if they actually won the election, the Liberals came up with what Kirby himself calls "an old-style, promise-something-to-everyone," scattershot platform that included pledges to reduce taxes, take over 100 percent of the cost of education, construct a new superhighway through the Annapolis Valley, increase old age pensions, provide property tax breaks for municipalities, and offer long-term loans to encourage new housing.

None of it made the slightest bit of difference. The Tories barely bothered with a platform of their own, simply pointing to their own record as more than ample reason for the voters to re-elect them. The premier himself airily dismissed the Liberal platform as something the Liberals themselves didn't believe in, "so why should I?"

The Tories, of course, traded unashamedly on the Stanfield myth, running Stanfield men on the Stanfield ticket for the Stanfield government. And Tories missed few opportunities to contrast that mythical figure with the garrulous, motor-mouthed former sportscaster in the cheap suit who wanted to take his place.

The tactic worked, even among many Liberals. Walton Cook, who was running for the party in Lunenburg, says he "wouldn't allow Regan to come down and campaign here. I felt his presence would be detrimental to my campaign. People here called him 'Gabby.' It seemed at that time as if he was just the leader by default and he'd soon be gone." In the end, Cook failed to win the seat, even without Regan's presence.

In fact, when the ballots had been counted, the Tories took a total of forty seats in the expanded House of Assembly, the Liberals just six. Although Regan narrowly won his own riding of Halifax Needham by 102 votes — the first time a Liberal leader had won his own seat since 1956 — and even though Regan managed to increase the party's share of the popular vote by a respectable 2 percent, the overall outcome was a major disappointment for the Liberals.

And for Gerald Regan.

DURING THIS PERIOD, Gerald Regan was trying to establish a public reputation as a legitimate political contender. But allegations that eventually contributed to a reputation of a different kind can also be traced back to these same years.

At least half a dozen teenaged girls in the west-end Halifax neighbourhood where Regan lived — all of them members of the same St. Theresa's Roman Catholic Church the Regan family attended — have testified that they shared a secret so secret none of them knew the others shared it too. They were members-in-good-standing of a kind of babysitters' club that didn't exist, a club of girls who would all later claim they had been attacked by Gerald Regan after babysitting his children.

Why didn't they say anything at the time?

Gerald Regan, they would explain many years later, was a pillar of St. Theresa's Roman Catholic Church, leader of the Liberal Party of Nova Scotia, devoted husband of Carole and father of Gerald, Geoff, Miriam, and baby Nancy.

One of them told the court it was not something people "discussed back then." Another said it was "a very different time. I was brought up to show respect for people in [a public] position."

Patricia MacDonald told the court her mother warned her not to tell anyone.

In March 1995, Gerald Regan was charged with sexually assaulting her. On April 2, 1998, Justice Michael MacDonald stayed the charge. The Crown is appealing.

According to Patricia's testimony, her mother and Carole Regan had become friends through the church, so Patricia wasn't especially surprised when Carole called one day in the spring of 1967 to ask if she might be available to babysit her children. She was. An eighteen-year-old Grade Eleven student, Patricia was well-known in the neighbourhood as a dependable, cheerful, helpful babysitter. "People called me Mary Poppins," she remembered years later. "I would always clean up. Most babysitters didn't do that. But I'd wash the dishes if they were there. I just did." Patricia was delighted to babysit the Regans; she knew from her girlfriends that they paid well and their kids were usually well-behaved.

The third time she babysat for them, Gerry and Carole needed her because they were going out for dinner. When she arrived, Mrs. Regan was still in the bedroom getting dressed, Gerald Regan was in the living room having a drink. He and Patricia exchanged small talk, but she can't remember the conversation — only that he made her nervous.

After the Regans left, Patricia cleaned up the house, checked on the children, and settled in to watch television for the evening. When the Regans returned a few hours later, Carole Regan came into the house alone.

"Mr. Regan will drive you home," Patricia would later claim Carole told her. "He's waiting in the car for you."

Patricia testified that she got into the front seat of the station wagon beside Regan, who then backed the car out of the driveway and began to drive slowly west along Berlin Street toward Oxford. Suddenly, she told the court during the 1996 preliminary hearing, Regan reached across with his right hand and grabbed Patricia's breast. He lunged at her and began to kiss her — even though the car was still in motion! She felt the car veer wildly to the right and bang hard into a curb. They had, she could see, just missed hitting a lamp post. Regan saw it too. "That seemed to bring him back to reality," Patricia said in court. Although she could smell liquor on his breath, she didn't think he was drunk. "He seemed to realize what he was doing."

He drove her the rest of the way to her house without incident, but Patricia described it as "the longest drive I ever put up with." When she finally got in her house, she ran immediately to the bathroom and used a facecloth to "wipe my lips until they were almost raw . . . because I wanted him off me."

Her parents were at a party at a friend's home when Patricia got home. She testified that she telephoned her mother and pleaded with her to come home right away. Something awful had happened, she said. When she told her mother what Regan had done, her mother warned her not to say anything to anyone, especially not to her father. "He would have gone over and punched him in the face," Patricia told the preliminary hearing. But that wasn't the only reason her mother counselled her to keep quiet. Her father worked for the federal government and Patricia's mother worried he might lose his job if anyone found out his daughter was saying such nasty things about such a powerful man.

Carole Regan called Patricia the next day to ask her to babysit her children again. A photographer was coming by to take pictures of the family, and she needed someone to look after the younger ones. Could Patricia come over? Patricia couldn't tell Carole Regan what happened the night before, she said in court, but she couldn't babysit either. "My mother went over instead," she says now. "I never went over there again."

But she did give a friend's name to Carole Regan as a possible babysitter — without ever telling the friend what she said Gerald Regan had done to her. The friend soon passed on Susie Woods's name without making it clear to her why she'd stopped babysitting at the Regans' too.

In March 1995, Regan was charged with sexually assaulting Susie Woods. In April 1998, Justice Michael MacDonald stayed the charge. The Crown is appealing.

Though Susie encountered no problems during her first baby-sitting assignment at the Regans', she said in court that she wasn't so lucky a week or two later when Carole Regan called on a Saturday afternoon to ask her to look after the children. Mrs. Regan had an appointment at the hairdresser's and Mr. Regan had been called in to meet some people at his office. By the time Susie got to the Regans' house, Mrs. Regan had already left. Gerald Regan, however, was still there, and he helpfully pointed out the television set in the Regans' master bedroom off the kitchen and suggested she might want to watch a little TV.

She did. She lay down on the bed and began to watch a show. She assumed Regan had gone to his office. But a few minutes later, he appeared again in the bedroom. She didn't see him come in. But when she looked up, she testified at his 1996 preliminary hearing, he was there. Then suddenly, "he sort of pounced on me, jumped on me."

Susie, who had six brothers — "when you grow up with six brothers, you're pretty squirmy and squiggly" — managed to squeeze out from under him and escape.

Through it all, she says, Regan never said a word.

And neither did Susie. Not then. And not when she returned home. Not to her sister. Not to her parents. Not to anyone. Not for a long time. "I was a little ashamed," she told Regan's preliminary inquiry. "I don't know, maybe there was some fear they wouldn't believe me."

IN THE SUMMER OF 1967, Robert Stanfield finally had a credibility problem of his own. After having insisted to Nova Scotia voters during the spring election campaign that he would as likely seek the leadership of the federal Conservative party as take up ski-jumping, Stanfield called a press conference for July 19 to announce that, "after much earnest discussion during the past fortnight with my colleagues in the Nova Scotia government and with provincial and federal members of the Progressive Conservative Party of Canada, I have come to a decision to declare myself as a candidate for the leadership of the Progressive Conservative Party of Canada."

Nova Scotians should have been angry with Stanfield and the Tories for deceiving them — it was difficult to believe he hadn't at least been considering the switch since November 1966 when the federal Tories had decided to hold a leadership vote — but they didn't seem to be. In fact, over the next eighteen months, the Tories, under Stanfield's successor, the finance minister G. I. "Ike" Smith, won three by-elections in a row, including one from the Liberals, after Gordon Hart resigned his Dartmouth North seat to become a Nova Scotia Supreme Court justice.

In 1968, the *Canadian Annual Review* summed up another *annus horribilis* for Gerald Regan this way: "Despite the attempt of Gerald Regan . . . to create a number of contentious issues out of the stuff of government, the public remained largely indifferent. Perhaps this was because of Mr. Regan's personality, his over-eager brashness in presenting issues, or because the issues themselves do not appear to be overwhelming. Nevertheless, in spite of Mr. Regan's energy, there was some underground dissatisfaction in the ranks with his leadership, and the suggestion once more was growing that the provincial Liberal party was facing another leadership crisis."

Though Regan was indeed facing still muted calls from within the party for him to step aside before the next election, the truth was the Conservatives were the ones in trouble. It just wasn't obvious yet. In fact, the eleven-year-old Stanfield-Smith government had become, as the legislature's chief clerk, Roy Lawrence, would describe it graphically to the Canadian Press reporter John Soosaar one day in the late sixties, "like a frayed rope. It will get extremely frayed and then one day, suddenly, it will snap."

The frays were certainly beginning to show.

For starters, Ike Smith was no Stanfield. Everyone agreed he was a hard-working, decent man, but he was more suited to his original role as Stanfield's able lieutenant and partisan hatchet man than he was to political leadership and vision.

Stanfield had been gone less than three months when Smith faced his first full-blown crisis. On October 13, 1967, Hawker Siddeley Canada, the Canadian arm of the British-based Dominion Steel and Coal Company, announced it was walking away from its aging, money-losing Sydney steel plant and putting thousands of Cape Breton workers out of their jobs. While Smith moved quickly to have the government buy and operate the plant, a decision that defused an explosive situation, the consequences were disastrous. The government was saddled with a voracious albatross it could neither fix nor get rid of.

But most of the problems Smith faced in the late sixties had their roots in Stanfield's own lofty industrial development ambitions. Stanfield had been determined to drag Nova Scotians, kicking and screaming if need be, into the twentieth century. While some of his ideas, such as convincing the Swedish Volvo automobile manufacturer to set up shop in Nova Scotia to build cars in order to market to North America, had borne fruit, others had not.

Like Regan after him, Stanfield sometimes proved a sucker for dream-sellers, especially high technology dream-sellers. Take Peter Munk. Munk, who later went on to earn fame and fortune as the head of American Barrick Resources, earned his MBA in how *not* to run a business during his years in Nova Scotia, compliments of the province's taxpayers.

In the early sixties, Munk and his partner David Gilmour had created Clairtone Sound Corporation, a successful Ontario-based business producing spiffy-looking hi-fi equipment that could easily double as designer furniture. They scored a coup in their first foray into the American market when Frank Sinatra bought half a dozen units to give away as Christmas presents. Plenty of others bought them too.

Industrial Estates Limited, the Nova Scotia government's industry promoting agency with a blue-chip board of directors that Stanfield had set up to help him lure industry to the province, convinced Munk and Gilmour to move their operations to Nova Scotia with a deal that, as Geoffrey Stevens put it mildly, was "too good to refuse." IEL agreed to buy $8 million dollars worth of company bonds, for which the company didn't have to pay a cent in interest for three years and from which the company agreed to spend about half on a new plant in Stellarton (which just happened to be where IEL president Frank Sobey was born and from which he operated his supermarket empire). In addition, IEL negotiated so many extra sweeteners and inducements for Clairtone from both the municipality and the federal government that the company essentially got a new Nova Scotia plant and working capital for nothing.

The bottom fell out of the glamorous company. It moved into producing expensive colour televisions, a business it knew nothing about, for the U.S. market just as consumers there began to resist high-priced TVs and the Japanese began to compete fiercely with American manufacturers for a bigger share of the market.

That's when the realization began to dawn that Munk and Gilmour, while first-rate promoters, didn't have a clue about how to manage a major manufacturing plant. The company's losses, modest in 1966, grew geometrically until the province, on the hook for nearly 20 million dollars, had to step in and take over the collapsing company.

By 1970 when it effectively went out of business, the company's shares, which had once traded briskly at $15.25 on the Toronto Stock Exchange, could command just forty-one cents each. The work force of 1,000, which was supposed to grow in time to 2,000,[*] totalled just forty by the time the operation was padlocked.

The government's romance with atomic power was even more costly. Though it knew it was moving into risky, uncharted waters, the Stanfield government decided to take a gamble on developing a heavy water plant it hoped would signal to the world that Nova

---

[*] Peter Munk had predicted his operation might become so big it would spawn an entire city to supply it with workers it would need. He had even come up with a name for the new entity: Clairtone City.

Scotia was in the front ranks when it came to high technology, and, not coincidentally, would provide jobs: 2,000 during the construction phase, 200 more highly skilled, highly paid permanent jobs when construction was complete and continuing work supplying coal to the new plant for 500 other out-of-work Cape Breton miners.

It didn't turn out that way. By the spring of 1967 when Robert Stanfield came to Glace Bay to officially "open" the plant during the election campaign, the original cost estimate of $30 million had ballooned to $83 million. And it wasn't really ready to open, officially or otherwise. The truth was the plant was already four years behind schedule and even the first phase of construction wasn't expected to be complete for another eighteen months. When it did finally open — briefly — the next year, engineers quickly discovered the salt water they'd intended to use in the plant's pipes caused corrosion and leaks of deadly hydrogen sulphide gas.

The cost to taxpayers: $180 million by 1969. "It was a decision that came naturally at its inception," former Tory cabinet minister E. D. Haliburton noted in his memoir, *My Years with Stanfield*. "The denouement later seemed incredible, unbelievable, incomprehensible as well as completely unexplainable."

To compound what began to seem like government incompetence, tales of corruption at other government ventures began to appear with increasing frequency in the newspapers, a sure sign of a tired government on its last, desperate legs.

Two people, including an official of the Nova Scotia Housing Commission, went to jail for their roles in flipping land for private profit in a land assembly scheme that was ostensibly intended to put together a bank of affordable land for housing in a Halifax suburb. And the provincial auditor general took the Smith government to task for allowing a slick American manager to mix up his private financial dealings with the accounts of a provincially funded strawberry farm he was supposed to be running in Digby. That boondoggle cost taxpayers another $500,000.

Gerald Regan, of course, did his best to keep reminding Nova Scotians of each of these scandals.

ALYSON MORRIS SAYS she can still remember the excited "buzz" among her fellow staff members in the summer of 1968 when they heard that Gerald Regan and his young family would be vacationing at the Mountain Gap Inn, a small private resort overlooking the Annapolis Basin.

In May 1995, Gerald Regan was charged with sexual assault of Alyson Morris. In April 1998, Justice Michael MacDonald stayed the charge. The Crown is appealing.

Alyson, a bright fifteen-year-old who was about to begin her senior year in high school, had a summer job at the Mountain Gap as a dishwasher. Her dad, who was the inn's chief groundskeeper and handyman, drove her to work each morning in time for the beginning of her 7:30 a.m. shift. After she finished work at three, she'd read a book or just enjoy the sunshine while she waited for her father to finish work at five.

According to her testimony at the 1996 preliminary inquiry, she was putting in time one bright sunny afternoon waiting for her father when she encountered Regan near the tennis courts. They struck up a conversation and he asked if she'd be interested in babysitting his children.

Though she'd never looked after the children of any hotel guests before — and, truth to tell, had very little experience at all as a babysitter — she said she might be interested.

"Why don't you come over and meet the kids?" Regan suggested. She followed him to the family's room, which was across from the resort's staff house. Inside, the room was dark. The children were napping. She stood at the foot of the beds, looking at them.

"They're lovely children," Alyson said, uncomfortably trying to make conversation.

Regan didn't answer. According to her testimony at the preliminary hearing, he grabbed her from behind, turned her around, and began to kiss her, his tongue, as she would describe it later, "searching for my tonsils."

But as suddenly as he began, he stopped. "He released me and continued on as if nothing had happened," she recalls. "I was very surprised. I didn't know what to do." When they left the room together a few moments later, they encountered Mrs. Regan. Regan introduced Alyson to her and explained to his wife that the girl was considering doing some babysitting for them.

She wasn't. Not anymore. When her father got off work at five,

Alyson says she told Regan, "I need to go home."

She did. She never babysat for the Regans that summer. And she didn't speak to anyone for another twenty-five years about what she said had happened between her and Gerald Regan that afternoon.

ALTHOUGH THE SMITH government seemed to be doing its best to self-destruct, two unrelated events of Gerald Regan's own making in the spring and summer of 1969 finally helped transform him from just another caretaker Liberal party leader into a legitimate contender for the hearts and minds of Nova Scotia voters.

The first was a nearly fifteen-hour legislative filibuster Regan staged in early April 1969 to protest measures that would have increased the provincial health services sales tax from 5 to 7 percent and make it apply to a broader range of goods, including automobiles, telephone service, and electricity. Regan said he was attempting only to convince the government to "remove the most odious aspects of its tax proposal," but his talkathon — the first filibuster in the Nova Scotia legislature in forty years — also helped position him in the public mind as a populist defender of the consumer against a government grown aloof and uncaring.

Although the tax measures were really designed to cover the increasing costs of medicare, Regan in his speech gave each new tax a name that would remind voters of a Tory scandal instead. The tax on gasoline, for example, became the Clairtone Tax, the motor vehicle tax the Heavy Water Tax, and the liquor tax — perhaps aptly — the Tory Patronage Tax.

More substantively, Regan argued the tax increase on electricity would play havoc with the budgets of low-income families and the extra costs for building materials and home furnishings would "add to the burden of the poor and the young just starting out and wanting a home of their own." To drive home his point — and to find something to say to allow him to keep talking — Regan used up a full hour at one point in his speech detailing piece-by-piece every table, chair, bed, dresser, and other item of furniture a newly married couple would need to set up housekeeping. After spelling out the cost of each individual piece of furniture, he would then add with a flourish the amount of tax that would have to be paid on it.

"I cannot see that any government who claims any concern for the working people of this province would have the audacity to come in here with a tax of this kind and for its members not even to question it," he thundered.

Not only did the acquiescent Tory MLAs not question the effects of the tax measures, they also maintained a stony silence, reading newspapers, dozing, and otherwise amusing themselves throughout Regan's marathon filibuster, which began shortly after two in the afternoon of April 2 and only ended at five the next morning. The only government interjection came in the middle of the eleventh hour of the filibuster when Peter Nicholson finally goaded G. I. Smith into a response. Nicholson chastised government members for failing to give Regan the respect he deserved. The premier looked up from his newspaper long enough to laconically declare that Regan's speech was "getting as much attention as it deserves," and then returned to his reading.

While the government's decision to allow Regan to talk himself out may have been good legislative tactics, it was lousy pre-election politics.

By the time an exhausted Regan finally slumped back into his seat near dawn and the government pushed its tax bills through final reading, the Liberal leader had become a kind of folk hero. A picture of Regan, in pyjamas and nightgown, apparently asleep on the couch in his living room, dominated the front page of the afternoon newspaper. And exultant party officials were quick to gloat that Regan's filibuster had saved consumers $116,000 in tax that couldn't be imposed while he talked. "Automobile dealers did a land office business," reported a new paper called *The 4th Estate*. "Cigarettes sold by the carton instead of the package. The bootleggers stocked up."

The Liberal leader seemed finally to have found his stride. In his memoirs, Jack Hawkins called the filibuster Regan's "finest hour."

GERALD REGAN WASN'T the only one to have cause to remember his famous filibuster. So too would Francetta Palermo, a slight, pretty, dark-haired seventeen-year-old who began work as a clerk in the Opposition leader's office the day after Regan's political triumph. Twenty-six years later, Regan was charged with the attempted rape of Francetta Palmero. In December 1998, the jury acquitted him, after cross-examination by Eddie Greenspan.

In truth, she testified at the trial, she had "no clue" at the time why everyone was so excited about the filibuster. She didn't follow politics. The only reason she'd gotten the job at all was that her father, Frank, a keen Liberal volunteer, had badgered party officials to hire his eldest daughter.

He may have felt he owed it to her.

The Christmas before, Francetta had dropped out of her secretarial course at Prince Andrew High School in Dartmouth after Frank, a sometime construction worker with a drinking problem, announced he had a line on a job in Montreal and would be moving the entire family — including Francetta, her mother, and younger brother and sister — there immediately. But the job didn't pan out and the family stayed in Dartmouth.

It wouldn't have been the first time the family followed Frank's jobs — or his whims — from community to community, even country to country. Born in Germany, Francetta had called Timmins, Sudbury, Montreal, and even Sicily home before Frank, on a barroom tip, relocated the family to Dartmouth in the spring of 1967.

Although she wasn't yet sixteen then, Francetta, who preferred her new Dartmouth friends to call her Fran or Frannie because it sounded less "foreign," had already been out of school for two years. She and her younger sister didn't bother to go to school at all while the family was in Sicily. When the family returned to Canada, Francetta was too embarrassed to go into Grade Nine with kids two years younger than herself. So she carefully changed the "8" on her school record to show a "9." It didn't matter much at the time — she was smart enough that she passed her Grade Ten subjects anyway — but the deception came back to haunt her in a courtroom nearly thirty years later, when Gerald Regan's lawyer used her failure to tell the truth about her school records as evidence she was a liar and a perjurer. But at the time it just seemed like an easy way to avoid the social stigma of being the oldest girl in her class.

Francetta didn't like school very much anyway and was just as happy to abandon it entirely in anticipation of the family's move back to Montreal. When that move failed to materialize, and Francetta needed work, she says her father traded on his political connections to get her the job in the Opposition leader's office.

Her job involved mainly typing and filing, although she was also responsible for combing the newspapers each day in search of the name of anyone celebrating a milestone birthday or wedding anniversary so Regan could send them his personal greetings.

When other people were in the office, Regan was "professional" in his dealings with her. But when she was alone, she testified, he would come up behind her and put his hands on her shoulders as he asked her how she was doing. The hands, she told the jury at Regan's 1998 trial on charges of attempted rape, soon moved from her shoulder to her breast. After a few weeks, he would sometimes cup her breast with his hand while he talked. "I tried to shrug it off," she said, "but it made me feel uncomfortable."

She told the court that one day, after everyone else had left for lunch, Regan buzzed her on the intercom from his private office. He asked her to come into his office and bring her steno pad. Damn, she thought, she was hoping he would leave her alone today. Then again, perhaps he did really intend to have her take dictation.

As she approached his office, Regan opened the door and ushered her inside. She walked past him, planning to sit in the chair beside his desk so she could write down whatever he planned to dictate, but then realized suddenly that he was still standing by the door. She turned around. "I looked at his face," she testified during the preliminary hearing. "He had this ridiculous looking grin on his face, and he was looking down. I looked down and I could see his erect penis. He had it exposed." She had never seen a man's penis before, she said.

Before she could react, Regan strode quickly over to where she was standing, grabbed her, and pushed her down on a powder blue shag rug. He used his weight to pin her beneath him. "I was struggling, he was on top of me," she told the court. "His legs were between my legs. He was using his left hand to support himself. And with his right hand, he reached down to take off my panties. He got my panties below my hip and then he put his penis up against my panties."

Suddenly, he stopped moving. "Shit," he said. He had ejaculated.

And then, as suddenly as it began, it was over. She testified that Regan got up off her, rearranged his clothing, and used a tissue to wipe the semen from the carpet.

Palermo was stunned, she said. She'd been wearing a "squaw-style" mini-dress with a leather fringe on the bottom. Half the fringes had been ripped off in the struggle on the floor. She looked up at Regan, unaccountably at that moment as angry at the destruction of her dress as at the assault on her person.

"Look what you did to my dress."

He threw her a twenty-dollar bill. "Buy yourself a new dress," she claims he told her.

She testified that she doesn't remember what happened after that. "The rest of the day is a complete blank." But her neighbours in the Dartmouth duplex where the Palermos lived, David Rent and his wife, would testify at Regan's 1998 trial that Francetta's mother came down to see them that evening. She was very upset and, though her command of English was weak, she made them understand something had happened to her daughter. She wanted them to come upstairs and talk with her. They found Francetta in her bedroom, crying. She told them what she said Regan had done to her. Although she didn't go into detail, she made it clear she didn't want Rent, a Halifax police officer, to do anything officially about Regan's alleged attack. Rent was just as happy. Gerald Regan was already a very powerful man.

Although she wouldn't recall it either, Francetta also allegedly told her younger sister what Regan had done. Maria had seen her sister's torn dress — a dress she liked very much — hanging in the closet and asked her what had happened to it. Francetta told her.

When Francetta returned to the office the next morning, she says Len Giffen, the Liberal party's executive director, called her into his office and fired her. "He didn't give me any reason, he just said I was fired. But I was relieved," she said in court. "I wouldn't have to face [Gerald Regan] again."

UNTIL THE FILIBUSTER finally began to shake them out of their arrogant lethargy, Tory strategists believed they would not have to face Regan very much longer either. If another by-election defeat didn't do him in sooner, the next provincial election would certainly take care of him for good. Like Connolly, Hicks, and Urquhart before him, Regan seemed destined to be an inconsequential footnote to an unbroken string of Conservative administrations.

Many Liberals felt the same way. A few may even have quietly hoped that if the Liberals were to lose a by-election Premier Smith called for Halifax Eastern Shore on July 8, 1969 — as seemed entirely likely — Regan could be persuaded, or pushed, to quit the leadership so someone else could establish himself as a credible alternative to the Tories in time to prepare for the next general election.

The by-election was necessary because the sitting member, a Liberal named Dr. Duncan Macmillan, had died. By rights, the Halifax Eastern Shore seat should have been an easy Liberal victory. The Liberals had held the constituency for thirty-five of the previous thirty-eight years. In 1967, even running against the Stanfield tide, Macmillan had won by nearly 500 votes over his nearest rival. Still, given that the Liberals had also won traditionally Liberal Dartmouth North by roughly the same margin in 1967 only to lose it in a by-election, Regan couldn't afford to take any chances this time. If he failed to hold the seat, the party would slip back to just four MLAs in the legislature, the same number it had when he became leader in 1965.

The party's candidate this time was Garnet Brown, an affable, backslapping thirty-nine-year-old president of his own food brokerage business. Brown had managed Regan's successful 1965 leadership campaign, after which Regan handpicked him to be his eyes and ears on the party as president of the provincial Liberal association. Brown was not only a frequent drinking and partying companion of Regan's but also a fierce Regan loyalist who poured plenty of his own — as well as the party's — resources into trying to win the critical Eastern Shore seat.

On the eve of the vote, Brown and Regan emptied the party's coffers of its few remaining dollars to buy television time. No wonder. As the Halifax *Mail-Star* reported on election day, "the Liberal party's future could hang on the outcome."

So, of course, could Regan's. Although the newspaper described the summer campaign as "one of the dullest contests in many years," it turned out to have been effective for Gerald Regan. With strong support from the growing urban areas of the riding near Dartmouth where the Liberals were gaining strength, Brown doubled the party's 1967 margin of victory to nearly a thousand votes and gave Regan the club he needed to keep the party wolves at bay while the Tories crumbled under the considerable weight of their own ineptitude.

WITH THE TORIES IN TURMOIL, it had become even more important for Regan to keep up his relentless pace of appearances around the province. To ease the burden on Carole, who was now at home with five young children under the age of twelve — Gerry, Jr., eleven, Geoff, eight, Miriam, seven, Nancy, three, and the new baby, David — the Regans placed a classified ad in the Halifax *Chronicle-Herald* in the late spring of 1969 seeking a live-in nanny/housekeeper.

The person they hired that summer was little more than a girl herself. Fourteen-year-old Catharine Schnare, a Grade Nine student from Cook's Brook on Halifax's Eastern Shore, took up her duties in the Regan household — vacuuming, washing dishes, making beds, and occasionally helping out with the children — in mid-June 1969. She can pinpoint when she started, she later testified, because she celebrated her fifteenth birthday on June 19, 1969, just a few days after she moved in, and the family "had a cake for me."

In March 1995, Gerald Regan was charged with indecent assault of Catharine Schnare. In April 1998, Justice Michael MacDonald stayed the charge. The Crown is appealing.

Cathy, as she was known to the family, remembered meeting Gerald Regan — "he was nice enough to me then" — shortly after she began work but didn't recall seeing him often during her first few weeks on the job, a period when he would have still been busy electioneering for the Eastern Shore by-election.

But one morning shortly after the Liberal victory, Regan — who'd spent the previous night attending a celebratory boxing match with Garnie Brown — was not only at home but also busily directing family social activities. Normally, Cathy would have taken the four older Regan children to the Waegwoltic, a boating and social club favoured by Halifax's upper middle class families, for their morning swimming lessons in order to give Carole a break. But on that day, Cathy told the court, Regan insisted Carole herself accompany the children to the Waeg. He and Cathy could look after David, a six-week-old baby who was asleep in his bassinet in the Regan bedroom.

"[Carole] really didn't want to go," Cathy said, "but he insisted. He wasn't usually there, he said, so now she had the opportunity [to spend time with the older children] and she should take it. I was in the kitchen. They were in the dining room. I could tell from the tone and her reply that she didn't want to go. I knew it wasn't a pleasant conversation."

Shortly after his wife had left with the children, Regan came into the kitchen where Cathy was just finishing washing the breakfast dishes. He'd had a piece of cake with his breakfast and now he wanted another.

"Do you know where Carole keeps it?" he asked.

Cathy did. She'd put the cake away in a cupboard near the sink a few minutes earlier. She went to get it for him. He followed her, joking that he'd better watch his waistline. She testified at the 1996 preliminary inquiry that he said, "You wouldn't have to worry about that, a tiny little thing like you," and reached out his hand as if to pat her tummy as she placed the cake on the kitchen counter. Surprised, she stepped back. But he was faster. She had backed herself up into a corner. Suddenly, "he was kissing me. It was forceful, invasive and wet," she told the court, "as if he was invading the inside of my mouth. His tongue was everywhere it could possibly be within my mouth." With one hand, she said at the preliminary hearing, he grabbed her left breast. Finally he stopped kissing her and picked up a piece of the cake. "Such a sweet little thing," she claimed he told her. "Give me another kiss." As his hands reached up, she ducked out from under his arms and ran into the Regans' bedroom next to the kitchen. She grabbed the baby from the bassinet and held it in her arms as a shield against any further advances. She saw him watching from the kitchen. "He was standing there smirking at me," she said.

A short while later, Regan left the house and Cathy, in tears, telephoned her mother to come and get her. She was still packing her suitcase when Mrs. Regan returned with the children to prepare for a previously scheduled meeting with the parish priest to discuss Baby David's christening.

"What's wrong?" she asked.

"I'm going home," Cathy said.

"But why?"

"Nothing," she replied. "I just have to go." She says she never told Mrs. Regan why she was leaving.

About an hour later, her brother and a friend arrived in a car to take her home. She couldn't bring herself, she testified, to describe to them the details of what happened, saying only that Regan "got smart with me in the kitchen." Because they had to detour to Bedford to pick up Cathy's sister, the normal hour-long drive from Halifax to Cook's Brook took considerably longer that day and, when they pulled into the driveway, Cathy was astonished to see Gerald Regan there already. He was calmly talking with her father, a superintendent for a local construction company. She brushed past them and went into the house. "I had nothing to say to him," she said in court. "I was still very upset."

Later, she asked her mother what Regan had said to her father. Her mother reported that Regan said Cathy must have misunderstood his intentions. She was a "shy, little country girl" who had recoiled at a little peck on the cheek, he'd explained.

"It was damn more than a little kiss on the cheek," she retorted and stormed off to her room. But she didn't say how much more. "I was embarrassed," she explained to the court. So eventually, after a telephone call to her parents from Mrs. Regan, Cathy reluctantly agreed to return to work and even accompanied the Regans on a vacation to Prince Edward Island later that summer. Gerald Regan accompanied them too, but he kept his distance from Cathy. After a week on the Island, Cathy left to return to Nova Scotia to write a supplementary exam in a school subject she'd failed in June. It was the last time she would see Gerald Regan, except on television, for twenty-seven years. When they finally met again, it was in a courtroom.

GISELLE SUTHERLAND was another babysitter who lived in the Regans' neighbourhood. In March 1995, Gerald Regan was charged with sexually assaulting her. Justice Michael MacDonald stayed this charge in April 1998. The Crown is appealing.

Giselle wasn't surprised when Carole Regan called her mother one Wednesday afternoon in November 1969 to ask if Giselle would be available to babysit the Regan children that evening. Though only fourteen, she was already an experienced babysitter. She was bright and organized and responsible, which made her a popular choice for families in the neighbourhood. Giselle had even babysat for the Regans one evening a few months before when their usual sitter wasn't available. They weren't among her regular customers but the

Regans and the Sutherlands did know each other — both families were members of St. Theresa's Roman Catholic Church — and Mr. Regan was a prominent man in the province. So Louise Sutherland had no qualms about allowing her daughter to babysit for the family. Her only concern was that it was a school night and she wanted her daughter home by ten. Carole Regan agreed.

Just before 7:30, Gerry Regan arrived by car to pick her up. "He was early," Giselle testified. "I wasn't ready and I can remember scrambling to get my school books to take with me. Mr. Regan made a big deal of opening the passenger door for me and he almost picked my legs up off the ground putting me into the car," she said.

After driving her the few blocks between houses, Regan followed her into the house, "took my coat, and hung it in the vestibule. His wife wasn't ready. She was in the master bedroom, which was just down the hall from the kitchen. That surprised me. I'd never been in a house then with the master bedroom on the main floor."

Giselle went into the kitchen where she noticed a baby's bottle being warmed on the stove and young David sitting quietly in his high chair. She scooped him up in her arms and began to talk softly to him.

"All of a sudden, I had this funny sensation that the baby was moving," she testified during Regan's 1996 preliminary hearing. "But it wasn't. Mr. Regan was beside me. His hand was between me and the baby. He had his right hand on my left breast, palm on my breast, the back of his hand next to the baby. I was completely startled. I felt myself getting flushed, sick to my stomach, and I turned to him and said, 'What are you doing?'"

"I'll just put the baby down," Regan answered smoothly, and he moved his hand from her breast, took the baby from her, and went into the bedroom where his wife was getting dressed. A few minutes later, the Regans left the house together. The older Regan children were upstairs in their bedrooms, Mrs. Regan had said. Gerry, Jr., was studying. And the baby was now sleeping in the Regans' first-floor bedroom.

Giselle told the court she was "pretty stressed, very unsettled" by what had just happened. She sat on the sofa, turned on the television, got up, turned it off, paced back and forth in the living room, turned the TV back on, turned it off. What really had just happened to her?

And why? She thought about the baby. She should check on the baby. She was just going back toward the kitchen on her way to the master bedroom when, according to her testimony, Gerald Regan suddenly appeared again back in the kitchen.

"I put in my appearance," Regan told her, "and now I'm home for the evening. So why don't you get ready and I'll drive you home."

Mrs. Regan, Giselle noted, was not with him. "I felt a little sense of panic." She also worried about the baby.

"We can't just leave the baby alone," she told him. "I'll call my father. He'll come and get me."

"No, no, don't worry," he said. "I'll drive you home. There's no need to disturb your family." He handed her a ten-dollar bill that had been folded in half and then in quarters. Her normal babysitting rate at the time was twenty-five to thirty-five cents an hour. And she'd been at the Regans' tonight for no more than an hour. "I couldn't accept that," she protested. "It's too much."

But he wouldn't take it back. And he insisted on driving her home.

Frightened, she got in the car but stayed as close to the door on the passenger side as she could manage. Regan began to drive but, she realized with a start, he was going in the opposite direction to her house. "We're going for a little drive," she claimed that Regan answered when she tried to protest. On a dark side street, he pulled over to the wrong side of the street, shut off the lights, and turned off the engine. "Then he reached over and pulled me over to his side of the car very quickly," Giselle testified. "There was no conversation. He tried to kiss me. I moved my head and I could feel his lips on my cheek." She could smell alcohol on his breath. Trapped between the steering wheel and Regan, "a man who had a hundred pounds on me," Giselle told the court she was "terrified. I didn't want to be kissed. I tried to break away. I reached for the door handle."

Suddenly, Regan stopped what he was doing and started the car again. Appearing to her "angry, almost belligerent," he drove down the wrong side of the street and through a stop sign on to Windsor Street, a major thoroughfare. "It wasn't until then that he turned his lights back on," she testified. "He was driving very fast, in the wrong lane and very erratic." Pulling up in front of the house, Regan ignored her as she got out of the car. Before she was inside her parents' home, Regan's car was long gone. It was only then that she realized she'd left the folded ten-dollar bill on the car seat.

She brushed past her mother who was surprised to see her home so early. The Regans were tired and came home sooner than they planned, she explained as she hurried through the kitchen — she noticed the clock said 8:20 p.m. — and up the stairs, discarding her school books in her bedroom. She decided to take a hot shower and try to forget what had just happened to her.

When Mrs. Regan called Giselle's mother a few weeks later to ask if she would be available to babysit again, Giselle made excuses. She still couldn't bring herself to tell Mrs. Regan or her mother the real reason she didn't want to babysit, she later explained "but, whenever I talked about him to [my mother], I did refer to him sarcastically as Prince Charming."

GERALD REGAN'S POLITICAL STOCK had finally begun to seem charmed during this period. While he hammered away at Tory scandals large and small, the party's backroom strategists carefully re-cast Regan's public image from the frenetic Gabby to a more statesman-like Mr. Regan. Aides were instructed to stop referring to him by his nickname or even Gerry. He was Mr. Regan or simply the Leader. Conversely, Regan changed the way he referred to his Tory opponent. Smith, who had been universally known by the familiar G. I. or "Ike" during his long political career, suddenly became a nondescript and less avuncular "Premier George Smith."

But Regan's makeover went beyond semantics. "He had one or two shiny, depressing suits; several deadly tired or sick-looking neckties; shirts with paper-thin, dingy collars and run-down, dirty shoes; and he always seemed to need a haircut," Donald Ripley, at the time a Liberal constituency president, would recall in *Bagman*. "Irv Barrow, Bill Simpson, and Garnet Brown decided to spruce him up. They took him to Montreal, fitted him properly in dark, flattering suits that didn't shine or sag, bought him ties that probably cost more than his old suits, and put good shoes on him. On top of that, they arranged for a Halifax barber to style and clip his almost unmanageable hair."

To complete Regan's transition to premier-in-waiting, the party staged a series of testimonial dinners around the province to demonstrate to skeptical voters that the party's rank and file supported their leader.

Much of this was illusion. Regan's plan "to present himself as a credible alternative to Premier G. I. Smith [was] something even members of the Liberal establishment doubted," J. Murray Beck, the pre-eminent Nova Scotia political historian, wrote later in the *Atlantic Advocate*.

The party, in fact, had reached a crisis point by the summer of 1970 after the Liberal brain trust got the results of an in-depth survey it had commissioned to get a handle on how voters felt about the party and its leader. Despite Regan's best efforts, recalls David Mann, the party's 1970 election campaign committee chair, "the poll showed we were down by five or six points [against the Tories]. And, in those days, it was unheard-of to pick up five points over the course of a campaign."

"The results shocked everyone," remembers Michael Belliveau, a fresh-from-university researcher who joined the pre-campaign team that winter. Even though Nova Scotians were clearly fed up with the Smith government and anxious for a change, the survey showed a surprisingly large number of them didn't think the Liberals — and especially Regan — were up to the job of governing. "It was clear to people that if we didn't find a way to change our focus, we were going to lose," Belliveau says. "And we didn't have much time. If we were going to win, it was going to have to be won during the campaign itself."

That wouldn't be easy.

The 4th Estate, a new Halifax-based alternative weekly newspaper, described Regan's own Needham nominating convention as a "dismal" event. "Of the 125 to 150 people present, there were probably no more than four under thirty. Many of those present were women in their fifties and sixties who had worked for the party for decades, no matter who the candidates were. There was no rapport between Regan and the audience."

And Regan was having difficulty exercising control over the rest of the party's rank and file too. When he tried to parachute those he believed would be star candidates into local constituencies, party members often simply ignored his wishes. His choice for Hants East, for example, was a Truro lawyer, later a judge, named Bill Grant. Although Regan urged him to run and then showed up for what was supposed to be his coronation, Jack Hawkins, a right-wing academic from the nearby Nova Scotia Agricultural College who could barely mask his disdain for his leader, won the convention by a more than two-to-one margin. "I paid careful attention to Gerald Regan who was on the platform while I was on the floor awaiting the announcement of the count," Hawkins later wrote. "At the instant it was read I glanced up to record his reaction. For a second, our eyes met and he broke into a broad smile, apparently indicating his pleasure at the decision. As well as possessing oratorical ability," Hawkins concluded, "[Regan] was a consummate actor."

Still, Regan did manage to bring together plenty of bright young Liberal talent to contest the 1970 election. Allan Sullivan, the energetic, passionately liberal young lawyer who had led the party's rebellious young Turks in the mid-sixties, ran again in Cape Breton West; Bill Gillis, a brilliant but self-effacing geology professor who'd lost by just twenty-six votes in his first try at elective office in 1967, offered himself in the university town of Antigonish; Scott MacNutt, the debonair welfare director for Dartmouth, was talked into contesting Dartmouth South against the former mayor and Tory cabinet minister I. W. Akerley; and Ralph Fiske, a successful, self-made businessman, was recruited for Pictou Centre.

As impressive as his candidates were, Regan's backroom campaign team was even more so. "Perhaps the smartest thing Gerald Regan ever did politically was to find a group of talented young people to handle the campaign of 1970," the Liberal advertising man Ned Belliveau wrote in his memoirs. The group — many of whom would stay on to serve as advisers during Regan's first term — included Michael Kirby, the brilliant, twenty-nine-year-old mathematics professor who'd just been named assistant dean of arts and science at Dalhousie University, and a sparkling collection of the city's brightest young legal talent: David Mann, who'd only recently returned to Halifax after earning his master of law degree in England, Gerry Godsoe, an Ontario-born Rhodes scholar who'd graduated from Dalhousie Law School in 1968 and immediately been recruited to the city's largest and most powerful law firm, and Brian Flemming, a

sophisticated and worldly thirty-one-year-old Halifax-born expert on
the law of the sea, who'd studied at the University College of London
and The Hague before returning home to teach and practise law.

By the time G. I. Smith finally announced the election date on a
Saturday in the middle of the Labour Day weekend, when most
Nova Scotians were thinking of other things, the Liberals were well-
prepared. By Monday, two days after the call and three days before
the Conservative campaign team had even met, the Liberal committee had already approved an advertising and promotion strategy, and
laid out everything from Regan's itinerary for the next six weeks to
how and when the party platform would be unveiled.

The new strategy, developed after studying the survey results,
depended on changing the public perception of the Liberals — and
especially Regan — from a bunch of carpers and scandal mongers to
a confident, competent government-in-waiting.

"We discovered that people weren't angry at the Tories over
Clairtone and heavy water," Michael Kirby says. "They thought that
at least they'd tried. They thought governments should be in the
business of industrial development but that they should do it better.
That's why we came up with the phrase, 'Industrial development is a
science not a lottery,' to convince people we could do a better job
than the Tories. That's what the numbers were telling us people
wanted to hear."

Still, the change came as a shock for many, inside and outside the
party. "There is some indication that many grassroots voters are confused and disappointed at the demise of the old, fiery, battling Gerry
Regan," noted *The 4th Estate* midway through the campaign, "and
puzzled by the new smiling 'positive' man on the platform at political meetings."

"It was not the same Gerald Regan who went swashbuckling
about Nova Scotia in the 1967 campaign turning on, or turning off
voters with fire and brimstone condemnations of the Tory government," agreed the political reporter Max Keddy, writing in the
Halifax *Chronicle-Herald*. "Nova Scotians saw a new Mr. Regan, a
quiet, pensive individual creating the impression of a man who could
govern the province."

"The people know all about the scandals already," Regan told
Doug Harkness, a reporter for CJCH-TV. "Now it's time to talk

about all the positive things a Liberal government will do." The full Liberal platform, published just four days before voting day in the October 9, 1970, edition of the Halifax *Chronicle-Herald*, was both ambitious and progressive. Regan promised to create new provincial departments of development and tourism, establish a provincial legal aid service, set up drug treatment centres, and provide funding for everything from child care to municipal sewage treatment. He also pledged to not only eliminate the 7 percent tax on building materials — one of his key complaints during his 1969 filibuster — but also provide help so those on low incomes could afford to buy a home. He reiterated his commitment to eliminate Nova Scotia's archaic poll tax and debtors' prisons. And he promised to create a new post of ombudsman to give recourse to those who felt ill-treated by government officials.

For the 1970 campaign, Regan traded in his battered station wagon for a chauffeur-driven Lincoln. The arrangement not only added a touch of professionalism to the Liberal campaign but it also gave Regan the opportunity for catnaps between speaking engagements. "He was one of the greatest guys for going to sleep just like that," recalls Harkness. "He'd get in the car, bullshit for twenty minutes about baseball or whatever, and then, suddenly, he'd be asleep. By the time he got to the next stop, he'd be all rested and ready to go again."

While Regan relentlessly criss-crossed the province delivering the message, Mann, the campaign chair, and his team — numbers and policy adviser Kirby, image-maker Bill Belliveau, and logistics expert David Thompson, another young Halifax lawyer — "met every single morning at seven a.m. at Liberal party headquarters on Barrington Street" to talk about what had happened the day before and what they wanted to happen today. "It was just like we were going to war," says Mann.

Unlike Smith, Regan and his advisers understood the growing importance of the media generally, and of television in particular. Regan assiduously courted key reporters like Harkness, who joined the government after the election, and Jim Robson, the Halifax *Chronicle-Herald* reporter who travelled with Regan throughout the campaign and became his press secretary after it. The Liberals even hired Ron Roberts, a well-known Halifax radio announcer, to accompany Regan during one frenetic trip he took in a small plane. The flight path hopscotched the province, touching down in almost every constituency. At each stop, Roberts's job was to find a phone and call in "news" reports to the newsrooms of local radio stations across the province. "He'd be reporting from Bridgewater one hour and Yarmouth the next," recalls Doug Harkness. "It made it seem like Regan was everywhere." And, of course, the reporting itself, paid for by the party, was always positive and upbeat.

Harkness himself played a critical role in the Liberals' media strategy for the election. Having broken several of the scandals that had dogged the Tories during their last term, Harkness had a reputation as a tough-minded, independent journalist. So the Liberal advertising guru Bill Belliveau hired him to be the moderator for a televised bear pit session that showcased a young, energetic Regan answering "tough" questions from a handpicked studio audience. Clips from the "bear pit" featured prominently in Liberal TV advertising during the last few weeks of the campaign.

Regan was, as usual, an indefatigable campaigner. While Smith was lamenting to reporters that electioneering was keeping him from his favourite Thanksgiving Day activity — partridge hunting amid the fall foliage in the pastoral woods of his beloved Colchester County — Regan continued his own whirlwind of hand-shaking, baby-kissing, and speech-making.

"Gerry was an incredible campaigner," recalls David Mann admiringly. "He could consume huge amounts of information very quickly, and then re-form it in his own mind and put his own spin on it when he spoke to groups." More impressive still, he seemed to have a knack for connecting with people on an individual basis. "No matter where you went or who you were with — a Valley farmer, or a *Herald* reporter, or some fisherman on a wharf on the Eastern Shore — Gerry had this way of, right away, beginning to talk to them about the issues that concerned them in a way that showed he really understood their issues."

On the final weekend of the campaign, Regan made a highly publicized helicopter tour of central and southwestern Nova Scotia. He spent Thanksgiving Day, the day before the vote, back in his own constituency, knocking on doors from nine in the morning to six at night, stopping only for a quick Thanksgiving dinner — and more campaigning — at a black Baptist church hall in the heart of his riding before returning to his door-knocking until after dark.*

By election eve Regan was confident he would win. "In canvassing today," he told the *Chronicle-Herald* reporter Jim Robson, "I find that almost all the previously undecided votes are swinging in our favour."†

This was a far different Gerald Regan from the man who, only a few months before, had confessed privately to friends that he didn't think he'd be around after this campaign. He had given it his best shot for more than four years, he said despondently, but the electorate seemed unwilling to listen to what he had to say. The best he thought he could hope for — a modest increase in the number of Liberal seats — probably wouldn't be enough to allow him to remain as leader.

Now, on the night before the vote, he fairly bubbled over with confidence. "Our reports from across the province make us confident that we will win a clear-cut majority of seats and launch Nova Scotia on a new era of job expansion and social reform," he predicted to Robson with his usual rhetorical flourish.

Others were still not so sure. David Mann, the campaign chair, was privately hoping to double the party's number of seats in the legislature to ten. "That to me would have been the beginning of the road to a comeback. If we had a reasonable result, we'd be in a position to prevail *next* time." But in the last few days of the campaign, Mann himself was picking up signals — tangible and intangible — that things were moving much faster than he had dared hope. "One night someone called me from Guysborough. He didn't identify himself, but he told me he worked for the Department of Highways and he wanted to know if he could keep his job if the government changed. That's when I realized something important was happening."

---

* While Gerry had spent most of the campaign on the road, his wife, Carole Regan — despite the demands of her still young family — tended to the electoral home fires, knocking on most doors in the riding. "I've never seen the wife of a politician who put more into the electoral success of her husband than Carole," says an admiring David Mann. "She worked like hell, pounding on doors, day and night. Someone would say, 'This poll's weak,' and she'd be there banging on the doors. And not just in Needham. She'd go all over the province, into some of the most difficult areas. People loved her."

† Regan's confidence was partly public bravado. Two days before, he'd had lunch with candidate Scott MacNutt at the Halifax Club, and predicted the Liberals would win just fourteen seats.

Regan's forecast, it turned out, was almost right. The Liberals did not win a clear majority; it was, in fact, a cliff-hanging minority with Regan's Liberals winning twenty-three seats — including nine of ten in the Halifax urban area — the Tories twenty-one and the New Democrats holding the balance of power with two seats.

Still, it was enough. As soon as the results were confirmed, Regan, who'd gathered in a suite at the Citadel Inn with his closest advisers to await the outcome, placed a call to his father. "He was just like a kid," remembers one of his aides. "He was so happy."

5

Time Out:
Gerry and Me 1

Gerry Regan and I have a history. It began sometime between two and three o'clock on the morning of October 13, 1970. Gerry Regan was not there at the time. I was sitting alone in a cramped recording booth in the empty newsroom at CJCH Radio, trying to make sense of a groaning table piled high with unlabelled tape reels and the sprawl of my open stenographer's notepads. The floor around the battered old Remington typewriter where I worked was littered with crumpled balls of yellow paper, false starts on a story I desperately wanted to get right. I had just rolled another sheet of paper into the machine when the telephone rang. It was Bill Ozard, the station manager. He was calling to tell me to go home. The station wouldn't be running my story that morning. Or any other morning for that matter.

"Sorry," he said.

I was twenty-one years old. I was crushed.

The story I had been working on was about Gerald Regan.

And I thought it was a good one.

I'd come to the mainstream media with a naively sixties view of journalism as holy mission, my sense of my personal role in that glorious mission having been puffed up by a stint as the editor of *The Gazette*, Dalhousie University's weekly student newspaper. *The Gazette*, in truth, was a run-of-the-mill, pseudo-leftist college paper, a mishmash of comfortably Canadian, down-with-the-American-war-machine, running-dogs-of-imperialism cant; snidely condescending coverage of most campus events; outraged letters from engineering students who wanted to know why their student union fees should be used to pay for this commie crap; adulatory puff pieces parading as sports reporting; and the occasional, almost incidental, bit of journalism. The best of the last was a special issue published shortly after I became editor. It meticulously drew the dot-to-dot connections among a series of lucrative university construction contracts and companies in which members of the university's board of governors had business interests. While I am, to this day, unreasonably proud to claim credit for the supplement, the reality is that most of the research was prepared by an independent group on campus, and almost all of it was completed before I became editor. Still, the mere experience of being the editor who published it made me realize this was the kind of journalism I badly wanted to do in the real world.

The real world, alas, was less interested than I in my holy mission.

I spent my last year of university dividing my time between *The Gazette* and my first professional job — as a reporter for CFDR, a fledgling Dartmouth radio station whose signal was so weak it couldn't be heard clearly across the harbour in some low-lying neighbourhoods of Halifax, including the one in which I lived. How small was CFDR? Small enough that it could have passed for Ted Baxter's proverbial 5,000-watt radio station, complete with an eccentric cast of characters. Small enough that I could be appointed news director after only nine months on the job. And small enough that being the news director didn't mean much.

The real news director was the station owner, a charming, glad-handing reporter-turned-PR-man-turned-wannabe-broadcast-baron named Arnie Patterson, who had once run unsuccessfully as a federal Liberal candidate, who would later serve as a press secretary to Prime Minister Pierre Trudeau, and who always knew just who to call to get the inside scoop on any good story relating to Liberals in Ottawa or Nova Scotia. Despite his impeccable establishment credentials, Patterson still thought of himself as a swashbuckling young reporter — he'd worked briefly for *The Toronto Star* in its *Front Page* heyday — and he enjoyed surrounding himself with a motley collection of fresh-off-the-campus reporters like me. It didn't

hurt, of course, that he could hire us for a fraction of the salary he'd
have to pay more experienced journalists. CFDR was a small radio
station. And it was Arnie's radio station.

His station was quintessentially down-home Nova Scotian. Its
news values were best epitomized by *Arnie Patterson's News at Five*,
a personalized daily newscast that consisted largely of gossip Arnie
had picked up that afternoon at the Brightwood Golf and Country
Club or over dinner the night before with Liberal party insiders. Still,
his *News at Five* was a staple of our broadcast day. And the highlight
of each year was the New Year's Day broadcast in which Arnie
would announce the winner — and *nine* runners-up — in his annual
Metro's Best Dressed Man contest.

I am now more sympathetic to Arnie's obsession with "people"
journalism (though perhaps I would choose different people than
Arnie), but he and I, needless to say, didn't see eye to eye then. There
was the time, for example, when we disagreed over his orders to the
newsroom to abandon work on a story exposing a local slum land-
lord who was violating new minimum housing standards so we
could all appear at a live broadcast of the official opening of the
second Halifax harbour bridge. We argued. I lost.

Just as I lost frequent battles to make our news reporting less . . .
well, less Liberal. Thanks to Arnie's connections, we could occasionally scoop our competition with news of an impending federal
Liberal government announcement — inevitably positive — or an
equally upbeat item from the provincial opposition Liberal caucus.
But there was rarely room for a discouraging word about a Liberal
of any stripe, and especially not about Gerry Regan, who was then
gearing up for what many were then predicting would be his final,
doomed battle as party leader in the upcoming election. CFDR most
assuredly was not among those predicting such a dire outcome.

I didn't last long enough at Arnie's CFDR to cover that election
campaign for his station. Arnie fired me in the summer of 1970 after
I refused to agree to his plan to dismiss several other reporters who'd
been involved in a union-organizing drive.*

---

* To this day, Arnie insists he didn't fire me. In fact, two days after I'd been let go and local
labour leaders were attempting to make a public issue out of Patterson's union-busting tactics, he told a local newspaper reporter that I hadn't been fired. I'd resigned. He understood
I'd lined up a better job in Toronto, he said. He wished me well.

Just as the 1970 provincial election campaign was getting under way, however, I landed on my feet: a reporter's job at CJCH Radio, the then top-rated station in the metro market. Unlike CFDR, CJCH seemed to take its news seriously, competing fiercely for scoops with CHNS, an equally news-conscious cross-town rival where Mike Duffy was the star reporter.*

When G. I. Smith called the provincial election for October 13, 1970, the CJCH news director, Bruce Graham, decided he wanted to do more than simply offer our listeners the traditional follow-the-leader coverage of legion hall rallies, senior citizen's home visits, and bean supper photo-ops. He wanted to expose vote-buying.

Three years earlier, during Robert Stanfield's last provincial campaign, *The Toronto Star* had turned our quaint local custom of "treating," as it was euphemistically known, into a national embarrassment with an election eve story entitled "Dollars and Booze Still Buy Votes in Nova Scotia." The story quoted Finlay MacDonald, the Tory provincial campaign manager, candidly explaining how voters in some ridings even stayed home from their jobs on election day so they could drink their fill of the free liquor the parties offered in return for their promises to vote the right way. At one constituency meeting, MacDonald told the *Star*, he'd overheard a Tory worker advising some others not to "buy those niggers too soon or they won't stay bought."

As the 1970 campaign began, both Tory and Liberal campaign organizers insisted vote-buying had really, absolutely, truly, finally become a quaint souvenir from the province's suddenly dusty political history; none of their workers, perish the thought, would indulge in such undemocratic practices. Indeed, they pointed out, the new 1969 *Provincial Election Act* officially made it illegal to give or accept gifts to induce a person to vote or not to vote. How could anyone doubt their sincerity?

Bruce Graham, who'd grown up in rural Nova Scotia, didn't find

---

* Duffy, who went on to become a well-known national news reporter for CBC radio and television, was so good at turning even hints of news into complete stories almost instantly he forced CJCH to stop touting its own scoops in advance. The station used to promote its upcoming newscast fifteen minutes before it aired by broadcasting the top headline followed by the invitation for listeners to get the details on "*Contemporary News* at five to the hour." The problem was that Duffy regularly monitored the headlines and not only matched the story before his hourly newscast but also often added new information we didn't know about.

it all that difficult. He assigned me and another young reporter, Andrew Cochran,* to find out if the politicians were telling the truth: Was vote-buying really a thing of the past?

For a number of reasons, we decided to focus our research on Halifax Needham, a constituency in the city's north-end. For starters, most politicians — even those rare ones who acknowledged vote-buying's existence — insisted it was exclusively a rural phenomenon. As an urban radio station, we couldn't afford to deploy reporters to spend weeks in a rural community we didn't know in order to develop a story that might or might not exist. Needham seemed to us a reasonable facsimile. Although it was poor and economically depressed — home to a large indigenous black community and the city's two biggest public housing complexes — it was also a very stable area where people knew each other in the easily familiar way often associated with small towns. That made it seem like a rural community to us. Besides, poor voters, even those in cities, we reasoned, would be among the most vulnerable to bribes. If the politicians were, in fact, targeting poor voters for their election day payoffs, it would put the lie to the popular argument that vote-buying was simply a harmless traditional game in which voters who planned to vote for a particular candidate anyway would hold out until they'd received their treat. Needham was convenient too because it was located in the same neighbourhood as the radio station, and because I'd grown up and had contacts there. Finally, of course, Needham was the home constituency of one Gerald A. Regan, the only provincial party leader running in Halifax and the man who could, if he got lucky, become the next premier.

Our assignment turned out to be far easier than we could have imagined. Despite the official pledges of allegiance to fair play and good sportsmanship, party workers openly went about their old vote-buying ways as if they'd never even heard the pious pronouncements of their leaders.

On the weekend before the election, we followed a pick up truck filled with groceries, perfume, and nylons as it made its Santa-like

---

*   Cochran, now a successful feature film and television producer in Halifax, had his own run-in with Regan several years later. By then a television interviewer, Cochran made the mistake of referring to Regan during a live interview as a "former sportscaster." As soon as the interview ended, Regan rushed up to Cochran, grabbed him by the lapels, and shouted that he was a "fat little pig" before aides could restrain him.

journey through Mulgrave Park, a large public housing project near Halifax harbour, distributing its collection of presents and Liberal party pamphlets to selected residents. We traced the truck's owner-ship to a senior Regan campaign organizer and identified the driver as one of his workers.* To pin down how liquor was going to be dis-tributed on election day, we enlisted the assistance of a young black wheeler-dealer who agreed to pretend to Needham Liberal party campaign organizers that he controlled a block of votes he could deliver on election day if the price was right. On the day before the vote, we listened in, tape recorder rolling, when he telephoned party headquarters and asked to speak to the constituency campaign man-ager. When our man explained his reason for calling, the manager indicated neither surprise nor shock. In fact, he seemed to treat the request as routine.

"No problem," he told the young man while the VU meter on the battered Ampex reel-to-reel tape machine let us know we were recording their conversation for posterity. "No problem at all. Just tell your people to see Buddy —"

"Buddy?"

"Yeah, Buddy. Buddy Daye. Buddy's handling the liquor for us tomorrow. You tell 'em to see Buddy and Buddy'll take care of them."

Buddy Daye! This was a stunning bit of information. Daye was one of Halifax's best-known civil rights leaders, a highly respected former Canadian boxing champ who'd become a community activist and had run for the NDP in Needham in 1967. Though I knew he'd switched allegiance to the Liberals this time out, I was shocked he'd be involved in such blatant vote-buying.† Still, we had the evidence on tape, so we prepared our story.

We planned to run the piece the following morning, the day of the election. Our report would simply detail what we had uncovered: the involvement of key Regan campaign organizers in a scheme to trade votes for everything from groceries to five-dollar bills to booze.

---

*   I learned later from a Liberal party campaign worker that senior campaign officials were so blasé about vote-buying they even stored all the rum, nylons, chocolates, and crisp new five-dollar bills used as treats in a room at campaign headquarters.

†   Shortly after Regan took office, Daye was named the legislature's chief page. He was later appointed Sergeant-at-Arms by the Buchanan government.

But we had to piece the final version of the story together without Bruce Graham. The day before, he'd gone home to his apartment to discover that his wife had left him — and town — with his best friend, making Graham a single parent to two small children.

In his absence, the job of overseeing our story fell to the station manager, a former talk show host named Bill Ozard. The story put Ozard on the horns of a dilemma. It was a delicate time for the radio station, whose new owners — CHUM Ltd. of Toronto — were in the process of buying CJCH Radio's former sister station, CJCH-TV. The deal needed the approval of the Canadian Radio-Television Commission. Given that the CRTC was dominated by Liberal appointees, Ozard was keen to have the support of Nova Scotia's most powerful provincial Liberal politician for the transfer-of-ownership application. Regan, Ozard decided, might be less effusive in his praise of CJCH if it were to broadcast an election-day story linking his workers to illegal campaign activities.

Ozard killed the story.

Regan won the election, CHUM got its television station, and the young black man who'd helped us nail down the story lost his job at a local dance club, which was owned by some prominent Liberals.

I don't know to this day whether any of those developments is connected, or whether Regan ever knew about our story and why it was killed. I did know, however, that I had smacked face first into the incredible yet almost invisible power a politician wields in a small province like Nova Scotia.

And I knew I didn't like it.

6

"The Preem"

In 1970, the year Gerald Regan won the political prize he had been lusting after for so long, the world beyond Nova Scotia was caught in the heave of the dramatic social, political, and economic transformation that had begun a decade earlier with John F. Kennedy's election as president of the United States, with the Soviet cosmonaut Yuri Gagarin's first orbital space flight, and with the Beatles' sudden emergence as the new gods of rock and roll.

The sixties transformed Canada too. In 1963, the year Gerald Regan arrived in Ottawa as a freshman MP, the country was led by fusty old men with bow ties and shaking jowls, who had been born in the last century and now bickered endlessly over the language on cereal boxes and the importance of Canada's connections to the mother country. By the end of the decade, Canada boasted its own flag, the red Maple Leaf; had hosted the world at its own coming-out party, the 1967 World's Fair in Montreal; and finally felt more than ready — thanks to its dashing new prime minister, the cerebral, mysterious, and implausibly, impossibly romantic Pierre Trudeau — to take its rightful place on the world's stage and make good on Laurier's boast that the twentieth century would belong to Canada.

But then along came October 1970, the kidnapping of James Cross, the murder of Pierre Laporte, the imposition of the *War*

Measures Act, and the end of innocence here too.

Gerald Regan's new government was elected smack in the middle of the worst of what became known as the October Crisis: only three days after the FLQ had escalated its confrontation with the established order by grabbing the Quebec Labour Minister Pierre Laporte off the street in front of his Montreal home and just three days before Pierre Trudeau upped the ante by calling out the army.

If Nova Scotians' October provincial election seemed almost quaintly uninteresting when measured up against such drama, the province was in the throes of its own quiet revolution, transforming and being transformed both by all those larger forces being brought into everyone's living room by the magic of television and also by homegrown events as well.

The 1970 election, in fact, is a convenient marker for separating the old Nova Scotia — a quiescent, traditional place where one was deferential, one accepted, one went along — from the new — a vibrant, more worldly and modern place where one challenged, one argued, one didn't necessarily always go along to get along.

Gerald Regan seems a curiously appropriate leader to preside over this unfolding transition. On the one hand, he had been raised in, and accepted, most of what passed for politics-as-usual in Nova Scotia — patronage, privilege, and pump-priming. He could certainly practise that sort of politics with the best of them. But at the same time, he was an enthusiastic student of the new, more rational politics in which polling and pragmatism held sway. While Regan kept one foot solidly in the camp of the old politics — the Garnet Brown branch of the Liberal family, which never met a highway that didn't need paving at election time — he also managed to attract to the party others from among the smartest in the generation behind him, men like Michael Kirby, a coolly intellectual young technocrat who attempted to apply scientific reason to the passions of politics.

What brought the Kirbys and the Browns together was that they shared — with Regan — a love of politics for its own sake. "I could have been a Tory as easily as a Liberal," admits David Mann, a Kirby crony with a penchant for polling who ran most of Regan's electoral campaigns. "I never had any strong philosophical views, but I loved the fun of politics."

In fact, Mann, like most of the group that helped Regan win in

1970, is still far more comfortable discussing tactics and strategies than he is ruminating about what they wanted to do with that power when they got it. That's probably because, like Regan himself, they never bothered to think very much about the question.

To the extent that Regan had a political philosophy, it was mildly reformist. Having spent so long as an outsider among his own party's elite — the Windsor shopkeeper's son, the sportscaster, the loser who couldn't seem to buy an election, the accidental backbencher, the leader no one expected to last — Regan had a natural affinity for the little guy over the establishment, even if another part of him was desperately eager to join that establishment.

If there was a formative period in shaping the new premier's political views, it was the two years he spent in Ottawa collecting backbench blisters and sharpening his sense of Maritime alienation. While many of his contemporaries accepted the conventional wisdom that Nova Scotia could never be anything but a have-not province and saw their role as federal politicians as making the best of a bad historic bargain, Regan was eternally hopeful. He genuinely believed Nova Scotia could use its abundant natural resources and strategic location to reinvent itself as the prosperous place it had been before Confederation — and central Canada — robbed it of its future.

Regan brought his infectious optimism home to Nova Scotia with him when he took over the party leadership in 1965. By 1970, more and more people, especially in the capital city of Halifax, shared his confidence in the future.

Twenty-five years after the last angry sailors had trashed the city at the end of World War II to vent their frustration and anger at its small-town small-mindedness, Halifax was finally beginning to kick off the traces of its image as a smug, parochial, socially stratified, down-at-the-heels port city and tentatively beginning to make a new psychic space for itself as an even more smug but now cosmopolitan, not-too-big, not-too-small city eagerly adapting to the task of satisfying the needs and desires of the growing numbers of upwardly mobile residents of a rapidly expanding government, university, and financial services centre.

The transformation had been painfully slow in coming.

Harold Connolly, a failed Liberal leader who had gone on to his reward in the Senate, had once described Nova Scotia's business leaders as "the world's champion sitters. . . . The older among us smoked our pipes, sat upon the front stoops and said to one another, 'What a great people we are! Isn't Canada a fortunate country to have Nova Scotia from which to draw its grey matter.'"

But by the dawning of the century's — and his own — seventh decade, Connolly sensed a sea change in his native province's self-perception. "A small core of younger men have finally realized that unless we do things for ourselves, the chances of someone else doing them is remote. So, for the first time in my more than seventy years here, there is real growth."

Halifax's once crumbling downtown core — which retailers and businesses had been abandoning in droves for more than a decade in favour of more prized selling space in suburban shopping malls — offered mute testimony in support of Connolly's thesis. In 1969, it got a new lease on life when the province's most powerful business families came together to transform a seventeen-acre slum neigh-bourhood in the heart of the downtown into a massive new concrete-and-brick shopping centre, office tower, apartment and hotel complex known as Scotia Square. Its promoters claimed Scotia Square would be the anchor as well as the catalyst for a vibrant new downtown bursting with shops, offices, restaurants, and night life. *Maclean's* took that prediction one step further, arguing the new development not only "revitalized a gloomy, decaying downtown" but its mere existence had also "perhaps changed the lives of all Maritimers because it generates an excitement about tomorrow that Canada east of Quebec hasn't felt since the death of sail a cen-tury ago."

Even as these "modernists" happily touted their new Halifax, a small but even more determined group of heritage preservationists, led by a Halifax school teacher and amateur historian named Lou Collins, was waging its own campaign to prevent other too-eager downtown real estate developers and city planners from flattening the city's historic waterfront to build "Harbour Drive," an urban superhighway that was supposed to circle the city.*

---

* As a result of citizen protests, the city abandoned plans for the new urban highway but not before constructing a huge interchange that was supposed to channel traffic on and off the superhighway. The incongruous cloverleaf still exists, now separating Scotia Square from the Historic Properties.

During its heyday in the 1800s, the stretch of Halifax's waterfront the developers wanted to wipe out had bustled with commercial activity and life. Privateers stored their ill-gotten booty in warehouses that dotted the harbour's edge, while ambitious young entrepreneurs probably used some of that ill-gotten gain to lay the groundwork for a variety of businesses, including British North America's first chartered bank.

By 1970, however, what remained of the shipping business was moving south along the harbour toward Point Pleasant Park, where a new container pier had just opened, and the old downtown waterfront area had become little more than a dowdy collection of derelict warehouses, piers, and abandoned office buildings where few were willing to venture, especially at night.

The preservationists argued these buildings should not be demolished, but saved, refurbished, and put to innovative use as a new home for the city's almost-as-historic Nova Scotia College of Art and Design.

Their new Historic Properties, they claimed with a fervour that was certainly the equal of the champions of Scotia Square, would become the anchor as well as the catalyst for a vibrant new downtown bursting with shops, offices, restaurants, and night life.

In the end, they were both right. The mix of old and new was potent, as Canada's national magazines were quick to note. The new Halifax, wrote *Chatelaine*, is "a beautiful city, a city fit for people to live in, big enough to compete successfully on just about any urban livability factor, small and personal enough for any individual to stay human." Its citizens had finally realized, added *The Star Weekly*, "that Halifax need no longer borrow from the styles of others but is quite able, thank you, to create its own."

This changing view of Halifax encouraged an influx of well-educated, well-paid come-from-aways to relocate to the city. Perhaps not surprisingly, they refused to accept much of what the locals had long taken as the city's inevitable, inviolable social givens. Separate Catholic and Protestant schools, for example. Men-only taverns. The obvious absence of black faces in local businesses. The dearth of good restaurants. The inordinate role party politics played in determining whether you got a job or an appointment, or even an invitation to a weekend dinner party.

Owing no allegiance or deference to the province's traditional power-brokers, these newcomers began to challenge the established order at every level, demanding change and a place at the decision-making table. By the late sixties, this conflict between old and new had become wrenching and traumatic for many.

In 1969, it spilled into the open when the city put itself on the psychiatrist's couch for a week in what was billed as an Encounter on the Urban Environment. This event was envisioned as a way of encouraging public discussion of the city's future. To lead that discussion, the province brought in a dozen high-powered international experts in various fields — from urban planning to the media to race relations — for an intense round of morning-to-night meetings, interviews, and workshops followed by nightly televised town hall gatherings.

Halifax certainly got more than it had bargained for from the week. The event not only exposed all sorts of previously hidden (or at least dismissed as inconsequential) divisions within the community — black versus white, young versus old, poor versus rich, business versus labour, newcomer versus old guard — but it also did it all in the full glare of CJCH-TV's live cameras, which brought all the bubbling anger and frustration into everyone's living room every night for the entire week.

The city was still reeling from that forced look into the mirror when it was brought up short by another confrontation, this one between the city's conservative political establishment and a coalition of labour and human rights groups. The issue: the appointment of a new city manager. City Council had secretly decided to hire an American named Robert Oldland, who'd served in a similar capacity in Oklahoma City. But before it could meet to rubber-stamp that decision, Edmund Morris,* the city's most popular and outspoken radio and TV commentator, announced that he'd learned labour and civil rights groups back in Oklahoma City regarded Oldland as an anti-labour bigot they were delighted to see gone. Morris's inflammatory daily radio and TV commentaries — at one point he

---

* Morris was a Tory member of Parliament during the Diefenbaker era. He abstained on the confidence motion that defeated Diefenbaker's government in 1963. He later became the city's mayor.

predicted blood would flow in the streets if the city hired Oldland — generated a firestorm of protests and, eventually, a mass march on City Hall by thousands of blacks, trade unionists, and other social activists.

The city backed down. Oldland didn't come.

It was a heady, volatile time for both race and labour relations in Halifax. City Council was still dealing with the fallout from its decision in the early sixties to raze Africville, a poor black community on the edge of town. Some coveted the strategically situated community for industrial development, others saw it as one more link in the dream of the Harbour Drive superhighway. But even most of those whites — and some blacks — who had no economic interest in its fate initially thought of Africville as nothing more than a slum and a blight, and assumed the people who'd lived there would be happy if the city wiped it off the map.

They weren't. Most of Africville's 400 residents regarded what whites saw as progress as the forced destruction of their community and the only way of life they had ever known. Worse, many later came to believe they'd been hoodwinked into selling their properties for far less than they were worth by smooth-talking city officials, often aided and abetted by some of their own black leaders. Most ended up in soulless concrete public housing projects that lacked any hint of the community spirit they'd known in Africville. Because so many established black leaders had been intimately involved in the wheeling and dealing over Africville's fate, they lost credibility — and influence — among many younger, poorer blacks.

Enter Rocky Jones, a darkly handsome black man who'd grown up in Truro but discovered the civil rights movement while working in Toronto in the early sixties. After Jones settled in Halifax in 1965, he and his wife Joan began to channel some of that frustration and anger, especially among younger blacks, into political action. In 1965, they opened Kwacha* House, a Company of Young Canadians project to encourage inner city youth to take control of their own lives. Although the young people's major projects — turning a vacant lot into a co-op playground for poor kids and organizing

---

* Kwacha means freedom.

local opposition to the city's plans for yet another massive public housing complex in their neighbourhood — may seem tame, almost civics-lesson-mundane by contemporary standards, their activism scared the hell out of local politicians and law enforcement officials. The RCMP put Jones and his wife under surveillance as dangerous revolutionaries.* City fathers lobbied Ottawa to cut funding for their subversive project. Kwacha House closed in 1968.

Two years later, Jones turned the city's power structure inside out by talking loudly about Black Power and inviting a few members of the U.S. Black Panther Party to visit Halifax.

Shortly after their rather uneventful visit — and just before the 1970 provincial election — the federal health minister John Munro flew to Halifax to announce major federal funding for a new organization called the Black United Front. Officially, it was created to serve as an umbrella for the province's various established black organizations; unofficially, authorities hoped it would provide a shield against the potent message of Jones and Black Power.

As Gerald Regan's Liberals were preparing to take over the province, the trade union establishment also came under fire from within, largely because of its inept handling of a bitter fourteen-month strike by Canso fishermen.

For centuries, fishing had been the economic lifeblood of much of rural Nova Scotia. But since World War II, it had been transformed into an economically potent, vertically integrated, highly profitable industry. The traditional picture of the independent inshore fisherman venturing out each morning in his own small boat to fish the waters near his home and then returning to his family at the end of the day with his catch, had been replaced by a much more Dickensian image. The new fisherman was a hired-hand, slaving sixteen to twenty hours a day for a week to ten days at a time at sea aboard a company-owned trawler. The vessel's huge trawl vacuumed the sea clean of fish, which would then be processed in a company-owned plant, packaged under

---

* Jones eventually returned to university, earning an MA and then a law degree. He is currently a staff lawyer with Dalhousie Legal Aid. Using the federal *Freedom of Information Act*, Jones and his now former wife managed to get access to thousands of pages of RCMP surveillance reports that documented their activities in the sixties.

a corporate brand name, and shipped to market in company-owned trucks. All, of course, for the greater profit of the company's shareholders, most of whom didn't live in Nova Scotia.

Often, the fishermen took home pitifully little for their effort. When a Canso fisherman, Everett Richardson, showed the writer Silver Donald Cameron his financial records for one year, for example, he pointed to one trip lasting more than a week for which he was paid a grand total of $2.01. "The one cent was in the envelope too," Richardson said with a laugh. Even in a good year when a fisherman might work 5,000 hours — three times as many as the average industrial worker works — he would often end up earning $3,000–$5,000 for the whole year. On an hourly basis, that was less than minimum wage.

But the fishermen weren't actually officially paid a wage.

Thanks to a 1947 Nova Scotia Supreme Court ruling, fishermen were, in the court's almost romantic turn of phrase, "co-adventurers" who supposedly shared in good times and bad with their fellow co-adventurers, the fishing boat owners. That made them — conveniently — ineligible to belong to a trade union although, by the late sixties, most of those fishing boat owners had become, in fact, powerful multinational companies, and their real relationship with their co-adventurers was essentially that of master to slave.

Despite simmering frustration among fishermen, Nova Scotia's trade union leadership remained remarkably uninterested in challenging the outdated legal status quo by attempting to organize them.

That left an opening Homer Stevens was more than eager to fill. Stevens was the president of the militant, British Columbia–based United Fishermen and Allied Workers Union, whose organizers began visiting Nova Scotia fishing communities in the late sixties. Within a few months, they'd signed up seventy of the eighty fishermen in Mulgrave, and formed organizing committees in a half dozen other communities all along the coast.

In the spring of 1970, fishermen in Canso, Mulgrave, Arichat, and Petit de Grat walked off the boats and began what would turn out to be a protracted, bitter, and landmark illegal strike against their co-adventurers: Chicago-based Booth Fisheries and the British-owned Acadia Fisheries.

If the fishermen saw Stevens as a kind of working-class hero whose own salary was automatically reduced to strike pay during work stoppages and who had gone to jail in British Columbia to defend the interests of his members, Nova Scotia fishing companies, politicians, newspaper editorialists, and even other trade union leaders saw Stevens and his union much differently. To them, he was the devil incarnate, threatening the future of the fish companies, the fishing communities, the province, and the Western world as they knew it.

For starters, Stevens was an unashamed member of the Communist Party of Canada and his union had been thrown out of the predecessor organization of the Canadian Labour Congress, in part over an accusation it had raided the membership of another union but also, in part, because of the Communist affiliations of some of its leaders. When the union failed to gain re-admittance during an annual convention nineteen years later — in the middle of its strike in Nova Scotia — the CLC president, Donald MacDonald, used the occasion to attack "sinister forces, particularly the Communist Party of Canada."

The Halifax *Chronicle-Herald*, which rarely took much interest in union politics, picked up on the story and carried it prominently. The companies, perhaps not surprisingly, also used it to discredit the union. Booth Fisheries, for example, declared in one of its newspaper ads that the company would willingly recognize any responsible union, but that the UFAWU had demonstrated that it was "irresponsible, unreliable, and contemptuous of Canadian law." The company then threatened to shut down its Petit de Grat plant if the fishermen didn't soon come to their senses.

The fishermen not only refused to be cowed by such threats, they also stood up to the province's justice system too. When the companies won injunctions prohibiting picketing at the fish plants, the fishermen ignored them. When modest legal penalties failed to shake the fishermen's resolve, Judge Gordon Cowan shocked many in the province — even some who didn't support the fishermen's cause — by sentencing one of the Canso fishermen, Everett Richardson, to nine months in the Halifax County Correction Centre for carrying a picket sign.

While all of this was going on, the province's politicians and labour leaders maintained a curious, careful distance from the dispute. The Smith government, gearing up for re-election, tried to defuse the issue by appointing Judge Nathan Green to look into the dispute and report on ways to resolve it.

Even Gerald Regan, who liked to trade on his reputation as a friend of working people, only finally — and timidly — suggested calling the legislature into special session to give the fishermen full bargaining rights after 7,000 miners and construction workers had already spontaneously walked off their jobs across the province the day after Cowan sentenced Richardson to jail.

Regan's concern for the strike, wrote Silver Donald Cameron in *The Education of Everett Richardson*, his 1977 account of the dispute, "could be measured by a July 29 [1970] speech to the Sydney Rotary Club on the subject of labour-management relations in which he managed not to mention the fishermen at all. Regan's most memorable comment had been a wintry expression of distaste after Everett Richardson's sentence: the government, he said, was 'paying too much attention to legal technicalities in contradistinction to social realities.'"

Huh?

Regan was able to look the other way during the strike, in part because his allies in the labour movement were doing their best to ignore it as well. Although the Nova Scotia Federation of Labour did emerge from its cone of silence occasionally to bluster it would really, truly, absolutely call a general strike if something wasn't done soon, it was usually only playing catch-up to the independent actions of some of its more militant locals and individual trade unionists.

The other main pillar of the Nova Scotia establishment, the mainstream media, naturally weighed in against the fishermen too. The headlines in the Halifax *Chronicle-Herald*, the province's largest and, by far, most influential daily, amounted to a drumbeat against Stevens and his United Fishermen's union: "Ultimatum: Work or Face Closure"; "No 'Viable Operation' with Stevens, UFAWU"; "B.C. Union Lacks Top CLC Blessing"; "Trawlermen Disclose Plans to Quit UFAWU"; etc. The newspaper harped on Stevens's Communist connections and, in a province where outsiders were still sometimes regarded as untrustworthy, continually referred to the UFAWU as a "west coast union" or a "B.C. union."

What is intriguing in all this is that, in spite of the might of the combined forces allied against them, the fishermen ultimately won the battle for the hearts and minds of the public, and they *almost* won the larger war to be allowed to freely choose which union they wanted to represent them too.*

They had plenty of help, of course: from the miners and construction workers who walked off their jobs to protest Richardson's jailing; members of the Halifax School Maintenance Union, and dozens of other union locals across the province and country who mailed in modest but meaningful cheques for seventy-five or one hundred dollars to supplement the fishermen's strike pay; the town council in their home town of Canso, which voted to contribute one hundred dollars a month for each family affected by the strike; Ron Parsons, a local Anglican parish priest who not only walked the picket line with the strikers but also put his own job on the line by joining the fishermen's wives in occupying the local welfare office when officials refused to issue cheques to the strikers' families; the young, middle-class radicals of the Halifax-based New Democratic Youth who passed out leaflets and led marches and sold fish on the streets of Halifax to support the strikers; and, perhaps especially, from *The 4th Estate*, a fledgling Halifax-based alternative newspaper,† which provided a much different perspective on the strike — a clearly pro-worker viewpoint — to readers fed up with the often blinkered conservatism of the *Herald*.

The crusading, twice-monthly publication was the brainchild of Frank and Nick Fillmore, a father-son team whose first issue landed on newsstands on April 17, 1969, shortly after Gerald Regan staged his famous filibuster.‡ It quickly attracted a following not only among politicians and officials who worried what it might say next but also among the growing numbers of those who felt left out by the *Herald*'s establishment positions. By the end of the first year, it had a paid circulation of more than 8,000 and had increased its publishing frequency to weekly.

Frank Fillmore, an eccentric, larger-than-life character who wore

---

* Although the new Liberal government did bring in legislation to amend the trade union act, making it legal for the fishermen to unionize, the companies "voluntarily" agreed to recognize other unions days before the new legislation became law, effectively preventing the UFAWU from organizing.

† More full disclosure. I wrote for *The 4th Estate* during the early seventies.

‡ The filibuster, in fact, was the paper's first lead story under the headline: "Regan Stock Up; Smith Criticized."

a black patch over his left eye and often showed up at press conferences sporting a black cape, was the paper's associate editor and its most visible figure. A horticulturalist by trade, he'd begun his journalism career writing gardening columns for the Halifax *Chronicle-Herald*, and then spent ten years as a staff writer before joining forces with his twenty-five-year-old son to start the paper. Nick, the managing editor, had recently returned from stints at Canadian Press in Toronto and Reuters in London, England.*

Like many alternative papers of the era, *The 4th Estate* offered a direct challenge to the local establishment. But, unlike many of its contemporaries such as Vancouver's *Georgia Strait*, which took an interest in drugs, the counterculture, and international issues like Vietnam, *The 4th Estate* was relatively mainstream and parochial. Nick and Frank, in fact, could most appropriately be characterized as populist reformers whose social views were summed up in an Upton Sinclair quote on their paper's masthead: "If I was not always right, I was looking for the right."

The paper's first major crusade was against slum landlords: "*The 4th Estate*, published in a city where a clear majority of politicians and civil servants don't seem to give a damn about cracking down on anyone except those who cannot defend themselves, is declaring war on those who profit from human misery," the paper thundered in its first Christmas edition. The crusade's unusual tactics — the paper promised *not* to print the names of offending landlords if they agreed to fix up their properties within a week of being contacted by the paper but threatened to publish photos both of their slum properties and their own residences if they didn't — attracted national attention.

The paper also shocked many in the community when it publicly disclosed that the city's former police chief, Verdun Mitchell, had killed himself in his office with his service revolver. The local media, led by the Halifax *Chronicle-Herald*, had quietly covered up the suicide, describing his death only as sudden and unexpected. Before *The 4th Estate* arrived on the scene, in fact, the local media had a kind of gentlemen's agreement to screen out unpleasant news. After

---

*   Nick and Frank later had a falling out, and Frank launched his own paper, *The Scotian Journalist*, in competition with *The 4th Estate*.

racial tensions exploded into violence in many American cities during the late sixties, representatives from other local media outlets met and secretly agreed to downplay any unfortunate racial incidents that might happen in their city.

The *4th Estate* took an almost perverse delight in chiding the Dennis family–owned morning Halifax *Chronicle-Herald* and its afternoon sister, the *Mail-Star* for its coverage — and lack of coverage — of local issues and events. The papers, which *The 4th Estate* skewered as "the Old Women of Argyle Street," were an easy target.

The newspaper monopoly had been created by the merger of the Liberal *Chronicle* and *Star* with the Conservative *Herald* and *Mail* in 1949. The merger, as the author Thomas Raddall put it in *Warden of the North*, his history of Halifax, eliminated the fierce competition that once had generated the "thunder and lightning that kept everyone aware of all the news all the time. . . . It soon became apparent that the new monolith of the daily press was set on a new monotonous course, with much attention to advertising and to filler, and a spotty attention to hard news."

In late 1970, just two months after Gerald Regan's Liberals took office and eighteen months after *The 4th Estate* began publishing, a special Senate committee investigating the mass media in Canada published a report, which included a damning indictment of the Halifax dailies. They were guilty of "uncaring, lazy journalism," the report declared, adding: "There is probably no large Canadian city that is so badly served by its newspapers [and] probably no news organization in the country that has managed to achieve such an intimate and uncritical relationship with the local power structure, or has grown so indifferent to the needs of its readers."*

The 4th Estate had helped the committee reach those unflattering conclusions by documenting for the senators dozens of major local stories it had uncovered — ranging from the results of an important study on harnessing the Fundy tides, which showed the project was

---

* In what might be seen as unintended evidence for the report's conclusions, the two Nova Scotia senators on the committee disassociated themselves from the report's criticism of the newspapers. "In the view of Senator J. M. MacDonald and Senator Frank Welsh, the *Chronicle-Herald* and *Mail-Star* are serving their province competently, honestly, and independently in the public interest," noted the report. "They point out that the majority of the committee, personally unfamiliar with Nova Scotia history and Nova Scotia practice, may apply a yardstick that is inapplicable to Nova Scotia conditions."

technically feasible but financially impractical, to an exposé of irreg-
ularities in how Liverpool's police committee chairman handled a
quantity of seized liquor — that the Dennis papers had either ignored
completely or only reported much later. "It seems odd," the senators
noted, "that a two-man operation like *The 4th Estate* could scoop an
organization with the resources of the *Chronicle-Herald* and the
Mail-Star. . . . It seems even stranger that the Dennis newspapers,
once scooped, didn't follow up these stories immediately — either to
enlarge on them or to knock them down.

"This may be," the report concluded, "because the Dennis newspapers appear reluctant to publish anything that might embarrass the
government. At the hearings, L. F. Daley, vice-president of the
Halifax Herald Limited . . . was questioned about the charge — contained in the December 20, 1969, issue of the *Globe Magazine* —
that 'in the twelve years in which Robert Stanfield was premier, there
wasn't one word of criticism of his administration in the Halifax
papers. But it was that way even before Nova Scotia turned
Conservative with Stanfield. While Henry Hicks was premier, he too
was the apple of their eye.' Mr. Daley told us he found that charge
'pretty hard to believe.' But he didn't offer the Committee any
instances of the *Mail-Star* or *Chronicle-Herald* mounting editorial
campaigns against government policies. Nor were our researchers
able to discover any."

Gerald Regan would soon come to regret the senators' stinging
attack on the largest newspapers in his province. Wounded by
criticism of its unwillingness to take on government, the Dennis
newspapers soon found their editorial voice, albeit in anguished
defence of the already powerful and privileged. In the winter of
1972, the paper would launch two major editorial campaigns against
the government of the day — Regan's government — for what it saw
as its "socialistic" government buyout of Nova Scotia Light & Power
and its draconian decision to impose "confiscatory" succession
duties on the estates of the wealthy.

If Regan's fortunes had been buoyed by the arrival of *The 4th
Estate* during his final days as Opposition leader, he quickly found
himself and his government in its editorial gun sights after he took
office. The paper was an equal opportunity critic. Having slammed
the Smith government during its last days in office, it just as eagerly

turned the tables and skewered the Regan administration after it assumed power.

But *The 4th Estate* was at its best — and most effective — when it was speaking out on behalf of those who had no power, those who'd been ignored or dismissed for so long by the Dennis papers. Including, of course, the Canso fishermen.

After the courts had come down hard on the strikers for refusing to obey the injunctions against picketing — and after the *Herald* had fulminated that it was "disturbing . . . when the system of law and order is so often abused and when people, insisting on their own rights, ignore those of others" — *The 4th Estate* published a full-page commentary under the title: "Contempt for the Law: What Else Could an Honest Man Have?"

Thanks to the efforts of *The 4th Estate* and others, the fishermen's strike became more than just another labour dispute. By the time it was over, Robert Chodos wrote in *The Last Post*, a magazine published in Montreal, "it had taken its place among the classic labour struggles of recent times. Like the Newfoundland loggers' strike of 1959 and the Asbestos strike of 1949, it had torn a society apart so that the society could never be quite the same again."

The fishermen, added Silver Donald Cameron, "demonstrated the real relationships between Nova Scotia's most powerful institutions with startling clarity, while revealing that a handful of people, strengthened by their insistence on justice, could bring an entire province to a halt."

The strike became more important than the outcome precisely because it challenged the status quo at a time when many others in the province were also beginning to question it. "It is the political nature of the whole conflict which made it so central, for a season, to Nova Scotia's public life," argued Silver Donald Cameron. "The political implications of the strike brought the fishermen the support of the NDP, brought the young radicals down to the picket lines, brought the opposition journalists to Canso Strait from Halifax, Toronto, and Fredericton. It is the political significance of the strike which made Nova Scotia's establishment so determined to break it."

The strike, in an odd, backhanded way, also helped make Gerald Regan premier. The NDP, which had spoken out strongly in favour of the strikers, picked up two seats in the labour stronghold of industrial Cape Breton and, in Halifax, "a coalition of Liberals, left-ists, and students submerged their differences in a joint effort to get rid of Attorney General Richard Donahoe," the Conservative government's most reactionary cabinet minister.

Those three seats were the difference between victory and defeat for Gerald Regan.

But it wasn't until after the votes had been counted that people finally began to come to terms with the depth of the antipathy so many in the province felt not only toward the defeated Tory government but also toward the politics-as-usual it had come to represent. The question now was whether Gerald Regan, the almost accidental beneficiary of all the changes that had taken place in the province in the last decade, would be capable of harnessing the forces that had brought him to power.

ON THE MORNING AFTER October 13, Michael Kirby, still running on the crazy adrenaline of that incredible election night, stopped by the Regan house on Berlin Street for a quiet wake-up-and-ask-yourself-if-this-is-really-real cup of coffee with the man he'd help make . . . Premier-elect Gerald Regan!

Sitting across from him at the kitchen table, Regan raised his cup in mock toast and grinned. "All right, wise guy, what now?"

Kirby was momentarily nonplussed. "I don't know," he confessed finally. He prided himself on being a rationalist who always considered all of the possible combinations and permutations of even the unthinkable, but this had been, well, too unimaginable. "I never thought that far ahead," he told Regan sheepishly.

"I was still stunned," Kirby admitted later. "I knew in the last few days that we were making gains and I think we were all hoping to do better — like thirteen, fourteen, maybe fifteen seats at the outside — but nobody thought we were going to win. We were all absolutely stunned."

But they had won. And now they had to quickly sort through what to do next.

"Mike, what do you know about how they run the premier's office in New Brunswick?" Regan asked.

Kirby didn't.

"Why don't you call them and see how they do things there and then put together a report for when I come back," Regan suggested. A Cincinnati Reds baseball fan, Regan had already made plans to celebrate the end of the election campaign — and now his victory — with a trip to Baltimore to take in the first two games of that year's World Series.

By the time Regan returned, Kirby had recovered from the shock sufficiently to have travelled to three provincial capitals as well as Ottawa to scope out how those offices were run. When they met again, Kirby was ready with a carefully crafted organizational chart for a new, prime ministerial Office of the Premier, which would include a chief of staff, an executive assistant, a press secretary, a researcher, and a personal secretary for the premier, as well as providing for an executive assistant for each cabinet minister. Though positively spartan by the standards of later Nova Scotia administrations, Kirby's proposal — which Regan adopted — quickly came under fire from the media and the Opposition as extravagant empire-building.

Kirby didn't care; he was planning to return to his teaching duties anyway. In fact, he was walking across the campus to his office a few days after delivering his report to Regan when he ran into the former Liberal leader Henry Hicks, by now president of Dalhousie University.

"Don't worry," Hicks assured him. "It's all taken care of."

"What's all taken care of?" Kirby asked.

"Your leave of absence," Hicks answered. "Gerry called to tell me he wanted you to run his office, so we took care of the paperwork. You're free to go."

"We laughed about it later," Kirby says today. "Gerry clearly thought he'd asked me to take the job, but he hadn't. So the first I know that I'd been hired as his chief of staff is when Henry Hicks tells me I've got my leave of absence."

Besides Kirby, who took responsibility for policy development and political strategy, Regan's office staff included many key members of the election campaign team. Michael Belliveau became the director of research. David Thompson, who took on the job of Regan's executive assistant, handled logistics and travelled with the premier. Peter Green, a young lawyer and the former president of the Young Liberals who'd invited Kirby to his first Liberal party meeting in the mid-sixties, became legislative adviser. Regan also hired the Halifax

Herald reporter Jim Robson as his press secretary, and lured Fred Drummie, an experienced Liberal bureaucrat from New Brunswick Premier Louis Robichaud's office to act as secretary to the cabinet.

Considering that only five of his MLAs had any legislative experience at all, Regan wisely kept his first cabinet lean. There were just nine members, including Regan himself. Their average age was forty-one — a full ten years younger than the last Smith cabinet — and its membership was a comfortable mix of experience and youth, pragmatism and idealism, left and right, insiders and neophytes.*

Its political and emotional anchor — Regan's too — was Peter Nicholson, an Annapolis Valley lawyer who became minister of finance and minister of education, as well as the de facto deputy premier. Nicholson was first elected in the 1956 campaign that brought Stanfield to office, and had beaten back the Tory tide in every subsequent election until the Liberals finally regained power fourteen years later. He was Regan's kinder, gentler version of Stanfield's G. I. Smith — a politician's politician who was not only universally respected by colleagues and opponents alike for his intelligence and integrity but who also seemed content, even ideally suited, to beavering away quietly in the background far from the limelight that belonged to the leader.

"Peter was the rock on which the government was founded," says Jeremy Akerman, who led the two-member NDP caucus after the 1970 election. "He was the one who was able to stop the boys from chasing off madly in all directions. He was the one who understood what things cost and what could be afforded, and he would say, 'This is as far as we can go at this time, boys.'"

"His general pitch," agrees Bill Gillis, "was always, 'We can't do that. It will be written up in the auditor general's report.'"

"We called him the wise old owl," recalls Doug Harkness, a television reporter who had joined the government as executive assistant

---

* According to Jack Hawkins, who joined the cabinet in the middle of the government's first term, Regan "loved" the weekly cabinet meetings — which Hawkins described as "something of a discussion club, like one might expect in an eighteenth-century coffee house or men's club." Regan liked those discussions so much he often prolonged meetings for hours longer than necessary. The meetings usually began at ten in the morning, would break briefly for a takeout lunch from Kentucky Fried Chicken around one and then continue until past six in the evening. By the time the meeting concluded, the formal Cabinet Room would be thick with stale cigar smoke and the smell of greasy chicken.

to Garnet Brown, the minister of highways and minister of public works.

If Nicholson was one personality extreme of the first cabinet, Brown, a onetime local baseball star who'd made his fortune in the family wholesale grocery business, occupied the other.

Loud, backslapping, and eccentric, Brown was chief among those eager to chase off madly in all directions — establishing new departments of tourism and recreation here, carving up part of his Eastern Shore constituency for a national park there, and flying off to California with an entourage of friends and hangers on to watch the province's petal-covered float pass by in the annual Rose Bowl parade.

He loved to talk, but occasionally, in the heat of verbal jousting, mangled the language. Once, when under fire in the legislature for some alleged lapse or other, Brown declared hotly that he resented the Honourable Member's "insinnuendo."

Brown's work habits were equally odd — he'd begin his days at six in the morning, but then hurry home in the afternoon so he could watch his favourite soap operas on television.

But Brown, a fierce Regan loyalist who'd won that critical 1969 by-election that saved Regan's political life and had served as president of the party during the rebuilding years, was more than just a loveable buffoon. He was close to key members of the party's old guard, including the bagman Irv Barrow, and "he knew what the party was thinking better than anyone else in the cabinet," says Michael Kirby. "When it came to how the party would react to this issue or that one, Brown was the one we all looked to for advice."

If Nicholson and Brown corresponded to two very different extremes of Regan's own persona — the diligent, driven workaholic and the happy-go-lucky party animal — Allan Sullivan, Regan's new minister of public welfare and minister of mines, offered up both an even greater love of a good time than Brown and also a more intense version of Regan's mildly reformist social conscience.

Michael Kirby maintains that Sullivan, a Cape Breton lawyer and cousin of Peter Nicholson — along with Nicholson himself, Regan, and the attorney general and minister of labour Leonard Pace — were primarily responsible for the government's early reformist bent. "They all shared, to a greater or lesser degree, a similar left-of-centre orientation, and they were very driven to do things that were socially progressive."

Pace, a gruff, often acerbic Halifax lawyer who would later become notorious for his role as an appeal court judge in the Donald Marshall, Jr., case,* seemed unlikely in the role of progressive, but Kirby and others argue he had an intellectual fascination with law reform and with the minutiae of legislation to achieve social policy, and spearheaded the updating of many of the province's archaic statutes.

Scott MacNutt, a handsome, perpetually tanned thirty-five-year-old former director of welfare for Dartmouth, rounded out the progressive wing in that first cabinet. MacNutt fancied himself a bon vivant who enjoyed good food and drink. "He might have stepped unadulterated from a play by Noel Coward," suggested Jack Hawkins. Regan, who enjoyed MacNutt's company, appointed him minister of health and minister of housing. Despite his lack of previous political experience, he had earned his place at the table by defeating I. W. Akerley, the Tories' powerful minister of highways, in Dartmouth South.

MacNutt's conservative counterweight, Ralph Fiske, was another impressive rookie cabinet minister. A thoughtful former banker turned self-made businessman with a reputation for unassailable integrity, Fiske was destined to be an outsider in the tight circle of the Regan cabinet, largely because he had come to partisan politics late and almost by accident, and never seemed comfortable with its social mores, or with his more liberal, more partisan colleagues.

The centrepiece of his business empire was the Heather Motel in Stellarton, which he'd built in the late sixties strategically close to a planned exit to the soon-to-be completed TransCanada Highway. He

---

* During Pace's term as attorney general, Donald Marshall, Jr., a young Cape Breton Micmac, was convicted of a 1971 murder he didn't commit and spent the next eleven years in prison. By the time the miscarriage was discovered, Pace was a member of the provincial court of appeal. He was a member of the panel that quashed Marshall's initial conviction but claimed — in words allegedly written by Pace — that Marshall had been "the author of his own misfortune." The court's decision, concluded a later royal commission inquiry into Marshall's wrongful conviction, "amounted to a defence of the criminal justice system at the expense of Donald Marshall, Jr., in spite of overwhelming evidence that the system itself had failed." The inquiry's report criticized Pace, saying that, as the attorney general at the time of Marshall's conviction and initial appeal, he "should not have sat as a member of panel hearing the reference."

says he had no time for politics — he was happy making money — until the Smith government began musing about allowing restaurants and other services to be developed directly beside the TransCanada Highway in competition with his facilities. "I tore hell out of [the Tories] for it," he says with a laugh. "And, well, one thing led to another and, before I knew it I'd talked myself into being a candidate. And Christ, to everyone's surprise, the Liberals won." Regan chose Fiske as his minister of industry.

Bill Gillis, the youngest member of the new cabinet at thirty-three and its only bachelor, was probably the least "swinging" of the lot of them. In the freewheeling, fun-loving Regan cabinet, Gillis, a geology professor from St. Francis Xavier University in Antigonish who became minister of agriculture and minister of municipal affairs, stood out as modest, shy, and, above all, frugal. He was often the butt of jokes from his colleagues, who would marvel when he not only insisted on taking the bus back and forth to his constituency each week, even after he was appointed to the cabinet, but also inevitably "ordered the six-dollar special when at dinner on government business."

Benoit Comeau, the new minister of fisheries and minister of lands and forests, was the cabinet's oldest — and least impressive — member at fifty-four. Although he'd first been elected with Regan in the 1967 campaign, Comeau, the son of a longtime MLA and senator, had done nothing to distinguish himself during his three years in opposition and was appointed to cabinet because he was an Acadian who represented the otherwise unrepresented area of southwestern Nova Scotia. Though he remained a cabinet minister for the entire eight years of the Regan administration, he rarely spoke in the House.*

Even after Regan's newly selected cabinet ministers were officially sworn in on October 28, 1970, it was not clear how long they would be able to govern. The election-night results had left the Liberals and combined Tory-NDP opposition in a dead heat, meaning the two-member NDP caucus would have a lot to say about the longevity of Regan's new government.

---

* Comeau, a friendly man who was well liked by colleagues and opponents alike, became famous for his brief, usually not very illuminating, answers to the Opposition in Question Period. "I will study it, Mr. Speaker," was his most usual answer to any request for information or comment.

Whom would they support?

From the outset — thanks, in no small part to Gerald Regan's considerable personal charm — the outcome was not in doubt.

Two years before the election, at the official opening of an expansion at the Stora Forest Industries plant in Port Hawkesbury, Regan had introduced himself to Jeremy Akerman, a young archaeologist who'd recently been elected NDP leader. "Regan was one of the few people who even noticed me that day," Akerman would later recall. "He came up to me and introduced himself and said I should give him a call the next time I was in Halifax." Akerman did, and Regan immediately invited him to dinner at his home. Despite their occasional political differences, they became fast friends. "I formed a pretty favourable opinion of him," Akerman remembers. "Number one, of course, he was great company. No dinner party of which Gerald Regan was a member could ever be dull. He was a great storyteller but he also was very good at encouraging other people to talk. And he listened to what they had to say."

In the first days after the Liberals won, Regan and Akerman talked frequently by phone. "He asked me what kind of office space we were looking for, what kind of legislation we were interested in, that sort of thing." But he insists Regan didn't offer him — as was rumoured at the time — the post of labour minister in his new government. He didn't have to. "He and we saw ourselves as basically on the same side," says Akerman. Besides, after fighting mainly Tories for seats in Cape Breton, he was loath to do anything to keep the Conservatives in power.

In the end, Regan didn't need the NDP's support to survive. G. I. Smith had suffered a heart attack while on a post-election vacation in Bermuda in November. That kept him away from the legislature. Meanwhile, the courts overturned a close Tory victory in another riding, reducing the effective Tory strength to just nineteen seats.* Even after appointing a Liberal MLA as Speaker of the House, Regan was confident he could survive any challenges to his new government.

Although many of his detractors still dismissed him — in the words of *The 4th Estate* — as an "accidental premier," Regan almost

---

* The Liberals won the subsequent by-election.

immediately began to act as if he had been born to the job. No longer good old Gabby, he began to call himself — and soon became known among his cabinet colleagues, staff, MLAs, and even the press and Opposition members as — "The Preem." When Regan's staff presented him with a sports jersey emblazoned with his nickname on the back, he wore it at work all that day.

As The Preem, he moved quickly to begin making good on his platform promises. The Liberals' initial legislative agenda mirrored Regan's own modestly reformist tendencies. "His was always very much an underdog approach," says Jeremy Akerman.

And Hilton Jarvis was Gerald Regan's favourite underdog.

Regan probably never met Jarvis, a poor black man from Weymouth Falls near Digby. During the sixties, Jarvis ended up in jail for the crime of not having enough money to pay his poll tax. The poll tax was an archaic "head tax" imposed on those who would otherwise pay no property or municipal taxes. It was, in effect, a tax for being too poor to have anything worth taxing. Although those who couldn't afford to pay it could theoretically be sent to jail, that rarely happened — except in cases where the offender was black. And then it was commonplace. "No white man was ever put in jail in Digby for not paying his poll tax," says Phillip Woolaver.

Woolaver, a Digby lawyer who'd developed a local reputation for taking on indigent black and native clients, remembers getting a call one day from the local jailer. "We got a nigger up here wants to talk to you," he said. The "nigger" was Hilton Jarvis. Given the tenor of the times, Woolaver ended up using his political clout rather than his legal smarts to get Jarvis out of jail. "The warden was a Liberal," Woolaver explains, "and he owed his position to being a Liberal. He knew I was a Liberal. And I had a reputation around the area for knowing some important Liberals — I knew Winters and MacEachen quite well, and I was with them whenever they were in town — so the warden knew what he should do."

The warden freed Jarvis.

But Woolaver, who thought the poll tax was offensive as well as discriminatory, complained about Jarvis's jailing to another well-connected Liberal friend, Opposition leader Gerald Regan. Regan soon began invoking Jarvis's name in his speeches and promised that, if elected, no more Hilton Jarvises would end up in jail for the crime of being poor.

During his new administration's first legislative session, Regan wasted little time in making good on that promise. And plenty of others too: his government created a new position of ombudsman to deal with complaints from individuals who believed they'd been treated unfairly by bureaucrats;* established a provincial law reform commission to bring the province's antiquated justice system at least into the beginnings of the twentieth century; reduced the age of majority from twenty-one to nineteen to bring more young people into the political process; set up night courts to make the legal system more accessible for working people; extended human rights protection to women by banning discrimination on the basis of gender;† ended the traditional practice of setting separate minimum wage levels for men and women; and provided, in theory at least, for modest levels of public funding for child care.

Regan also kept his promise to abolish the 7 percent sales tax on building materials that had been the central focus of his 1969 filibuster. And his government went even further to encourage more new home construction, including promoting development of affordable, serviced land in the suburbs outside Halifax, providing grants for new home construction, and launching a program to subsidize mortgage interest so families earning less than $4,000 a year could afford a home of their own.

Regan's personal interest in labour law was the driving force behind the government's efforts to overhaul the province's regressive Trade Union Act. Though his government took a tough line on the illegal strikes that had begun to wreak havoc in the construction industry, Regan also introduced changes designed to get labour and management in that volatile industry talking to one another *before* trouble developed. And he moved to give fishermen recognition as workers under the Trade Union Act.

---

*   Although Regan won plaudits for creating the post, he disappointed many when he appointed Harry Smith, a prominent Liberal who'd backed him for the leadership, as the first ombudsman. People were even more upset when Smith, in his first major test, refused to stand up against Garnet Brown, the highways minister, when a road worker claimed he'd been dismissed simply because he was a Tory.

†   The victory for women was by no means complete, however. The law did not apply to credit-granting or rentals where women were still regarded as second-class citizens.

As he had promised in his election platform, Regan set up a Royal Commission on Education, Public Services, and Provincial-Municipal Relations, which he described at the time as "the most comprehensive study of its type ever undertaken in Canada."

But the most controversial decision of Regan's first term in office — and one that would cost him his hope for a third term — had never even been mentioned in his 1970 platform.

On December 3, 1971, the government stunned the province's business community by announcing it was offering to buy all of the shares of the province's largest privately owned electric power utility, the venerable Nova Scotia Light & Power, and fold it into the much smaller and publicly owned crown corporation, the Nova Scotia Power Commission.

Nova Scotia Light & Power was perhaps the most establishment of Nova Scotia's establishment companies. Its chairman, Colonel J. C. MacKeen, was a celebrated industrialist, a key player in the development of Scotia Square and the honorary chair of Nova Scotia's Industrial Estates Limited. At one point or another in its history, the NSLP board had boasted virtually every member of the province's corporate elite — from industrialist Roy Jodrey to super-market tycoon Frank Sobey to real estate developer Charles McCulloch to lawyer and dealmaker Frank Covert.

Over the years, the company had become profitable by concentrating its efforts on providing electricity to the easy-to-service urban areas of the province, leaving the more expensive and difficult-to-serve rural areas to the publicly funded NSPC. During the previous decade, in fact, the Crown corporation had been forced to swallow one small, unprofitable local utility after another — in Pictou, Glace Bay, Bridgewater, Dominion, Amherst, and Glace Bay — simply so the people in those communities could continue to have electricity.

Now, the Power Commission was facing the prospect of having to spend millions more to upgrade the provincial power grid to serve those communities, but without the benefit of the profits NSLP was generating as a result of its urban monopoly.

Given the critical importance of electric power to everyday life — and the reality that governments could use electricity rates as an industrial development lever — most other provinces had already long since nationalized their private power companies. By 1970, in fact, 90 percent of Canadians were served by public utilities. Nova Scotia, too, had considered complete public ownership back in the 1930s when Angus L. Macdonald had legislation drafted to accomplish a complete takeover. He abandoned the idea after intense lobbying from private interests.

Regan didn't give those private interests the chance to change his mind. With a secrecy and cleverness that Frank Covert, one of the takeover's most implacable foes, would later describe as "magnificent," Regan quietly assembled a block of about 35 percent of the company's 5,000,000 outstanding shares — giving the government effective control of the company anyway — and then simply announced what amounted to a take-it-or-leave-it proposition to shareholders. The government-owned utility offered shareholders thirteen dollars a share, about four dollars above market value, and gave them until January 24, 1972, to decide.

The takeover outraged the company. The NSLP president, Russell Harrington, denounced it as "socialistic." Major shareholders publicly accused Regan of "a high-handed assault on the free enterprise system." In private, says Harry Bruce, who has written biographies of several of the principals, their criticisms were even more barbed. "They called [Regan] everything from a liar to a Communist."

Regan and his advisers, on the other hand, saw the decision as simple common sense.* The province's power grid needed a major upgrade. One strong utility would have the clout to carry it out; two smaller rivals wouldn't. Regan himself says he would have been just as happy if Nova Scotia Light & Power had taken over Nova Scotia Power, but he didn't see that as likely, so the government decided to go ahead on its own.

The issue created major splits in the Liberal party. Frank Covert, for one, had reason to be angry at what he considered Regan's ingratitude. "What was particularly galling" to the Liberal insider, writes Harry Bruce in *Corporate Navigator*, "was that Regan would not have sought the Liberal leadership, which he parlayed into the

---

* Although it was probably not a determining factor, a number of Regan's associates say his antipathy to Nova Scotia Light & Power dated back to his childhood in the Depression, when the local private utility cut off electricity to his father's store on several occasions.

premiership, if Frank hadn't set up a trust fund to give him a decent salary."

While that is debatable, what is beyond dispute is how personal the battle became. It certainly "spilled a lot of blood" between Regan and Covert. As Gerry Godsoe, a Regan adviser and Covert law partner, put it in an interview with Bruce, Regan bitterly came to regard his onetime benefactor "as part of the Halifax establishment, as one of those guys who gathered at the Halifax Club every day for lunch and thought the world of Bob Stanfield."

Although most of the wounds eventually healed, the takeover generated such hostilities during that holiday season Michael Kirby remembers he stopped accepting invitations to Christmas parties because he got tired of being accosted by angry business friends.

Perhaps predictably, the Halifax *Chronicle-Herald* finally found its voice, fuelling public anger by claiming wrongly that provincial taxpayers would be on the hook for the full $66 million the takeover was expected to cost, hinting darkly that the government wouldn't compensate municipalities for any losses when the newly nationalized utilities stopped paying property taxes and wondering loudly where all this socialism was leading. The paper even published coupons for outraged readers to fill out and mail to the premier to let him know how much they opposed the takeover.

In fact, most of the general public didn't seem all that exercised by the takeover at the time. The premier's office reported it received slightly more than one hundred of the coupons in the mail. The public's anger with the takeover — and with Regan — would only finally manifest itself much later, after the 1973 Arab oil embargo forced Nova Scotia Power to dramatically increase electricity rates. Because the province was so heavily dependent on oil to generate electricity, it wouldn't have made any difference who ran the utility; prices would have gone up anyway. But the fact that Regan had taken over the power company shortly before rates had gone through the roof would eventually make his government a convenient scapegoat for public anger.

The only other issue that generated such an editorial outcry during Regan's first term also involved what the formerly quiescent Halifax *Herald*'s editorial board saw as another socialistic money grab by Regan and his government.

The background was fairly straightforward. As part of its 1971 tax reform package, Ottawa had decided to give up imposing inheritance taxes on the estates of the wealthy and replace it with what it claimed would be a fairer tax, on capital gains. The problem for provincial governments was that the federal government had shared revenues from estate taxes with the provinces. Although it planned to share the take from the capital gains tax too, it planned to phase the new tax in over a period of time. Like a number of other provinces, Regan's government decided to step into the breach with a transitory succession duty and gift tax on the estates of the wealthy in order to make sure the province didn't lose tax revenues during the period before the capital gains tax was fully in force.

Although the actual number of people who would be affected by the new tax was expected to be ridiculously few — about 200 a year, according to the province's Department of Finance — the *Herald* was apoplectic. "Canadians were led to believe they had seen the last of the dreadful, confiscatory estate tax system, which deprived a man's children of that which he had worked all his life to provide," the newspaper raged. Now the Regan government had decided "to smuggle the estate tax back under the guise of a new name. . . . The government is imposing on itself the onerous, perhaps impossible task of explaining to and convincing people inside and outside Nova Scotia that, despite the government's actions in respect of these taxes, private investment is needed and is welcome in this province."

In the end, Regan's Liberals weathered the newspaper's attacks and the tax legislation became law. Few in the province noticed; fewer still were affected.

WHILE MUCH OF WHAT the Liberals did in their first term would certainly qualify as progressive, there certainly were several important exceptions.

Perhaps none was more puzzling than the government's relationship with Allen Stockall and his Nova Scotia Operators, Journeymen, and Labourers' Union. Stockall, a onetime Dartmouth alderman, was among the most intriguing and mysterious characters in Nova Scotia politics in the seventies. The Operators' Union was his creation, and it became the underpinning for his own unlikely career as a municipal politician and a businessman.

His story begins in the late fifties when the International Association of Machinists decided to try to organize Nova Scotia highways workers. At the time, those low-paid, mostly seasonal workers who cleared the snow after storms, spread the sand and salt, carried the gravel, and otherwise made sure the province's roads were in good repair in winter and summer, were pawns of whatever party was in power. When governments changed, so did the district highway foreman, whose chief qualification inevitably was being a supporter of the government of the day. Then the foreman, in cahoots with the government MLA or road committee, fired every known or suspected supporter of the previous government and replaced each of them with one of their own party loyalists.

The IAM sent one of its Moncton field representatives to Halifax soon after Robert Stanfield's Tories took power in 1956 to scout out the prospects for organizing the highways workers. At the Fairview Garage of the Department of Highways, the union field rep met an ambitious, enthusiastic young stock clerk named Allen Stockall who agreed to help him recruit new members.

Although the two men successfully signed up a significant number of the more than one thousand highways department workers, there was no provision in the province's Trade Union Act to permit government employees to join a union. Instead, the IAM hoped to use its success in recruiting the workers to convince the Tories to agree ' to some sort of voluntary recognition. But the Stanfield government balked at the idea. It was leery of making a deal with what it saw as a powerful international union.

So Stockall decided to make his own deal. He had a lawyer draw up a constitution for a new independent union — the Nova Scotia Operators, Journeymen, and Labourers' Union — which vested virtually all power in his hands. He convinced workers who had signed cards with the machinists to join his fledgling union instead and then secretly negotiated an arrangement under which the government agreed to recognize his new union as the workers' representative. In return, the cabinet order-in-council that sealed the deal forbade the workers from striking to back up their new so-called bargaining powers.

In April 1971, shortly after the Liberals came to power, Stockall unilaterally more than doubled union dues to $10.50 per month, ostensibly to fund investigations if the new Liberal administration decided to fire anyone.* When some workers complained they hadn't been consulted about the increase and asked Stockall to hold an annual meeting, he refused.

To make matters worse, the workers hadn't gotten a raise in years, either. Some had walked off their jobs in 1969 to protest what they claimed were wages so low they had to go on welfare in order to survive.

Stockall appeared to be thriving. In the early sixties, he won election to Dartmouth City Council, where he became a close personal and political ally of the town's Tory mayor, I. W. Akerley, who would later become the province's highways minister. And the provincial Tories appointed Stockall to the province's Liquor Licence Board, a powerful agency that decided who would get lucrative licences to operate bars or taverns.

Despite his position as president of the highways workers' union, Stockall took no role in the province's Federation of Labour and, in fact, publicly described himself as a "businessman" rather than a labour leader.

Questions about Stockall and his operation of the union finally bubbled over into the public prints in May 1971. During a legislature committee hearing, he said he had made some threatening statements attributed to him at a meeting with highways workers, but not — as had been alleged — in response to questions about the union's finances. "I anticipated something like this," he had told a group he had agreed to meet at the department's mechanical branch garage in Fairview on the outskirts of Halifax. He was accompanied to the meeting by two men apparently connected with the International Teamster's Union.

Stockall told the legislative committee, "A gentleman in the back of the room said something to the effect that he wanted a financial statement. Someone to the left said, 'Now we are going to get you.'" Stockall's reply had been directed to this latter speaker, he said.

A number of highways workers decided to start looking elsewhere

---

* The new government did fire twenty-nine of the thirty-two highways superintendents and an unknown number of workers, but Stockall did little to protest.

for representation; soon both the Canadian Union of Public Employees and the Nova Scotia Civil Service Association had launched campaigns to recruit Stockall's members to their unions.

Given Stockall's Tory connections and his intensifying battle with Regan's allies in organized labour, you might have expected Stockall would have been *persona non grata* with the new Liberal administration.

You would have been wrong.

Within days of the Regan victory, Stockall began distancing himself from the Tories and cozying up to the Liberals, including — especially — the new minister of highways, Garnet Brown. Stockall became one of the Liberal party's largest contributors, targeting key cabinet ministers, including Brown and Peter Nicholson, for large donations.

For whatever reason, Brown became Stockall's strongest champion at the cabinet table. Nicholson wasn't far behind.* Regan, for his part, tried his best to keep his distance from the growing dispute over the highways workers. That became more complicated after the Civil Service Association began signing up highways workers. The association was headed by Regan's good friend and first labour ally, Tom Shiers.

When CUPE officials sent Regan a telegram in late August 1971 claiming they had signed up the majority of highways workers and asking his government to pass an order-in-council similar to the deal it had with Stockall, Regan ignored them. Just as he did a second telegram asking for a meeting with Regan and Brown so the union could show them copies of the signed cards it had from the province's road workers.

Brown was not nearly as reticent. He insisted to reporters he'd seen no proof CUPE had signed up the workers but he refused to meet with its officials to examine the cards. "I judge the men on their past performance," Brown blandly told reporters. "If there's a big snowstorm or something and the roads are cleared promptly, that's

---

* Arnie Patterson, a prominent Dartmouth Liberal, says he remembers having dinner with Nicholson one night when the finance minister raised the question of why the media "were being so hard on poor Allen. I said, 'Oh no, not you too, Peter.' I couldn't understand why so many Liberals were taking up the Stockall cause."

how I judge the men. We've had pretty good performance out of the men under this union in the past and I'm going to continue to negotiate a contract with them." In fact, he began negotiating with Stockall for a new three-year contract to replace the union's current minimum-wage deal when it expired March 31, 1972. Stockall claimed to the press that he was demanding a 45 percent increase in the workers' $1.25 an hour wages; the government had already announced it wouldn't go higher than 5 percent in negotiations with other workers. It did. Brown and Stockall signed an agreement allegedly providing for a 42 percent wage increase.

The NDP's two-member caucus continued to pepper the government with embarrassing questions and stunning revelations. At one point, for example, Regan informed reporters he hadn't received "a single letter [from] a dissatisfied highways worker, even anonymously. If there is a highways worker with a grievance against this union," he added, "tell them to write me and I'll certainly look into the matter." A few days later, Akerman stood up in the house and tabled more than 500 signed letters from highways workers expressing dissatisfaction with Stockall's union. "Regan blanched noticeably," reported *The 4th Estate*.

In September 1972, with the issue refusing to disappear, Regan finally took action, shuffling Brown out of the highways portfolio, replacing him with the anti-Stockall Len Pace, and then announcing plans — at the annual meeting of the Nova Scotia Federation of Labour — for a free vote among highways workers on which union they wanted.

CUPE won the vote handily* and the government agreed to give it the same order-in-council recognition it had previously offered Stockall's union.

THE HIGHWAYS WORKERS dispute wasn't the only one in which Regan's personal relations with organized labour were put to a severe test during his first term. Early in 1971, Michelin Tire officials let his new government know they were upset about delays in constructing their

---

* The official results of the three-way race: CUPE, 882; Operators' Union, 297; Civil Service Association, 218.

new Nova Scotia tire-making plant, and began threatening to take their tires and their jobs and go elsewhere.

During the late sixties, the previous government had lured the giant French multinational to set up shop in Nova Scotia with a combination of low-interest loans, outright grants, and tax incentives so generous one economist later described the package as "an offer that could not be refused." But there'd been a spate of illegal work stoppages during construction of the plant that had delayed its opening, and Michelin officials now wanted the new government to take immediate action to get the project back on the rails.

Robert Manuge, the former head of Industrial Estates Limited who'd handled the original negotiations to bring Michelin to Nova Scotia, remembers being called to one Saturday morning meeting in the Cabinet Room near Regan's office. He, Regan, Peter Nicholson, and Michelin's Nova Scotia lawyer, Hector McInnes, tried to figure out what they could do to placate Michelin. Regan, Manuge says with obvious distaste even today, showed up for the session dishevelled, "with his shirt tail out," and joked that he'd spent the night playing poker at a well-known private gambling den on Quinpool Road. Whatever his successes at poker the night before, Regan certainly knew better than to gamble on calling the French tiremaker's bluff.

A few months later, in May 1971, Regan flew to France to meet face to face with François Michelin. A month after that, he called an emergency session of the legislature to push through a new law outlawing picketing at construction projects valued at over $5 million and forcing unions to submit any unresolved disputes to arbitration after thirty days. Regan acknowledged that the law — which also required "pre-start" bargaining on future major construction projects — had been written specifically for Michelin, but he managed to defuse an open confrontation with labour both by appealing personally to his friends in the leadership and also by making the point — rightly, as even many labour leaders agreed — that continuing disruptions in the province's volatile construction industry were beginning to scare off investment.

But the emergency session turned out to be just the first of several occasions when Regan would appear to go out of his way to do

Michelin's union-bashing. Michelin, which London's *Financial Times* once described as "anti-union by instinct and paternalistic by practice," wanted as little as possible to do with any union at its new Nova Scotia operation. In 1970, it even paid Nova Scotia tradesmen $250,000 to stay away from the company's construction site while it brought in its own non-union workers from France to install proprietary equipment.

Trade unionists, not surprisingly, saw Michelin's anti-unionism as a challenge, and its several thousand well-paid employees as an organizing opportunity. The labour movement's initial strategy was to organize each specialty unit within each plant separately, using its success among those units to help it spread the good word to the rest of the plant's employees. By mid-1973, the International Operating Engineers' Union, which had quietly signed up a majority of the company's twenty power plant operators, prepared to ask the province's Labour Relations Board to formally certify the union as the stationary engineers' bargaining agent. Just before the union could present its case, however, the Regan cabinet rushed through a special order-in-council, making it impossible for any union to be certified unless it had signed up a majority of all the workers in the plant. Later, again to insulate Michelin — but this time against the possibility a union might actually succeed in signing up a majority of workers in one plant — Regan changed the rules once more to eliminate provisions in the Trade Union Act providing for automatic certification of a union that could demonstrate it had signed up a majority of workers.

REGAN'S DEFERENTIAL, almost reverential treatment of the Michelins following his 1971 meeting with François Michelin highlighted an important aspect of his character: he took an obsequious, almost groupie-like delight in cultivating — and then bragging about — his friendships with the world's wealthiest and most powerful figures. Regan, as his onetime adviser Brian Flemming once said, "prided himself on being able to talk with kings and commoners and say both of them are 'my kind of guys.'"

And gals. Robert Manuge remembers how badly Regan, during a trip to Asia, wanted to meet Indira Gandhi, the Indian prime minister. "He got me to prevail upon Mr. Jolly [an India-based entre-preneur whom IEL had convinced to establish a hardboard plant in Chester during the sixties] to find some way to get him in to see Mrs. Gandhi," Manuge remembers. "He did, and Gerry was very excited."

Regan was also "a big project guy" who, Flemming says, served as his own minister of development "no matter who held the title." That gave him plenty of opportunity to cultivate the rich and powerful. And he did. He combined his 1971 visit to the Michelins, for example, with a globe-trotting industrial development promotion tour that allowed him to rub shoulders with the likes of international financier Baron Edmond de Rothschild. Regan, says Jeremy Akerman, often referred later to the baron in conversation as "Eddie." By the spring of the following year, Regan was holding secret meetings to talk about plans for a "multi-million-dollar chem-ical processing operation in the Strait of Canso" with John Shaheen, a flamboyant New York wheeler-dealer-developer, who was in the process of building an oil refinery project for Joey Smallwood in Newfoundland. The next year, he flew to Skorpios, Aristotle Onassis's private island, for a personal meeting with the Greek shipping tycoon to discuss whether he might invest in industrial development in Nova Scotia. Photographs showing the premier and his wife hobnobbing with Ari and his wife Jackie, the glamorous widow of John Kennedy, eventually found their way into the Australian edition of *Women's Day*.

Regan, of course, wasn't unique among politicians of his era, especially among politicians from have-not regions, in his conviction that he could find economic salvation for his province in the arms of the maker of the latest mega-project. "It was the mentality of the country at the time," points out Michael Kirby, "a view that government could solve anything if it put enough money into it, and that mega-projects were the way to go in economic development."

While that was certainly true — one only needs to look at Stanfield's heavy water and Clairtone disasters for evidence close at hand — Regan stood apart, even among the political crowd of his day, just because of how much he seemed to personally revel in his connections with the world's movers and shakers.

"He was a superb salesman and he knew the importance of

personal relationships in getting things done," insists Kirby, but even he is forced to concede that "obviously, Gerry had a hell of a lot of fun doing it too."

Despite the Liberals' 1970 campaign slogan that industrial development should be a science and not a lottery, the Regan government's approach to attracting industry was haphazard and whimsical, more the result of Regan's inspirations and chance meetings than of any organized approach to developing the province economically. The problem was that none of it produced the desired results; certainly nothing of substance in the way of industry or jobs.

Take tidal power, for example. "It sometimes seemed that Fundy Tidal Power and Gerald Regan had been waiting all these years only for one another," wrote Harry Bruce in a tongue-in-cheek debunking of Regan's "Great Fundy Hot Air Project" in the August 1971 issue of *Saturday Night.*

There was nothing new about Maritime politicians dreaming of harnessing the powerful tides of the Bay of Fundy in order to generate pollution-free, inflation-proof electricity that could not only fuel the industrial development of their province but also serve as a kind of perpetual electrical cash crop that could be exported for profit to the power-hungry U.S. eastern seaboard.

But in late 1969, the federally funded Atlantic Tidal Power Programming Board reluctantly concluded, after a three-year feasibility study, that the project wasn't viable.

None of that daunted Gerald Regan, who continued to describe Fundy Tidal Power grandly as a "horizontal Churchill Falls" and talked excitedly about "the inevitability of vast profits" that would flow from its development.

His ace in the hole in moving the project forward was to be his new-found "friendship" with Edmond de Rothschild.

In April 1971, Regan triumphantly appointed R. B. Cameron, a successful Nova Scotia industrialist who'd previously headed up the provincial rescue of the Sydney Steel Corporation, as president of a new $10 million Nova Scotia Tidal Power Corporation. Its role, Regan explained, would be to oversee development of the project, which Regan made sound close to a *fait accompli.* Hinting that some of the world's most important private financial interests were keen to get involved in the project, he informed reporters that negotiations had already reached the "deadly serious stage."

As if to underscore the point, Regan arranged for a highly publicized meeting with Rothschild in France during what the *Chronicle-Herald* described as Regan's "personal inspection tour of the world's major successful tidal power project"* at Little Rance River on the coast of Brittany. During the trip, he and his entourage — which included so many government ministers, officials, and their families, Bruce said, it "must have looked to the French like the entire government of a large country" — met with a number of what were described as potential tidal power investors, including Regan's good friend Eddie de Rothschild.

By the time he returned to North America, Regan was happy to tell American reporters in New York he was "extremely optimistic. . . . I would hope to place a target date of 1980 for major development of tide energy to come on stream."

Even before the ink was dry on those predictions, however, the Baron was doing his best to distance himself from his new-found friend. While conceding that the project sounded "interesting and feasible," he offered wisely in an interview from London that "a whole host of factors are unknown."

However one wanted to parse that phrase, the reality was that Regan's Big Plans for Fundy Tidal Power went nowhere.

Regan had no more luck persuading Aristotle Onassis to establish an oil refinery at the Strait of Canso. Despite a flurry of publicity, discussions between the province and the industrialist never got much beyond the what-if stage.

Negotiations with John Shaheen went much further than that, but they too collapsed without producing any refinery or, more importantly, any jobs.

Shaheen, the grandson of a Lebanese businessman who had migrated to the United States in 1863, was an ambitious fifty-seven-year-old entrepreneur. He'd built a successful business empire by employing his considerable salesman's charms, tapping his family's

---

* The Associated Press was less carried away with the project's success: It referred to the Rance River tidal power project as "a fine tourist attraction and a dandy bridge."

financial connections in the U.S., Britain, and the Middle East and establishing a personal pipeline to Middle Eastern oil suppliers. President Richard Nixon, who introduced him to Prime Minister Trudeau at a 1969 White House reception as "the world's greatest salesman," appointed him commissioner of the United States Petroleum Council. That same year he signed a controversial deal with Newfoundland Premier Joey Smallwood to build a $155-million refinery at Come-by-Chance. The day that deal was announced three key members of Smallwood's cabinet, including John Crosbie, resigned, claiming the agreement was bad for the province.

Shaheen's Newfoundland refinery was still in the final stages of construction when he visited Halifax in May 1972 to talk with Regan about his interest in building yet another refinery, this time at the Strait of Canso. The strait, which separates Cape Breton from the mainland, boasted one of the few ports on the eastern seaboard that could handle the new generation of giant, ocean-going oil tankers. Shaheen's plan was to import crude oil from the Middle East in huge tankers, refine it at this new refinery, and then ship the finished product in smaller vessels to markets in the U.S. and central Canada.

But, as in Newfoundland, Shaheen wanted to build his new refinery — which was to be capable of refining 200,000 barrels of oil a day and cost $200 million — with as little of his own money as possible.

Publicly, Regan insisted his government wasn't willing to provide any grants to Shaheen and would only agree to guarantee one-sixth of the cost — about $35 million — on a first-mortgage basis. Regan didn't bother to point out, of course, that the province had already agreed to ante up $30 million to build a new dock at Mulgrave, whose chief — and perhaps only — customer would be Shaheen.

For Regan, however, that investment seemed a fair trade for the jobs Shaheen promised he would create. During its two-year construction — conveniently expected to overlap with Regan's first re-election bid — the refinery project was supposed to generate 2,000 short-term jobs, while work on the dock would provide employment for another 300 construction workers. When the refinery was up and running, it would need a staff of more than 550 technicians and managers, most of them skilled and well-paid.

Even more important than the refinery itself, Shaheen suggested, could be the spin-offs that would naturally follow the development of the refinery and the wharf. During the November 1972 press conference to announce their refinery deal, a beaming Regan turned to Shaheen and asked him to paint reporters a word picture of what the Strait of Canso might look like in fifteen years. "Have you ever seen the strip running from New York to Pittsburgh, or the development from Dallas to Fort Worth?" an effusive Shaheen asked. "In fifteen years from now, you could see fifteen billion of investment in the Strait area."

That press conference was the closest the refinery — or any of the other possible projects touted by Regan and Shaheen — came to reality. There were delays while Shaheen's company argued with construction unions over the terms of a contract; seemingly inevitable cost escalations that forced Shaheen to go back to his various backers, including Regan, and re-jig his financing arrangements; just as inevitable political bickering over which level of government should pay for the common user dock Regan had pledged to build and who should get credit for its construction; and more than a few pointed questions about whether North America, in the suddenly energy-conserving, post-oil-embargo world of the mid-seventies, really needed another refinery to supply it with Middle Eastern petroleum products.

The real problem for Shaheen's Nova Scotia refinery, however, was Shaheen's Newfoundland refinery. When it officially opened in 1973, Shaheen chartered the luxury liner the *Queen Elizabeth II* to sail more than one thousand guests, including such luminaries as the conservative literary icon William F. Buckley, Jr., and the pollster George Gallup, from New York to Come-by-Chance for the lavish opening ceremony.

But the refinery was plagued from its start-up by a variety of technical and production gaffes that kept it from reaching peak production. At the same time, a worldwide glut of oil suddenly made the project uneconomic. In 1975, its creditors pushed the operation into receivership. With debts of more than $600 million, it was the biggest insolvency in Canada. While Shaheen spent most of the next decade caught up in a blizzard of lawsuits and court actions in an unsuccessful battle to win back control of the company, his troubles in Newfoundland ended any hope he might have had of moving forward with his Nova Scotia project.

And his friendship with Regan as well.

When Shaheen showed up in Halifax for a meeting with Regan in the summer of 1978, *Maclean's* magazine reports, Regan was at pains to distance himself from Shaheen. "Regan," the magazine reported, "flatly denied the province would in any way get tangled up with a man behind the multi-million-dollar flop in Newfoundland."

IF REGAN'S FIRST TERM as premier failed to produce prosperity, his own fortunes certainly improved. In the fall of 1970, he and Carole and their still growing family moved from their modest house on Berlin Street in the working-class west end of Halifax to fancy new quarters on fashionable Shore Drive. The rambling, six-bedroom house located on seven acres of prime real estate overlooking the Bedford Basin would eventually boast a tennis court and in-ground swimming pool.

Years later, in 1996, Tammy Connors testified that she babysat for the Regans in that period. In 1995, Gerald Regan was charged with sexually assaulting her. These charges were stayed in April 1998, by a decision that the Crown is appealing.

According to her evidence at the preliminary inquiry, Tammy Connors remembers being delighted when Carole Regan called to ask if she would babysit her children for a few hours one night in 1971. She was then a sixteen-year-old high school student, and had a major homework project she hoped the province's new premier might be willing to give her a few pointers on. Unfortunately, Mr. Regan wasn't at home when she arrived that night, so she made do with small talk with Mrs. Regan instead.

Though the Regans had only recently moved into the neighbourhood, this was the second time Tammy had been asked to babysit for them. Her first job for the family — for a few hours one summer afternoon when Mr. Regan was at work — had passed without incident, and she saw no reason why this assignment shouldn't go just as smoothly.

The *babysitting* did, at any rate. Since most of the Regan children were now old enough to take care of themselves — Gerry, Jr., was fifteen — Tammy's role was simply to act as a support person in case something went wrong. That meant she was able to spend most of the evening quietly watching television and doing her homework.

When Gerry and Carole Regan returned home shortly after 11:30, Mr. Regan was quick to offer Tammy a drive back to her home at the other end of Shore Drive.

She later described how Regan, with his right arm casually stretched across the top of the car's front seat and his left on the wheel, drove in the direction of Tammy's house, which was about a mile from the Regans'. But then, about midway down the dirt road — at a point where there were no street lights — he suddenly stopped the car and shifted the transmission into park.

"I couldn't figure out why," Tammy would testify at Regan's preliminary hearing, "so I looked behind to see what was wrong. All of a sudden, his left hand grabbed my chin and he was on top of me. He stuck his tongue down my throat and he grabbed my breast." She could smell alcohol on his breath. Though his legs stayed on the driver's side of the car, she felt the upper part of his body as an oppressive weight on her. "He was very driven, very aggressive, assaultive," she told the court. "There was something he wanted to accomplish."

Though she was only five-feet-four-inches tall and a little under 125 pounds at the time, there was something Tammy desperately wanted to accomplish too. Using the strength and agility that had helped earn her the title of female athlete of the year at Bedford's Sidney Stephen High School, Tammy managed to push Regan off her.

But then, as suddenly as he had come on to her, Regan stopped, and resumed driving her home as if nothing had happened. Tammy pressed herself as close as she could to the passenger side door, holding onto the door handle, just waiting for the moment when she could escape. When they did finally — it seemed to her to take forever — pull up in front of her house, Regan was almost eerily calm. She claims he handed her her payment for babysitting and told her: "This will be our little secret."

Tammy, upset and crying, immediately woke her parents to tell them what she claimed the premier had just done to her.

Then she went into the bathroom and, still crying, began to brush her teeth. Over and over again. She wanted desperately to brush away the smell and taste of Gerald Regan, she testified. She couldn't.

Though she didn't go into details about what she claimed Regan had done to her, Donald and Alma Connors were shocked by their daughter's elliptical description of Regan's behaviour. He was, after all, not simply a neighbour, not just a lawyer, not only a politician, but the premier of Nova Scotia — the most important and powerful politician in the province.

How could he?

They couldn't let him get away with it.

The next day, according to what he told Tammy and two other witnesses, Donald Connors himself telephoned Regan to demand an apology on his daughter's behalf. He didn't get one. In fact, he told police, Regan seemed almost blasé about the whole incident, which he didn't deny. "It's OK," Connors claims Regan told him. "I was drinking."

Still not satisfied but mindful that they didn't want to make an already bad situation worse for their daughter, Donald and Alma Connors sought out a family friend, Senator Fred Blois, a former Tory opposition leader in the pre-Stanfield era, and asked him for his advice. Blois directed them to G. I. Smith, the former Tory premier.

When they went to visit him at his office in Truro a month later, Smith was sympathetic but hardly encouraging. He took down the information they provided about what they said happened to Tammy, told them he would put it in a file "with all the other similar complaints" he'd received about Regan, and then advised them pointedly to forget it all. It would only end up blackening Tammy's reputation if it came out now, he said, but added prophetically: "Someday, these things will come to the surface."

It would take nearly twenty-five more years but Smith's prediction turned out to be correct.

For her part, Tammy never babysat for the Regans again. "A few weeks later, I was with some friends and Mrs. Regan drove by. She stopped the car and asked me to babysit. I told her I wasn't going to babysit again. Ever."

GERALD REGAN ENDED his first term in office much as he had begun it — with a visit to Dr. Clarence Gosse. But there were several important differences between the October 1970 post-victory visit to

Gosse's country estate to plot his new government's future and this February 1974 visit to Gosse's digs at Government House to ask him to issue the writ for a general election. For starters, of course, Gosse in 1970 was just one of many defeated Liberal candidates whose contributions needed to be recognized, or wounded egos restored. Now, thanks in no small part to Regan's urgings to Prime Minister Trudeau, Gosse was the province's lieutenant governor. And, whereas the 1970 meeting had involved an intense gathering of party insiders, the 1974 visit was merely an official fifteen-minute courtesy call to inform Gosse of his decision to call an election for April 2 and to ask him to formally sign the writ. If back in 1970 Regan was still getting over the shock of having been elected, he would have been even more shocked in 1974 if he did not win the upcoming campaign with a much increased majority.

There was one other important difference between the two meetings, though neither Regan nor Gosse would probably have noted it at the time. Donald Ripley, the Liberal fundraiser who'd been miffed by his treatment during the 1970 meeting, was not only not a party to the 1974 meeting he was no longer a Liberal. He'd become a key Tory fundraiser and he was seeking revenge.

But the taste of sweet revenge would not — as even Ripley knew — come in 1974. "Regan," as he wrote sadly in his memoirs, "could have won if he stayed at home."

For all its minor missteps, Regan and his ministers had provided Nova Scotians with generally competent government. The books were balanced, the economy was growing, and there was the promise — off in the ever-growing distance — that one of Gerald Regan's Grand Plans might still come to fruition. Although his government had already begun to lose the sense of direction it had in its first two years, Regan wisely ran on his government's overall record — he claimed to have added up his government's accomplishments during its first term and come up with a total of 300 of them — and on the mostly vague promise of more of the same to come.

Regan knew the next government would face serious financial difficulties because of the impact of the 1973 Arab oil embargo on world oil prices. Because Nova Scotia was almost entirely dependent on oil for its power generation and because Regan had taken over the private power utility just before prices began to gush upward, he knew he would ultimately — if unfairly — be blamed for increasing electrical costs. To put off that day of reckoning, Regan's government provided short-term subsidies to the power corporation in 1974 to help it keep rates down for the time being and then moved quickly to call an election before events — and costs — could catch up with him.

Regan's prospects in 1974 were undoubtedly helped by the Tories' internecine battles too. John Buchanan, a glad-handing Spryfield lawyer who'd served briefly as fisheries minister in the final days of the last Tory regime, had won the 1971 leadership convention called to replace Ike Smith. But his victory split the party badly. Buchanan finished third — and last — on the first ballot. But then the first-ballot runner-up, Roland Thornhill, the popular mayor of Dartmouth, suddenly withdrew his candidacy and surprised everyone by offering to support Buchanan in the next round. Their combined forces then defeated the first-ballot leader, Gerald Doucet, a bright young Cape Breton lawyer who'd served as Stanfield's minister of education.*

If the steady-as-she-goes theme of the Liberal campaign seemed in touch with the electoral mood, the Tory campaign — based on an upbeat Bobby-Gimby-like theme song, "Honest, It's John for Nova Scotia," and a confusing collection of extravagant promises — quickly turned into the butt of Liberal campaign jokes.

In the end, the Liberals only increased their share of the popular vote by 2 percent from 1970 but the NDP doubled its vote to 13 percent, and all of those votes came at the expense of Buchanan's Tories. When the votes were counted, Regan's Liberals, with thirty-one seats, had a comfortable majority; the NDP, with one additional seat, appeared to be on the upswing; and the Tories, their representation in the legislature having plummeted from twenty-one to twelve seats, were in disarray.

John Buchanan, like Gerald Regan before him, would soon have to fight off the wolves in own party who wanted to toss him aside

---

* Despite their political differences, Regan and Doucet were good friends. During Regan's sex crimes trial, Doucet, who had gone on to become an Ottawa-based lobbyist during the Mulroney era, became a continuing presence in the courtroom — offering advice to Regan's lawyer as well as comfort to the family and companionship to Regan himself — and one of the key organizers of Regan's legal defence fund.

for failing to lead them to immediate victory. Like Regan, Buchanan would also survive that challenge, and become stronger. And finally, like Regan again, he would win the next election, not so much because of anything he had done but because the party in power — in this case Gerald Regan's Liberals — had self-destructed for him.

7

Time Out: Gerry and Me 2

During his first term in office, Gerald Regan and I crossed paths a few times while he was trotting the globe promoting Nova Scotia as a great place for a petrochemical complex or a Fundy Tidal Power project and I was trotting the city from journalism joe-job to journalism joe-job in radio, print, and eventually television.

It wasn't until the fall of 1974 that I bumped up against that invisible power again. By then, I was one of the hosts of *Here Today*, CBC-TV's Halifax supper-hour news and current affairs program, and Regan, having been re-elected that spring with an increased majority, was beginning his second term as premier.

He'd come into the studio that evening for a routine, post-legislature session interview about the state of the province. I wasn't expecting much. Long before media consultants began teaching their clients how to morph difficult questions into softball serves for whatever company line the interviewee was pitching, Gerry Regan was already a past master of the art. He was, of course, a former professional sportscaster who knew better than most the limitations of the live interview and could usually out-talk even the most insistent of interviewers. He wasn't known as Gabby for nothing.

Before the interview began, Regan sat slouched in his chair, apparently distracted by matters more important than talking to me. He didn't seem any more interested in this interview than I was.

My first, rather rambling question had something to do with problems Regan was facing on the industrial development front. Despite the premier's best efforts at salesmanship, I pointed out, none of his Big Deals had been done and none seemed likely to come to fruition in the foreseeable future. What had gone wrong? I wanted to know.

I'm not sure whether it was my question that touched him off or if he'd simply been waiting for his opportunity to pounce. But pounce he did.

"You!" he said, sitting bolt upright in his chair and pointing a finger in my direction. "You and people like you, Steve, are what's wrong with this province." And he was off on a tirade about negative reporters, me especially, who had undermined his best efforts to bring development to the province. I was so surprised by the ferocity of his outburst I'm still not sure what I said in reply. I know I stammered. I know I smiled dumbly. I know we traded verbal blows for a while. It was, if nothing else, great television. In fact, the director was so pleased with it he quickly dropped other scheduled interviews and items from the show as it was going on to allow the dust-up to continue. When he was finally forced to break away for a commercial, the announcer, Frank Cameron, told viewers with a smile: "We'll be back with Round Two right after these messages."

If it was a boxing match, Regan had me on the ropes for most of it and certainly won on points. The CBC switchboard that night recorded twenty-seven calls about the interview, twenty-three of them criticizing me and expressing satisfaction, as one of them said, to "see Mr. Regan putting Kimber in his place."

When the interview mercifully ended and the cameras turned off, Regan was all smiles and good-natured bonhomie. "That was fun, Steve," he said to me. "We'll have to do that again soon."

Regan, I was beginning to realize, was no easy read.

His interest in being interviewed by me turned out to be short-lived.

In those immediate post-Watergate, post-Nixon resignation days, investigative reporting had developed a cachet, and I was as eager as anyone else to strut my stuff. Perhaps because of my earlier inability to tell the vote-buying story, I remained strangely intrigued by the seamy side of politics in Nova Scotia, including by the ways in which governments handed out contracts — usually without tender — to companies owned by friends of whatever party was in power.

I decided to take a look at the changing of the guard among suppliers that followed Regan's first victory in 1970. For the two years before the Liberals came to power and the two years after they took office, I examined the entries in the Supplement to the Public Accounts, an annual, publicly available department-by-department compilation of the names and billings of all suppliers of goods and services valued over a certain amount. By comparing those numbers, I figured I could get a handle on whether the government's favoured suppliers had changed dramatically between Tory and Liberal regimes.

They had.

According to the Supplement to the Public Accounts, the names of the companies doing business with the province in almost every category — from buying and leasing vehicles, to supplying meat and vegetables to local hospitals, to providing courier services, to offering legal and financial advice — changed in almost every government department between the 1969–70 report and the one for 1971–72, the Liberals' first full year in office. When we looked more closely at the companies involved, we discovered that the firms losing the business almost all had close ties to the Conservative party while those winning the business were — surprise, surprise — Liberal.

My research did confirm what virtually everyone in Nova Scotia already knew — that the Liberals were milking the system as ruthlessly and as systematically as the Tories had ever done, all the while claiming, like the Tories before them, to be cleaning up the system — but the reality was I didn't uncover anything especially shocking.*

Nonetheless, the Liberals — and especially Gerald Regan — weren't happy with me.

Regan had refused a number of requests for an interview. When he did not acknowledge a last pleading letter requesting the chance to ask him about his government's purchasing practices on-camera,

---

* We certainly didn't discover, for example, the tollgating scandal that came to light after the Liberals left office. After what was described as the "most extensive commercial crime investigation in Nova Scotia history," three prominent Liberal fundraisers were charged in July 1981 with demanding payoffs from liquor companies in exchange for having their products sold in Nova Scotia liquor stores. J. G. "Suitcase" Simpson pleaded guilty and was fined $75,000. Charles MacFadden and Senator Irvine Barrow were convicted in 1983 and fined $25,000 each. Barrow later successfully appealed his conviction.

I decided I at least needed to get him to turn us down with the cameras rolling.

Regan was scheduled to speak to the provincial party's annual meeting at Halifax's Hotel Nova Scotian a few weeks before our documentary was to air, so I showed up at that event with a TV crew and attempted to beard him in his lion's den. In those long-gone CBC salad days, my crew consisted of a cameraman, an assistant cameraman, a sound man, a lighting man, a director, and me. Not to forget a heavy camera, battery packs, Klieg lights, tape recorder, assorted microphones, clapboards, and the web of wires connecting us each to the other. As Regan spoke, we hovered near the side of the hotel ballroom, awaiting our chance to pose our questions. I could sense Regan nervously glancing our way, sizing up the situation even as he urged on the party faithful with an especially stirring speech. As soon as he finished, and with the crowd still on its feet cheering, we began to lumber up to the front of the hall en masse, hoping to catch Regan as he came down from the platform to begin his usual triumphant handshaking, backslapping procession back out through the hall. Instead, without even waiting for the applause to disappear, Regan turned on his heel and bolted out through a back door. "Let's go," roared our cameraman. The crew swung into action. Within seconds, the film and audio tracks had been synched and the lights flipped on as we ran — as one — through the door and after the premier.

It must have been like a scene from a bad movie. Regan strode purposefully, not once looking back, through the hotel kitchen, past startled cooks and servers, the six of us in hot pursuit. "Mr. Regan, Mr. Regan," I shouted above the din of pots and pans and the hiss of frying food. "We'd just like to ask you a few questions if we could." Regan made it to a service elevator, which happened to be open and empty. He quickly entered and pressed a button for another floor while we struggled to catch up with him. "Mr. Premier," I tried again as the elevator doors shut on us, "why won't you talk to us about political patronage? We only have a few —"

When it was broadcast, our finished documentary provoked a brief firestorm of debate — questions from the Opposition in the legislature, denunciations by a few Liberal cabinet ministers in the press — but, more important, it generated a freshet of new tips and leads. I believed we were on to something and that there would be plenty more stories I could do on this topic.

I was wrong.

A short time after that documentary aired, I was in the studio late one afternoon. I had just finished recording narration for a special on the energy crisis scheduled to air on that night's show when a voice from the control room paged me. I was wanted upstairs, the voice said, for an "urgent" meeting with the station's program director. Between the time I left the studio and arrived at his fourth-floor office, someone discovered the studio recording equipment had malfunctioned. My voice-over would need to re-done. My "urgent" meeting suddenly became less urgent. "Ah," he began, clearly nonplussed by the awkward turn of events. "Listen, why don't you . . . I mean why don't we . . . er, this can wait. It's not that important that it can't wait until the morning." The reality, as I discovered soon after, was that I had been called in to the office to be fired, even though I still had four months left on my contract. But my actual dismissal, embarrassingly for all concerned, had to be delayed because I was the only host available that day to record the voice-overs. And the show had to go on.

I was handed my severance cheque the next morning, and I was gone before noon.

There were undoubtedly all sorts of good reasons for the CBC to fire me, but I couldn't help wondering — then and later — if it had anything to do with that documentary, with my run-in with Gerald Regan. I have no evidence to support that suspicion, but I couldn't help recalling the story of the award-winning Canadian journalist Harry Bruce who'd publicly claimed he'd almost been fired years before after running afoul of Regan over a magazine story.

In the late sixties, Bruce, who had family roots in Nova Scotia, decided to abandon Toronto for Halifax. To make ends meet, he took a job editing a company magazine for Nova Scotia Light & Power, the privately owned electric power utility, while he freelanced for national magazines, mostly about his experiences as a newcomer to a place he desperately wanted to call home.

Shortly after arriving in the province, for example, he wrote an affectionate account of his first visit to the legislature, where he got to meet and shoot the breeze with all three party leaders, something, he noted, he couldn't likely have done in Ontario. But he soon discovered the down side to Nova Scotia's political familiarity. In August 1971, *Saturday Night* published Bruce's "The Great Fundy Hot Air Project," his tongue-in-cheek account of Regan's efforts to sell the mega-project and boost his own reputation. The article, Bruce wrote later, "was a documentation (hilarious, I thought) of a theory I had that, among all Maritime politicians, none had proved anywhere near so tiresomely inventive as the Honourable Gerald A. Regan in exploiting the Fundy Tidal Power project for publicity that was flattering to himself. I thought that the horny hands and mighty wrists and steel cable forearms of the best dairy farmer in Nova Scotia had never, ever managed to milk a cow's udder more dry than the Honourable Gerald A. Regan had milked the idea of Fundy Tidal Power and, shucks, I guess I made the mistake of letting this opinion show itself."

Regan was not amused.

As Bruce recounted it later in a column in *The 4th Estate*: "I wish to reveal to the part of the world in which I have chosen to live that late last summer, the premier of Nova Scotia, the Honourable Gerald A. Regan, signified to the man who was then my boss, A. R. Harrington, to fire me, insignificant Harry Bruce, right out on my goddamned ear. Or words exactly to that purpose.

"He not only wanted Harrington to dismiss me, he VERY MUCH wanted him to dismiss me. So much so that when Harrington said, in effect, 'Oh, well Gerry, I don't know, maybe that wouldn't be such a hot idea,' the Honourable Gerald A. Regan let his desires be known to the chairman of the board of the power company, the venerable and near-legendary Colonel J. C. MacKeen and, the next thing the president knew, he had not only the premier but the Colonel as well expressing this interest in seeing me — a newcomer of lowly stature, an outsider, an unknown, a humble wordsmith, a poor working stiff and perfect stranger to the gentlemen who run Nova Scotia — seeing me get the can."

Harrington refused to buckle under to the pressure, though he did warn Bruce that he now had two very powerful strikes against him, "and we all understand what three strikes mean, don't we, Bruce?"

After the province moved three months later to take over Nova Scotia Light & Power, Bruce tweaked Regan's nose, again in the public prints: "A grudge is a grudge, I thought, but surely he has gone too far this time," he wrote in *The 4th Estate*. "Tens upon tens of millions of dollars just to get at me. I had to admire his style."

I wasn't so sure.

8

Dumbly Horny in the Land of the MAGI

John Soosaar, a veteran Canadian Press reporter who covered three Nova Scotia administrations, says that, legislatively, Gerald Regan's first term in office "was as good as any I've covered. They had a real sense of direction and they met every one of their election promises from 1970. The second term? The second term, they went soft. There was lots of partying, and not very much got done."

Regan's government is far from the first — or last — to lose its way after only one term. Newly elected governments, having arrived in office after too many years on the outside looking longingly in and armed with plans and proposals they had the opportunity to propose and polish, revise and refine during their years in the wilderness, tend to be more than ready and eager to get on with the job they believe they were elected to do. But, once that initial legislative agenda is accomplished, they often become far too swamped by the day-to-day wash of events and the endless demands of the various interest groups to find the time to consider the larger picture or plan for the future. They come to believe that the real job of the government is to survive. And when events beyond their control make that seem unlikely, they cling to the perks of office, enjoying them while they can until the next set of new brooms comes in to sweep them away.

Regan's original lean and mean cabinet had ballooned to twenty members, and it no longer resembled an eighteenth-century coffee house, though it was still most definitely a men's club. "Cabinet meetings got to be a circus," says Doug Harkness. "Brown would be throwing peanuts at Sullivan for fun, and Allan Sullivan was 'fuck-this' and 'fuck-that' all the time just to shock people. One time, I remember Maynard MacAskill [a Cape Breton doctor elected in 1974 whom Regan had appointed minister of health] coming out of cabinet one day just shaking his head. 'Allan Sullivan said "fuck" fifty-two times,' he said."

The government's one major new initiative of its second term turned out to be an unmitigated disaster. Even the acronym for its official name, Metropolitan Area Growth Investments, quickly became a joke; newspaper editors delighted in coming up with variations on headlines like: "The Gift of the MAGI?" The MAGI's gift to the people of Nova Scotia turned out to be a Bahamas-registered, Thai-crewed cruise ship venture that sank on the shoals of scandal and bankruptcy without ever making its maiden cruise in Canadian waters.

The story actually began during the 1972 federal election campaign when the Trudeau Liberals announced vote-getting plans to create an ambitious new federal-provincial agency and give it $20 million to invest in businesses with growth potential in the Halifax-Dartmouth area. But when the Liberals barely limped back into office at the end of that campaign with a minority government, that plan was quietly shelved.

In the late spring of 1974, Scott MacNutt decided to dust it off. MacNutt, Regan's housing minister, had lost his seat in the legislature in the April 1974 election, and he was casting about for something new he could do to earn a living.

Ottawa was still willing to set up the agency but it didn't want MacNutt, a former Dartmouth welfare director and provincial cabinet minister who had never run a private business, to head the new venture. Ottawa and the province haggled for months over his role before finally agreeing to a compromise choice: Derek Haysom* — a South African administrator the former Tory government had

---

* After he left MAGI, Haysom and his wife were brutally murdered in Virginia. Their daughter and her boyfriend were eventually convicted of the killings.

hired to run its Sydney Steel plant and who still had a long-term, virtually unbreakable contract that bound the Regan government to keep paying him whether he worked or not — would become MAGI's president. MacNutt would be vice-president and general manager.

But Haysom and MacNutt didn't get along. Haysom was a secretive, backroom businessman who was so nervous about making a wrong investment move he rarely made any at all. MacNutt was an outgoing, gregarious type who enjoyed long expense-account lunches with friends and associates at the Henry House, the most expensive restaurant in town, and was developing what he claimed was a list of more than 200 potential clients he thought MAGI could invest in.

The friction between the two men generated a lot of table-pounding and loud arguments, but hardly any investments. In its first three years of operation, in fact, all MAGI had to show for its $20 million investment fund was one small loan to a bankrupt uniform supply shop.

Enter Joe Nugent, one of MacNutt's frequent luncheon companions. Nugent had started his career as a ship's purser, then opened a successful, Halifax-based ships' supply business called Mercator Enterprises. As a self-made entrepreneur, he ostentatiously drove a Rolls Royce around town and entertained friends, including MacNutt, with his dream of starting his own cruise ship line. He and MacNutt first seriously discussed the idea during a vacation the two men took in Costa Rica in 1976. MacNutt saw the venture as an exciting opportunity to encourage development of a cruise ship industry. He took the proposal to MAGI's board of directors who, stung by press criticism they hadn't invested in anything, agreed to let MacNutt pursue the venture without apparently giving much consideration of whether the idea of a government agency investing in a cruise ship made economic or logical — or any — sense.

In the fall of 1976, MacNutt and Nugent bought a small German-owned cruise ship called the *Regina Maris* with $5.2 million of MAGI funds. MacNutt's original plan was for MAGI to buy the vessel on Nugent's behalf and then farm the mortgage out to a conventional lender, but Nugent balked at paying 12 percent interest on the loan, so MAGI ended up holding the mortgage for the ship as well as paying the costs of a $100,000 refit and another

$300,000 for start-up and promotional costs.

When Gerry Regan discovered from a newspaper report what MacNutt and MAGI had done, he was upset. So was Ottawa, which threatened to take back its money and scuttle the agency. In the end, Regan and Nicholson persuaded a reluctant MacNutt to resign and accept another patronage job as the chair of the Workmen's Compensation Board instead.*

But the government's cruise ship embarrassments were far from over. To help Nugent avoid paying customs duties on the new ship — which he renamed *Mercator I* after his ship's chandlering company — MAGI's directors agreed to allow the taxpayer-funded ship to be registered in the Bahamas. To add insult to injury, Nugent hired more than half the ship's crew from Thailand. So much for creating employment in Halifax-Dartmouth, one of MAGI's goals. To protest the use of the Thai crew, the Seafarers' International Union announced plans to picket the ship at every Canadian port it docked.

It didn't have to. The 271-passenger ship launched what was supposed to be its inaugural spring Caribbean season in April 1977. By the end of its fourth cruise, Nugent had run out of money and the MAGI board out of patience.

The entire ill-starred venture provided lots of fodder for the Opposition and the media. When the *Mercator I* finally arrived in Nova Scotian waters, it was hidden in Shelburne harbour until it could be disposed of. It never made a single cruise in Nova Scotia.

MAGI, the taxpayers, and the Regan government all paid the price for the failure.

THE MAGI SCANDAL happened, in part, because no one was paying attention. By the second term, it seemed, everyone was having too much fun to sweat the details of governing. "Everybody worked hard," insists Doug Harkness, "but at the end of the day at around six or seven at night all the fellows would drop over to the premier's office and shoot the shit for a while. There'd be Brown and Pace, Sullivan, Nicholson, and others too, and usually some of their aides. We'd sit around, and the bottle would come out. The odd fellow

---

* After only fourteen days on the new job, MacNutt quit the board post too, claiming he wasn't being allowed to do anything useful.

might get full, but that was rare," Harkness says. "It was just a good time."

Regan's office on the Hollis Street floor of the legislature building wasn't huge but it was a comfortable gathering place with a couch and easy chairs across from the desk that had served Nova Scotia premiers for generations. There was a private bathroom to one side and an exit to Regan's secretary's office through a padded, sound-proofed door. Large windows, framed by rich green drapes overlooked Hollis Street to the east and the legislature garden to the south, where, Jack "the Hawk" Hawkins would recall, "office girls used to bask in the August sun at lunchtime, a practice Regan would not object to."

Everyone in Regan's entourage had a nickname. To their con-stituents and their minions, they might be Mr. Sullivan or Mr. Minister or Sir but inside Regan's office, they were Sully, Brownie, Nickel, the Hawk, and so on. After his 1974 re-election victory, Regan was promoted to the "Preem Supreme."

But Regan was no monarch after hours, says Hawkins, just the first among a group of equals, and "there was little order or deco-rum among the Happy Gang." As soon as they walked into Regan's office, he recalls, Garnet "Brownie" Brown or Glen "Bags" Bagnell, a Dartmouth MLA who joined the cabinet after the 1974 election, would quickly grab one of the expensive Havana cigars from the always full humidor Regan kept on his desk, and light up.

Despite the boys' club atmosphere, few claimed to know their boss well. "I don't think Gerry ever really confided in anyone," says David Mann, who ran the Liberals' campaign machine during the period and spent countless hours with the boss. "I don't know if he had a best friend."

But he clearly enjoyed the company of cronies — in his office after hours or at the hockey rink. Though he still wasn't an especially good player, Regan delighted in organizing a team of MLAs to tour the province playing charity games, often against the media. "Regan revelled in 'starring' in these games since they drew good crowds," says Hawkins. "I felt it was inappropriate to have a premier, balding, overweight, falling and making such a display. Yet he saw nothing wrong and it was probably good politics."

Besides the regular post-work gatherings in the premier's office, it wasn't unusual to find other impromptu parties going full-tilt in the Hansard office two floors above Regan's office, or in the Press Room on the main floor, or in the Executive Council Office nearby.

"In the early seventies, people did all sorts of things that simply wouldn't be possible today," says Jeremy Akerman. "It was freer, and there weren't so many things you couldn't do. My secretary could slap me on the arse and say, 'Get on with it,' and no one would think anything of it." He laughs. "Those were the times."

While the legislature was party central, there were plenty of other venues nearby where you could find politicians, their aides and officials, and not a few reporters socializing together: there was the Arrows Club, a popular nightclub owned by the Downey brothers, members of a prominent black north-end Halifax family that had been long-time supporters and close friends of the premier; the Misty Moon, a cavernous show bar on Gottingen Street; the Lobster Trap, a late-night dance bar in Scotia Square; and the Press Club, which was located in the basement of the nearby Carleton Hotel.

For the more adventurous, there were visits to after-hours poker games in everyone-knows-where-to-go downtown hotel rooms or, of course, late evening visits to Ada's.

Ada was Ada McCallum, the city's most notorious — and well-connected — madam.[*] Born Ada Jane Piper in Manitoba in 1909, she arrived in Halifax during World War II. By the seventies, she was operating a call-girl operation from her home on Windsor Street not far from where Gerald Regan's family had lived. Though it wasn't listed in the telephone book as anything but a private residence, her call-girl operation was so well-known you could apparently get the telephone number by dialing Information and asking for "Ada's." Or by asking any cab driver, as one national magazine noted in a story about Halifax in the late sixties.[†]

The police knew about Ada too; some, it's said, even used her

---

[*] When she died in 1986, even *The Globe and Mail* noted her passing with an obituary under the headline: "Woman a Halifax Legend in Four Decades as Madam."

[†] The fee for the services of one of her girls in the seventies was twenty dollars, plus five dollars more for cab fare if the client was located in Dartmouth. The fee was split evenly between Ada and the prostitute. For her share, Ada set up the liaison, took care of medical and legal expenses, tipped cabbies and others for steering business her way, and paid off whoever needed to be paid off to keep the business running smoothly. According to income tax officials' estimates later, she took in over $3 million from prostitution during the mid-seventies.

services from time to time. After one raid by the police, in fact, Ada confided to a friend that the officer who had come to arrest her was a regular customer. "He was always such a nice man," she said. No one considered the occasional police crackdown and subsequent court fine as anything more significant than a kind of licence to operate her business.

Politicians of all parties and persuasions were frequent users of her services. During political conventions, she apparently flew in additional women from Montreal or Boston to handle the increased demand and was rumoured to have a special line to handle calls from Ottawa politicians planning visits to Halifax. That last rumour isn't true, but it's a testament to her reputation among Halifax insiders that several people told me they'd heard the same story.

If you were looking for members of Regan's inner circle late at night in the mid-seventies, Ada's was a good place to start. Though a few cabinet ministers were customers, most were just friends or confidants. "She was up all night," notes Harkness, "so people would drop by after a function or whatever for a last drink. And then she'd make one of her big pork sandwiches and sit around and talk about the news events of the day."

Or play cards. Ada enjoyed playing but wasn't very good. One night, Garnet Brown won Ada's entire prized collection of two hundred Royal Doulton figurines. For the next year and a half, friends say Brown took particular delight in handing out the figurines as gifts to Halifax society ladies, never hinting at how — or from whom — he'd gotten them.*

As for Regan himself, he wasn't believed to be one of Ada's customers. "He was a good guy," NDP aide Marty Dolin told *the fifth estate* in 1994, "but he liked to chase young women. And he would press himself a little too aggressively on occasion. 'Ho, ho, ho,' you know. I mean that was the image Regan had."

He seemed especially interested in young women, or women who looked young. "Hey Premier," Doug Harkness once called out to the premier across a room, "I saw you with that thirteen-year-old." He paused a beat. "But don't worry. She had the body of a

---

* Although the story is well-known in Halifax and has been confirmed by others who say they were at Ada's that evening, Brown told researchers for *More Class Than Flash*, a 1998 film about Ada's life and times, that he didn't know her.

nine-year-old." People laughed. Today, Harkness insists it was all in good fun. "I'm not saying I'd be surprised if he was unfaithful to his wife, but I never saw him force himself on anyone. There's no doubt Regan was 'dumbly horny,'* but the girls at Province House would just laugh at him. I used to kid him, 'Preem, you couldn't get fucked in a whorehouse with a stack of credit cards and a thousand-dollar bill.'"

Anne Hines who worked at Hansard from 1973 to the mid-eighties, says women hired to work in the legislature were warned not to allow themselves to end up in a room alone with Regan. She too says at one level it was "all a big joke. We partied a lot — secretaries, cabinet ministers, MLAs, the press corps, everybody. Hansard and the press corps were upstairs, and at night the booze would flow freely, then we'd go disco dancing after the session was over. We had a great time." But she says she took the warnings to stay away from the premier seriously. "He was all hands."

SHEILA MURPHY HEARD NO such warnings. She'd only been a CBC radio reporter in Halifax for two weeks when she was assigned to cover the Liberal party's annual meeting one weekend at the Hotel Nova Scotian. According to unproven allegations by the Crown on a pre-trial motion, she was accosted when she innocently dropped in on the premier's hospitality suite to see if she could pick up any gossip about the convention or at least make some contacts who would be useful to her in her new job.

As Adrian Reid, who would eventually prosecute Regan for sex crimes, described that evening in court years later, Murphy ended up standing in one room of the two-room hospitality suite talking to someone when she felt a hand on her shoulder. It was the premier. After about thirty seconds, Regan finally propelled her into the adjoining bedroom where people had been putting their coats, pushed her down on the bed and climbed on top of her. Through the still-open door, Murphy claims she could see Regan's wife talking to other visitors. She managed to get away from him and get out of the suite without further incident. But it wasn't the last time she had to fight

---

* Harry Flemming, another former aide, first used the description of Regan as "dumbly horny" in a newspaper column defending his former boss after the RCMP announced it was investigating him for sexual misconduct.

him off. At a reception after the end of a legislature session, Regan allegedly grabbed her arm and dragged her to another room, ostensibly to see a new piece of art the province had acquired. Instead he chased her around the room until she finally managed to escape.

During their investigation, the mounties repeatedly questioned her about these incidents. Although she confirmed that they'd taken place, she refused to press charges. "If I didn't think they were serious enough to do anything about then, why would I go ahead twenty years later?" she told me.

DONNA JOHNSON WAS ANOTHER young female reporter who'd arrived in the press gallery in the mid-seventies. She was in her early twenties, fresh out of journalism school at the University of Western Ontario and rapidly advancing through the reporting ranks at her first journalism job at the Halifax *Chronicle-Herald*. By the spring of 1976, she was the junior — and only female — reporter on the *Herald*'s provincial political beat.

She enjoyed the casual, we're-all-in-this-together atmosphere in the legislative press gallery. More than twenty years later, Johnson can still remember fondly her conversations at those gatherings with MLAs like the venerable Liberal backbench MLA Joe Casey. "He was always so friendly." So, she says, was Premier Regan. "He was one of those hail-fellow well-met types," she says, "loud and hearty, and always quick with a joke."

In May 1976, she was covering the annual Maritime Premiers' Conference, which was taking place that year in Windsor, Regan's home town.

In April 1997, Gerald Regan was charged with sexual assault of Donna Johnson. She was not one of the original complainants in the case. After numerous meetings with police and prosecutors, she eventually agreed to become a complainant. But she never testified about what she says happened between Regan and herself, because the Crown decided to proceed by direct indictment. The judge stayed the charge in April 1998. The Crown is appealing. What follows is based on my interview with her as well as her statement to police and on the judge's later summary of the allegations.

Though the annual conference was usually as much a social event for the premiers — Regan, New Brunswick's Richard Hatfield, and

Prince Edward Island's Alex Campbell — as a working meeting, Johnson regarded the gathering as one of the first big political stories she'd been assigned to cover, so she was keen to impress her editors.

She'd seen Regan in the lobby earlier, joking with reporters that he had to leave the meetings for an hour to "crown Queen Hatfield* . . . oh sorry, I mean Queen Annapolisa" at the annual Annapolis Valley Apple Blossom Festival. By the time Regan returned, Johnson had already filed her first story for the next morning's *Herald*, and now she wanted to put together a second story that could run in its afternoon sister paper, the *Mail-Star*. She approached Regan who was standing talking with some aides, and asked him if she could have a few minutes of his time for an interview.

"Sure," Regan said, "but my briefing book and notes are back in my room. Why don't you go down and wait for me there?" She believes now he handed her the key to his room, "or else he said it was open."

She went to his room. Regan's briefing book was indeed there. "I even had a look through it while I was waiting for him to arrive," she confesses. When Regan did come into the room, Johnson told the RCMP in a 1993 statement later included as part of a defence abuse of process motion, he "tried to kiss me." Suddenly, she claims, she was on the bed and he was on top of her, kissing her. "He pushed me down on the bed. He had my skirt up and he was sort of pulling at my underwear." She could feel his erect penis against her. "I wasn't scared except for one moment when I could feel his dead weight on top of me and I thought I'm never going to get away from him." She says she finally managed to push him away and ran out of the room.

"I left the reception and I drove back to the other hotel where I was staying." She laughs. "I can't tell you today whether I wrote a story for the *Mail-Star*."

She says now she was shocked and angry that Regan would take such liberties with her. "He never mentioned it again. It was like he was above it, like he knew nothing would ever be said." Johnson says she never had any similar problem with any other politician, or indeed with anyone else she covered during her journalism career, but she adds quickly she regarded the whole incident as a minor

---

* Hatfield's sexual orientation, even then, was often a matter of conjecture and snide comment, though never in public.

matter, certainly not one worth going to the authorities about. "I mean I wasn't hurt or anything. My clothes were not ripped off. He'd put his hands up under my skirt but that was all."

She put the incident behind her. Despite the occasional urgings of other journalists and, later, police and prosecutors, she refused to go public with her story for more than twenty years.

HEATHER SNOW EVENTUALLY did go public with her story, which she told to *the fifth estate* in 1994. During the Regan era, she was a single mother who worked as a secretary in Peter Nicholson's office. Regan later sued the CBC for broadcasting allegations he said were false and defamatory, including some concerning Heather Snow. According to his statement of claim filed in court, she had alleged on television that one day, as she was working alone in a small office, Regan came into the room. "I thought that he would, to put it crudely, feel me up. I was afraid he would assault me, that he would touch me where I didn't want to be touched."

She says she screamed.

Nicholson arrived on the scene quickly from his office down the hall, sized up the situation, and, without even asking for an explanation, confronted Regan: "You keep your fucking hands off my staff," he said coldly.

Snow says she gratefully escaped from the room. "I was gone and I was very relieved to be gone."

REPORTERS AND SECRETARIES weren't the only ones who alleged that Regan had come on to them sexually. Several young women who sought him out for help getting jobs would claim the same thing. So would some who just happened to meet him casually.

Regan's lawsuit against the CBC about *the fifth estate* program also concerned allegations by Glenna Hanley that are similarly set out in his statement of claim, to specify what he objects to. Hanley was a young single mother who lived in Regan's north-end riding, who said she had heard the most direct route to a government job passed through the premier's office. So she wrote him a letter asking for his help. He called her back one evening around 9:30 p.m.

"I got your letter and résumé," Regan explained in a businesslike way. "And I'd like to come see you about it." Twenty minutes later he was at her door. Now, he was less businesslike, she told *the fifth estate*, inviting her to sit beside him on the sofa, leaning close to her, telling her she was attractive, kissing her on the cheek.

She managed to get away and get him out of the house without anything more happening. Two weeks later, he called back to say he had some information about a possible job. "Would you like me to come and see you when I have a little more information?"

"Well, no," she replied. "I think you can just phone me and let me know."

Regan, she told *the fifth estate*, never called again.

KATIE PRINCE, whose father was such good friends with Regan that Regan gave the eulogy at his 1992 funeral, says she grew up thinking of him as a kind of uncle.

In 1976, when she was twenty-two, according to the Crown's allegations during an abuse of process motion, she ran into Regan one night in the Jury Room, a downtown Halifax bar. She was drinking with some friends, she said, when Regan joined them at their table. Later that night, he invited them all back to his office so he could show them plans for what he described as the province's futuristic new heavy water plant. After they got there, Katie said she needed to use the washroom. Regan offered to show her the way but, as soon as they were out of sight of her friends, she claims he pushed her up against a wall and began fondling her. He was "groaning," she told police. She managed to get away from him, grab her coat, and leave. Though she told her mother, brother, and sisters what happened, she says she couldn't bring herself to tell her father what his friend had done to her.

No charges were laid in connection with her but the Crown prosecutor Adrian Reid included it in a long list of allegations he referred to during arguments on a defence motion claiming the Crown had abused the legal process in its obsession to "get" Regan. Reid countered that the police believed they had enough evidence to lay charges in connection with the Prince incident as well as a number of others, but had decided not to in the interests of fairness to Regan.

ACCORDING TO CROWN submissions in court, the mounties did want to lay charges against Regan in connection with Aileen Santos, but did not do so because of her precarious health.

She didn't know Gerry Regan, but Regan was friends with her boss, Bob Hayes, the athletic director at Saint Mary's University. Hayes had invited Regan, a SMU alumnus, to officiate at the opening ceremony of a university sports tournament. After the premier performed his official duties and while the game was under way, Hayes asked Santos to escort Regan to the tournament's VIP hospitality lounge. She says she wasn't keen because she still had plenty of work to do, but Hayes was her boss and the premier of the province an important guest.

The lounge was down an alley under the stands. The Crown prosecutor told the court that Santos remembered suddenly feeling Regan's hand on the centre of her back. His hand "propelled me forward like a rocket," she told police. "I nearly went face first into the cement. Then he took me by the arm and almost physically carried me into the hospitality suite."

The bar manager, who was still setting up the lounge and didn't notice the circumstances of their arrival, served Regan a drink and then left the room to get more supplies, leaving Santos and Regan alone in the room. Somehow, she says, Regan managed to get her boxed into a corner with a wall at one end and tables on either side of her. "I knew something was really wrong," she told police later. She claimed Regan pinned her against the wall "with his full weight, groping my breast, running his hands up and down, grabbing my crotch." She struggled. "I kept thinking, 'This is the premier? Why is this happening?'"

Suddenly, the bar manager returned to the room carrying boxes for the bar. Regan abandoned what he'd been doing and Santos fell to her knees and crawled under a table to safety.

DURING THE SAME COURT motion, Adrian Reid, the Crown prosecutor, also described an alleged incident involving Gerald Regan and Kelly Allan. Allan reportedly met Gerald Regan in a hospitality suite in a Toronto hotel. This location made a difference: investigators later decided not to pursue cases where the events were supposed to have happened outside Nova Scotia.

At the time, she was a twenty-seven-year-old employee of the Ontario Liberal party. The federal party was holding a fund raising dinner in the city and her bosses had asked her to host the Ontario party's post-dinner hospitality suite. After the dinner ended and the prime minister and most of the guests had left, Allan says she was getting ready to close the room when Gerald Regan approached her and began talking with her. Why didn't she come down to the Nova Scotia hospitality suite and meet the rest of the Nova Scotia delegation? he asked.

She agreed but when they got to the Nova Scotia suite, she says, no one else was there. She was about to leave when Regan asked her to wait in a chair while he went into the next room for a minute.

When he came back a moment later, he was completely naked according to the Crown's recounting of her statement to the police. Before she could react — or reach for the telephone, which had just begun to ring — he grabbed her and pushed her down on the bed. He ripped off her nylons and, then, putting one hand over her mouth, used the other to try and insert his penis in her vagina. During the struggle, she claims, he ejaculated without entering her.

As soon as he climaxed, he got off her and went into the other room to dress. Still too stunned to know what else to do, Allan answered the telephone. It was a mountie from the prime minister's security detail. He and another man, an assistant to the prime minister, had heard she'd left the Ontario suite with Regan and had decided to try to locate her. They were, allegedly, worried what Regan might do to her.

The prosecutor told the court that the police did speak to the two men who phoned the hospitality suite and that both had confirmed that part of Allan's account.

IN 1977, JENNIFER OULTON was a bubbly, gregarious, five-foot-two eighteen-year-old, who had worked part-time at the legislature for two years, first as a messenger and then as a page. Messengers delivered messages to and from the legislative chamber, but didn't go inside. Pages, who were more senior in the pecking order, delivered messages to and from MLAs in the chamber during legislative sessions. Sometimes, they delivered more than messages. Occasionally, on request, they'd discreetly bring liquor from a downstairs safe to a thirsty MLA in the chamber.

Oulton liked the job, liked the camaraderie and the friendly, relaxed atmosphere in the chamber. She also liked the fact that working at the legislature during house sessions could lead to contacts for summer jobs in government departments. One summer, she'd landed a job as a receptionist in the Department of Recreation.

In 1977, having graduated from high school and finished a secretarial course, Oulton knew it was time to find something more permanent. She figured Gerald Regan might be able to help her find that something.

As a result of what she testified happened when she went to see him, Gerald Regan was charged with sexually assaulting Oulton. The charge was stayed. The Crown is appealing.

Oulton told Regan's 1996 preliminary inquiry she'd seen him in the hallway of the legislative building and asked if she could come talk to him after the house session. Sure, he'd said. Given the casual atmosphere around Province House in those days, she says, it didn't seem like a big deal for a page to be asking for a meeting with the premier of the province. "I wasn't stigmatized by the idea that he was the king of England or anything," she told the preliminary hearing. "He was just an ordinary guy."

During the session that evening, Oulton made arrangements with two fellow pages to handle her share of the clean-up chores — washing the dishes and glasses the MLAs used — so she could go and see Regan as soon as the house rose. After quickly changing out of her uniform and into her street clothes, she went downstairs to the premier's office. There was an older woman at work in the outer office, she remembers, but she didn't speak to her. She entered Regan's private office in a corner beyond the outer public area and through a smaller office where his personal secretary worked in the day time. When Oulton entered the secretary's office, according to her evidence she saw Regan standing near the entrance to his inner office. He ushered her inside. She remembers noticing the burgundy-coloured leather padded door to his office. "There were buttons on the leather that created a diamond effect."

Inside the office, she took a seat in front of Regan's desk. The premier then sat at his desk and took out some paper. "What kind of a job are you looking for?" she said that he asked. As she talked, he made notes while she outlined her qualifications and talked about her interest in a full-time job. The ten-minute conversation was, according to her later account, friendly but businesslike. At one point when she'd finished her pitch and Regan appeared to have run out of questions, she decided it was probably time for her to leave. Two other pages were waiting for her upstairs; they'd agreed to all go home together. But as she got up to leave, Regan suddenly began talking again. "I got the sense it wasn't time to leave yet." She sat back down. As he spoke, she claims, Regan got up, came around to the front of his desk and stood behind her. "Now I assumed for sure it was time to go." She thanked him for his time, stood up and was about to turn to leave when — as she testified at Regan's preliminary inquiry — "the next thing I can recall is him driving his tongue down my throat." She was stunned. "The whole atmosphere had been so normal and then all of a sudden . . . I mean he was old enough to be my grandfather."

Panic-stricken and in tears, she said she bolted from the room and headed straight for the women's washroom down the hall. Alone, she tried to figure out what exactly had just happened to her and what she should do about it. Believing she had her tears under control, she left the washroom and went upstairs to meet her fellow pages. By the time she arrived at the second floor, it was clear she wouldn't be able to keep her emotions in check. She ran past Susan Randall, a page who had been stationed at the outer chamber doors of the legislature. "She was crying and shaking all over," Randall told investigators years later according to the Crown's allegations. "She said Regan had pushed her up against a wall, had put his tongue down her throat." The Crown also alleged in court that Susan Nugent, another page who happened on the scene at this time and heard Oulton's story, urged her to go and tell Buddy Daye, the legislature's chief page, what Regan had done.

Before she could, she ran into Harold Long, the sergeant-at-arms and Daye's boss. "Did Regan rape you?" he demanded.

She told him he hadn't. Long offered to drive her home. "He often did that," she testified. "He was an older man and he worried about us going home alone when it was so late."

By the next morning, the story of Regan and the page girl was already the buzz of the legislature. Doug Harkness, working as a reporter again but certainly "still as close to [Regan] then as anyone in the press gallery," says he asked Regan point blank about the rumours.

"He said [Oulton] had come to him for a job and, at the end, just as she was leaving, he said to her, 'Have you got a kiss for the premier now?' And he leaned over to kiss her. He was just being fatherly."

Jeremy Akerman, who says he wasn't in the legislature that night, says the first he heard of such an incident was several days later when a reporter "from Toronto came up to me and demanded to know what I knew about the premier and the page girl. So I went to see Peter Nicholson and he suggested to me that they'd called someone in to investigate — by which I understood him to mean the police* — and it was clear the story had been cooked up by the sergeant-at-arms, Harold Long, and [Conservative MLA] Don Cameron. Long was supposed to be upset because he hadn't gotten an invitation to a dinner for royalty some months before, and Cameron was just nasty." Although no one has corroborated these allegations, Akerman says he accepted that explanation at the time. "I had always known Peter Nicholson to be an honourable man and I had no reason to think he wasn't telling the truth about this."

BUT THE WORD was out very quickly that Regan had tried to kiss a page girl and that the sergeant-at-arms knew all about it. Though some reporters dismissed the gossip as irrelevant or unworthy of being reported, others, including the CP reporter John Soosaar, tried to follow it up: "Something had obviously happened so I decided to glean all the details I could and then figure where to go from there." After interviewing Long and a number of other aides and officials, Soosaar decided he had better talk to his bureau chief, Jack Brayley, before going any further. Brayley, too, immediately recognized the information as potential dynamite. Brayley sent a message to his bosses in Toronto, who immediately passed it on to J. J. Robinette, CP's chief legal counsel. Robinette's unsurprising advice: CP couldn't run the story without some documentation, including an affidavit from Oulton. Though no one told him to drop the story, Soosaar says "no one suggested I should bother to go out and get the documentation either." Soosaar got the message.

So did most other reporters. The page girl incident was great gossip for the newsroom, but no one was going to risk a lawsuit by

---

* There's no record that anyone in authority ever asked the police to investigate.

airing an allegation that the premier of the province had attacked a page girl.

Frustrated, CBC radio reporter Ray Aboud telephoned a friend at the Toronto *Globe and Mail*, the investigative reporter Peter Moon, and suggested he look into the incident. Moon did, flying into Halifax to interview Oulton, Long, and others. Regan refused to be interviewed. "After it happened, Regan went missing for a couple of days," Soosaar remembers. "Then, when he came back, Moon was there. There was this confrontation in the hall. I think Moon yelled some sort of question at him as he and [press secretary Jim] Robson were walking by in the hall. They immediately went into [executive assistant] David Thompson's office and didn't come out."

Undeterred, Moon showed up at Regan's Bedford home at six the next morning to try to confront him about the allegations. Moon apparently believed the *Globe* might be legally able to publish the story if he could get Regan to talk to him about the incident, even to deny it. But Regan refused to say anything at all, and an aide finally ushered Moon off Regan's property.

The next day, Ian Morrison, a former radio reporter who'd joined the civil service as a public information officer and whose bailiwick included the premier's office, went to see Regan's assistant Robbie Shaw to warn him about a rumour he'd picked up from some media contacts. "Peter Moon has an article nailed and ready to go," he told Shaw, "possibly as early as tomorrow."

"Really," replied Shaw. "That's not good, not good at all."

Meanwhile, Regan's lawyers were already calling the *Globe*'s lawyers to threaten them with a very expensive lawsuit if the paper published anything at all. It didn't.[*]

Bette Cahill, a radio reporter with CFDR, tried another tack. She approached Oulton — as a female rather than as a reporter. "She seemed like she was there to help, to be supportive," Oulton said in her testimony. Cahill urged her to sit down for an audio tape

---

[*] While no media outlet reported the alleged page girl incident at the time and no official reported it to the police, the episode certainly didn't go unremarked. In fact, the page girl became the punch line to sly, knowing jokes. During the 1978 press gallery dinner, in fact, the biggest laugh came when one wag suggested that Regan's government had improved in the last year — "It's turned a new page." Even the NDP in Halifax Citadel couldn't resist this line in its campaign leaflet: "It would take pages to tell the full story" of just how bad the Liberals had been, the pamphlet suggested.

interview of her recollections while her memories of what happened were clear. If Oulton decided to go public, Cahill would be able to use the taped interview to break the story.* In the meantime, they agreed, Oulton would keep the tape. She testified at Regan's preliminary inquiry that she kept it on her bureau in the bedroom of her apartment. Until, she told the court, it mysteriously disappeared.

Cahill had discussed the tape with her boss, CFDR president Arnie Patterson, and told him that Oulton was keeping the recording in case she decided to go public. As a result, its existence had become common knowledge among Liberal insiders and others. At any rate, soon after that, someone broke into Oulton's apartment. The only thing taken was the tape she'd made for Cahill. Though Oulton reported the break-in to the Halifax City Police and even explained to them why someone might have wanted to steal an audio tape, the police apparently didn't believe that the story behind the story — involving allegations against the premier as well as the possibility someone might have stolen the tape for blackmail purposes — was important enough for them to investigate.*

ANOTHER YOUNG WOMAN HAS alleged Regan came on to her just a few months after the page girl incident, according to Crown submissions in court. Regan had met Dana McDougall, an eighteen-year-old provincial champion tennis player, at the Waegwoltic Club. They discussed their shared passion for tennis and Regan told her he admired her forehand. So when she began looking for a summer job that year, she wrote to the premier. He invited her to come visit him in his office to talk about her job prospects. Once she was inside, she claims, he closed the door and pulled her against him, kissing her aggressively and forcing his tongue down her throat. Then he stopped suddenly, she told police later, and conducted the job interview as if nothing had happened. She didn't say anything to anyone at the time. Soon, she had a summer job in the province's recreation department.

No charges were filed in connection with this incident, but it was another of those raised by the Crown prosecutor, Adrian Reid,

---

* The police did ask Oulton to submit to a polygraph test. She passed. No one was ever charged in connection with the break-in.

to demonstrate the police had shown discretion in not charging Regan in a number of cases where they believed they had sufficient evidence to do so.

CLARE BENNETT RECOGNIZED the booming, scratchy voice on the speakerphone immediately, she told Regan's 1996 preliminary inquiry. It was Gerald Regan, the premier of Nova Scotia. Although it was two o'clock in the morning, Regan insisted he be allowed to speak to Yvette Surrette, Bennett's roommate. Surrette didn't want to speak to him. Neither did Bennett.

Regan was the kind of man who made Bennett "uncomfortable," she said.

In March 1995, Regan was charged with sexual assault of Clare Bennett. The charge was stayed in 1998; the Crown is appealing.

Clare Bennett was just nineteen at the time, and she and Surrette — both freshly graduated from the legal secretarial program at Mount Saint Vincent University — had been hired as secretaries in the Liberal party's legislative caucus office.

Though she didn't work directly for Regan, she'd met him several times. The first was at a reception after the house recessed that spring. Her boss, Shirley Williams, had introduced her. "He was very friendly, very pleasant," she testified. But more: "He came very close . . . and then he very casually put his arm around me."

Regan, she said, was the kind of man who went out of his way to "make sure you noticed him." And he noticed her. Like all the other women who worked in the office, Regan invariably added the suffix "-insky" when he referred to her by name. She was "Clare-insky." Surrette was "Yvette-insky."

Tonight, in fact, he asked to speak to Yvette-insky. It wasn't the first time he'd called late at night looking for Surrette, Bennett recalls. Tonight, Regan told her he and a few of the others were having a little get-together and she and Surrette should "come down" and join the party. He would send someone to get them, he said.

Even after Surrette told Bennett to tell Regan she wasn't interested and Bennett said she wasn't either, Regan insisted on being allowed to speak to Yvette. "Yvette was very upset," she remembered.

Because "it wasn't any secret how Mr. Regan carried on," Bennett testified that she did her best not to end up in a room alone with him.

That became more difficult when, in the summer of 1978, she landed a job as secretary to George Doucet, the Speaker of the legislature. Unlike the caucus office down the hall where there were almost always three or four secretaries and at least one or two MLAs present at any given time, she was now the only secretary in an out-of-the-way office where the Speaker — a high school principal — was rarely present when the house wasn't in session. "Most of my contact with him," she says, "was over the phone."

The office included an area for the secretary and private offices for the Speaker and his deputy as well as a small boardroom and a coffee room.

One afternoon, Bennett was returning to her desk from the coffee room when she says she was "surprised by Mr. Regan as I came around the filing cabinet." He asked if the Speaker was in. When she said he wasn't, Regan made no move to leave. In fact, she testified at Regan's preliminary inquiry, "he came closer to me. . . . He reached down and cupped my breast" and leaned over her as if to kiss her. Startled, she stepped back and attempted to push him away.

"You should leave," she told him.

Regan, she claimed, "laughed. He was nonchalant, like I shouldn't be bothered by it. . . . He was never violent or angry. He was still friendly. He acted as if I was being a silly girl not to take it that way. . . . He said, 'You don't know how things are done around here. You don't know how to get ahead.'"

He did leave. But Clare Bennett never forgot, she said in court. Or forgave herself for not having "the guts" to do anything about it. She eventually told her story to *the fifth estate* and then became a complainant in the criminal case.

BUT NEITHER THE MAGI mess, nor the page girl incident, nor Regan's alleged continuing come-ons to women were, in the end, what defeated the Regan government. One key event that was totally beyond its control — the 1973 Arab oil embargo — not only made every other problem pale in comparison but also made its 1978 defeat inevitable.

In the first days of its first term, the Regan government — and Nova Scotians generally — had dared to dream that offshore oil would prove to be the province's economic salvation. The dreaming reached its peak on October 5, 1971, when the Halifax *Chronicle-Herald*'s three-and-one-quarter-inch front page headline screamed "IT'S OIL." Below the bold red headline, there was a picture of a beaming Gerald Regan holding a vial of oil that Mobil Oil had supposedly discovered during exploratory drilling in the waters off the province's coast. Regan could barely contain himself, although he did try to sound a note of caution. "It is not the time to count chickens before they are hatched and fully grown," he told reporters, but then added quickly that this news was so promising "Nova Scotians will have trouble restraining their enthusiasm."

The *Herald* certainly did. In addition to its war-is-over-sized headline, *Herald* reporters found sources who claimed the discovery was "extensive" and there was so "little doubt about the commercial viability" of the find that Mobil was "merely deciding whether to run a pipeline to the coast or build a 'floating island' for offshore tankers."

Alas, it was not to be. Exploring for oil and gas in the treacherous North Atlantic off Nova Scotia was incredibly expensive and dangerous, and success far from guaranteed. In the end, Mobil and most of the other international oil companies exploring the offshore simply analyzed the results of their discoveries, marked the spots for future reference, and moved on to other more immediately promising territory.

But if another Big Dream was dead, or at least on ice for the foreseeable future, the province's oil-fired nightmare was about to come lurching to life. On October 5, 1973, Syria and Egypt attacked Israel in what became known as the Yom Kippur War. When the United States and other Western countries, including Canada, sided with Israel, oil-producing Arab nations retaliated. The Organization of Petroleum Exporting Countries, which controlled most of the world's oil supply, announced its members would no longer sell oil to the countries that had taken Israel's side. Prices for the oil still available on the open market skyrocketed — from three dollars a barrel before the boycott began to four times that much by the end of 1974 — and the Western world discovered to its shock and chagrin just how dependent it had become on a resource whose supply it did not control.

Nova Scotians had more reason to be shocked and chagrined than most. Ninety percent of its electricity was generated by burning imported oil. And there were no easy or quick fixes to change that. That meant electricity rates would have to go up quickly — and dramatically.

Gerald Regan knew that. He also knew he'd be blamed for those increases because of his government's 1972 takeover of Nova Scotia Light & Power. Even though there was clearly no connection, Regan knew truth couldn't save him. All of those shocked and appalled editorial writers and outraged opposition politicians and blustering business spokespeople, who had earlier predicted Gerald Regan's socialist takeover of a fine, privately owned and operated company would inevitably lead to increased energy prices, could now crow that they had been right all along. And they would.

Regan managed to delay the inevitable by refusing to allow the power corporation to increase rates before the 1974 provincial election, but it was, as historian J. Murray Beck argued later, "a Pyrrhic victory. The energy crisis simply would not go away." By the end of 1975, Regan — whose own political energies were increasingly dissipated in trying to find ways out of the box of the energy crisis — "had few grounds for optimism."

Regan's only hope was Ottawa. Regan cobbled together what amounted to a political rescue package. He asked Ottawa to give the province $144 million so it could keep power rates down long enough for the government to figure a way out of the mess. Regan, as always, was optimistic. "The biggest problem," he would explain to anyone who would listen, "is an interim one. If we can get over the next four years" — which, though he didn't mention it, would also see him safely through the next provincial election — "we'll be fine."

But the Trudeau Liberals, who had regained their electoral majority — and their cockiness — after 1974 weren't interested in solving Regan's problems. In February 1977, Ottawa agreed to ante up $63 million — not nearly as much as he was seeking and not as the direct subsidy he so desperately wanted. The money, Ottawa insisted, could only be used to help residents insulate their homes — an energy conservation subsidy for which Ottawa would also claim credit.

"There are those," a federal energy department official sniffed to an interviewer on CTV's *Canada AM*, "who believe Gerald Regan's political future is on the line."

Including, of course, Gerald Regan. And he knew now his future was almost certainly epilogue. When the province's Public Utilities Board, which he had assigned to monitor and approve requests for rate increases, gave the go-ahead to a 47 percent increase in electricity rates, Regan had to know that nothing could save his government.

In the early days of his administration, remembers Doug Harkness, Regan used to enjoy pointing to the portraits of former premiers hanging on the walls of the House of Assembly building and noting how many years each one had served. "'Harko,' he'd say to me, looking at the portrait of [George] Murray [who served as premier for twenty-seven years], 'I only need so many more years and I'll be the longest serving of the lot.'"

By 1978, he had given up counting those "years until."

Many of those who had been with him from the beginning had already jumped ship. Allan Sullivan opted for an appointment as a county court judge in 1976; two years later, Len Pace took his leave to become a Supreme Court judge. And his closest allies, Garnet Brown and Peter Nicholson, were in political trouble in their own ridings.

"It sapped our energy," remembers Bill Gillis, one of the government's few ministers whose seat still seemed safe. "We got down in the polls and there were all sorts of front-page editorials. They just kept piling [the power rate increases] on top of the takeover of Light & Power. It wasn't fair, of course, but it hurt."

Regan delayed calling an election through the spring of 1978 but then, apparently sensing time would not help his cause either, called the vote for September 19, 1978.

Like the Tories in 1970, Regan's Liberals tried to run on their record but the electorate clearly wasn't buying. According to their own polls, the Liberals were five percentage points behind the Conservatives when the campaign began. When the votes were counted, the Tories had climbed to 46 percent of the popular vote compared to 39 for the Liberals. John Buchanan's Tories took thirty-one of the now fifty-two seats in the House of Assembly, the Liberals just seventeen, and the NDP four. After surviving the entire Stanfield-Smith era, Peter Nicholson lost his own seat. So did seven other cabinet ministers, including Garnet Brown. Regan, who had increased his own margin of victory to more than 2,500 votes in 1974, could only barely hold on to his own seat by 137 votes.

9

"A Letter to
the Honourable
Gerald A. Regan..."

Brian Flemming could not believe his good fortune. He only wished he weren't stuck here in New York in his room at the Plaza Hotel, getting the dramatic news from Ottawa relayed to him in tantalizing bits and pieces in telephone calls from his wife and his political allies back in Halifax.

It was the morning of Friday, December 14, 1979. The night before in Ottawa, Joe Clark's six-month-old Conservative government had been defeated in the House of Commons, and Clark had already announced, "I will be calling on the Governor General in the morning." There would be another election, another opportunity for Brian Flemming to win a seat in the House of Commons. He had more than earned it. He had run for the federal Liberals in the Halifax riding in the 1974 election, losing — as everyone knew he would — to the Tory leader Robert Stanfield. But, even as a sacrificial lamb, he had cut Stanfield's margin of victory — roughly 8,000 votes in both 1968 and 1972 — to just 2,500 and helped hasten Stanfield's decision to resign as leader. In 1976, he'd left his successful Halifax law practice for some Ottawa seasoning, serving as an assistant principal secretary and policy adviser to Pierre Trudeau for three years until Trudeau called the May 1979 election. He ran again in Halifax, but this time anti-Trudeau sentiment was running high in the region and the country. He lost to George Cooper, another prominent local lawyer, by a few dozen votes. After that, Flemming had returned to his law firm to lick his wounds, resigned to the idea that he would have to bide his time for at least another two or three years before Clark decided to seek a majority government or the opposition parties combined to defeat him.

But now, just six months after they'd beaten the Liberals, the Tories had blundered into a defeat on their first budget. Worse for them, better for the Liberals and Flemming, the Tories were already in trouble with the voters. Their popularity had nose-dived since their almost-majority win in the May election; the November Gallup poll showed the Tories nineteen percentage points behind the Liberals. And their first budget, which included an eighteen-cents-per-gallon excise tax on transportation fuels, was sure to cause them to fall further. The Liberals, who had combined with the NDP to defeat the budget 139 to 133, could only gain from defeating it.

George Cooper, Flemming was convinced, could be beaten. And he was just the man to do it.

But it was not to be.

When he went down to breakfast in the hotel's Palm Court restaurant that morning, he was taken aback to see Gerald Regan, who happened to be in New York too, already seated, surrounded by stacks of newspapers. "Of all the people I wanted to talk to, here you are," said Regan, equally startled to see Flemming. "I've been thinking about it and I have an idea," he began.

Regan's pitch was straightforward — he would resign from the provincial party leadership and run for Parliament in the Halifax riding. In exchange, Regan would support Flemming for the provincial party leadership.

Since his 1978 defeat, Regan had seemed lost and distracted in opposition. Although he tried to put the best face on it — even telling a *Globe and Mail* reporter in December 1978 that "it's going to be fun to be in opposition" — he had clearly been there and done that, and he didn't relish waiting four more years for a chance at winning back his old job.

Regan's spirits had finally lifted in November 1979, when Pierre Trudeau announced he would be stepping down as federal Liberal leader. Perhaps he might make a run for national leadership, he suggested hopefully to aides. When the Tory government fell a few weeks later and Trudeau was persuaded to lead the party into one last election, Regan recognized his best hope to position himself for a run at the top job now would be to win a seat in Parliament.

Brian Flemming understood the logic of it all even if he wasn't convinced Regan could ever win the leadership. But he also understood there was no way he could refuse Regan's request to run in the seat, though he understood as well that Regan would probably never be able to deliver on his promise to support him for the provincial leadership.

So Flemming quietly abandoned his best chance of winning a seat in Parliament, loyally nominating Regan for the job instead. Regan won and was appointed to two junior portfolios — minister of labour and the minister responsible for fitness and amateur sport — in the new cabinet.* Despite what might have appeared to outsiders to be a rebuke to his lofty ambitions, Regan was undeterred. He began quietly assembling support for what he intended would be an eventual run for the Liberal leadership.

Though he wouldn't realize it for many years to come, that ambition would be his ultimate undoing.

IN 1980, PHILIP MATHIAS told Regan's 1996 preliminary inquiry, he was an investigative reporter for the CBC television program *the fifth estate* looking into financial problems at the Canadian Council of Christians and Jews. While he was talking to an official of the CCCJ, questions about Gerald Regan's relations with women happened to come up.

According to Mathias's testimony, the official told him of a rumour that Regan had sent flowers to a Cape Breton schoolgirl, perhaps fifteen or sixteen years old; her family had been worried, it was said.

Mathias already knew of his friend Peter Moon's unsuccessful investigation into the matter of the page girl. And he had heard gossip about Regan from time to time.

The sex lives of politicians were not exactly Mathias's specialty. He much preferred to devote his energies to exposing business fraud and government corruption. Still, he talked it over with his boss, Ron

---

* Regan was promoted to minister of international trade in 1982.

Haggart, then the executive producer of the program. Haggart was even more ambivalent than Mathias himself. He was uncomfortable with what seemed to him tabloid journalism. And he wondered about the relevance of going after Regan now that he was no longer the premier. It would take a lot of work. And for what?

They didn't exactly agree to dismiss the idea altogether but they didn't decide that Mathias would actively pursue it either. Like a lot of possible stories, it ended up in a kind of limbo, awaiting some trigger that would make it worth doing or slowly receding from attention until it finally disappeared from everyone's consciousness.

But this time Mathias couldn't quite let the story go. Something about it troubled him. As he often did, Mathias ruminated about the moral dimensions. At one point, he sought out Michael Robitaille, a Roman Catholic theologian and director of St. Michael's Cathedral in Toronto, for his advice. Robitaille counselled against writing a story but he suggested Mathias try to talk to Regan directly. "Absurd as it sounds," Mathias says now, "I seriously contemplated a private approach." When it became clear it didn't make sense for a journalist to approach a politician in such a personal way, Robitaille "finally, reluctantly agreed" that reporting the story might be the only sensible approach.

A woman friend from England, a housewife who happened to be staying with Mathias and his family at the time, was far less timid in her advice when Mathias explained his dilemma to her. She, in fact, was appalled that he could even contemplate *not* pursuing the story. "What right do you have to withhold that kind of information?" she demanded.

Mathias decided to go back to Haggart to push the project one more time. By this point, however, a new development had changed the story from being just a titillating peek into the closet of someone's private life. Mathias knew Regan had already quietly begun to sound out potential supporters for a run at the Liberal leadership when Pierre Trudeau stepped down. For Mathias and Haggart, this put a different spin on the story. If Regan wanted to be prime minister, his character was an issue. And his treatment of women who worked for him certainly could be considered a mark of character.

Although Haggart gave the green light to Mathias to see what he could uncover, they agreed the investigation should go beyond simply trying to finish the page girl story Peter Moon had started. They were convinced one of the reasons Moon's work had never seen the light of day was because it could be dismissed as one, out-of-character, isolated incident in an otherwise exemplary life. They decided to follow up other rumours and gossip to see if there was some continuing pattern of behaviour that would make the story significant.

They established other ground rules as well: Mathias wouldn't pursue any incidents that appeared to be based on consent. "That taboo was absolute," Mathias says. "We wanted to focus very clearly on the issue of abuse of authority for sexual ends. We also wanted to explore the question of how do you deal with alleged misconduct by someone like a premier who had control over the attorney general. And we also wanted to at least explore the journalistic issue — Moon's effort to report the story and the fact that it had been suppressed."

Not wanting it to leak out that Mathias was investigating Regan, Haggart and Mathias agreed on a bland code name for the investigation they hoped would serve as a logical cover for Mathias's trips to Halifax. They decided to call it "Halifax Harbour."*

Mathias began working the phones. He says he didn't have one particular technique he used to ferret out information. Like most investigative reporters, he based his approach to individual stories on some combination of experience and gut instinct.

Sometimes, he liked to only approach sources after digging up some snippet of information he could wave in their faces like a gloved fist, as if to make the point that he was already on to this story and they'd better not try to snow him. Out of each interview, he tried to gather some sliver of new information he could use on the next person.

At other times, he played "totally dumb" with his questions in hopes that the interviewee would, in attempting to set him straight, inadvertently let out some critical piece of information he otherwise wouldn't have known. Occasionally, he attempted to bully a source

---

* The ludicrousness of trying to keep such an explosive investigation a secret from colleagues in a program that prides itself on ferreting out secret information quickly became apparent when another producer in the unit sent a note to Mathias. "If 'Halifax Harbour' is really about Gerry Regan," it began disingenuously, "I can tell you the following . . ."

into giving up the goods; sometimes he even tried humour. Occasionally, his intuition was wrong. Once, he recalls, he was trying to get information he knew a Price Waterhouse accountant possessed. "I decided to start the conversation by telling him this joke about accountants," he recalls. "When I came to the punch line, there was silence. And then he said, 'Oh, I see, so you don't take our profession seriously. . . .'"

MATHIAS WAS KNOWN in the business as a "document man" rather than a "leg man." By contrast, Gerry McAuliffe, a fellow investigative reporter, was a leg man. "If you told Gerry that the prime minister had a mistress who was living somewhere on Yonge Street in Toronto," Mathias marvels, "he would knock on every door of every building on Yonge Street, which is the longest street in the world, and then go back a second time to any place where there was no answer the first time round."

Mathias preferred to spend his time rummaging around in the fine print of documents and papers, looking for the "fingernail" of information that could connect the dots of his research into a story.

But he could be just as tenacious at that as McAuliffe was at knocking on doors. "I have a kind of dogged persistence," he explains, "that a lot of journalists don't have. I will go on forever. Lots of times I have to be pulled off of stories when someone else decides the returns aren't worth it anymore. But it's a dimension of my personality — which can be a drawback in other professions but is useful for a journalist — that I have to keep going until I find something out. I'm a congenital analyst."

For this story, which would almost certainly involve more legwork than document-burrowing, Mathias began by calling people who seemed not only most likely to know things but also to be willing to share them: opposition politicians, disaffected Liberals, reporters.

Mathias knew Elmer MacKay, a Nova Scotia Tory MP, from some research he'd done for an earlier *fifth estate* program. When he called MacKay to ask for leads on Regan, MacKay recounted a story he'd heard from another well-known Nova Scotia Tory, Billy Joe MacLean. MacLean operated a motel in Port Hawkesbury, which Regan had visited during his time as premier, MacKay explained. Despite their political differences, MacLean, a glad-hander and local politician of note, had decided to put on a show for Regan. He got his entire staff to line up in the lobby to shake hands with the premier. But when MacLean tried to introduce Regan to a young waitress named Carly Sinclair, she blurted out "I hate you!" at the premier and ran off. When MacLean found her later, he demanded to know why she'd been so rude to Regan. "He's my father," she said.

Donald Ripley, then a Tory bagman, told Mathias about a number of different alleged incidents, including one in which Regan had supposedly tried to rape a Miss Canada.

Serena Renner, a former secretary to Garnet Brown who'd ended up working for the NDP caucus, offered up an incident in which she said Regan not-so-subtly tried to suggest to Renner's sister, Glenna Hanley, a single mother, that he would help her find a job if she'd agree to have sex with him.* The story Hanley eventually told *the fifth estate* was much less damning; that Regan had tried to put his arm around her while visiting her house to talk to her about a possible job.

Former MLA Walton Cook told Mathias a second-hand story he'd heard about somebody's sister in his community whom Regan had allegedly assaulted outside the local hockey arena.

He talked to one female reporter who told him she'd heard about another reporter who'd been attacked by Regan at a reception. The reporter, Mathias was surprised to discover, worked for the local CBC-TV outlet.

One source led to another, and then another and another until Mathias, according to his evidence at the preliminary inquiry, had come up with a shockingly long list of the names of thirty-seven different women Regan had allegedly assaulted.

The next step, he knew, was to talk to each of those thirty-seven women to see if they would provide first-hand confirmation for all the second- and third-hand accounts he had compiled. He decided to try to talk to each of them face to face rather than over the telephone.

During the spring and summer of 1980, Mathias flew to Halifax twice for a week each time, to try to track down the various women whose names he had uncovered. His approach was non-confrontational. As a television investigative reporter, he kept his pre-filming interviewing informal. If the woman seemed nervous, he might not even take notes, hurrying back to his hotel room as soon as it was over to write down everything he recollected about the conversation. Those initial interviews, Mathias explains, could be casual and conversational because they weren't designed to challenge what the women claimed happened to them so much as they were to get them to open up and tell Mathias concrete details about the incidents. If they agreed to be interviewed on camera, there would be plenty of opportunity to confront them over any inconsistencies in their stories.

But, in fact, as Mathias later testified, he was surprised at how consistent the stories were and how well what they told him tracked with the stories others had told him previously, and how quickly a pattern emerged: Regan would allegedly come on to a woman — usually young and vulnerable for one reason or another — force her on to a bed or shove his tongue down her throat, pulling back if she fought him off and then attempting to threaten or cajole the woman into silence.

Take Tammy Connors, for instance. Mathias got Connors to agree to talk to him by saying he was doing some background research on Regan and he understood that she'd had an "incident" with the former premier. She had, she said. Mathias arranged to meet with her and her father at the Halifax YWCA, where she now worked. Although she agreed to tell her story, she made him agree he wouldn't reveal her name to anyone without her permission. He made a note to himself: "Highly confidential. Promise not to reveal names," it said.

Describing that "still upsetting" night nearly ten years before when Regan had tried to force himself on her during a drive home after she'd babysat for his family on Shore Drive, Connors described Regan "driving" his tongue down her throat and then telling her later that "this will be our secret."

Connors was surprised at how unsurprised Mathias seemed to be at all her revelations. "He told me that seemed to be Regan's method — sticking his tongue down somebody's throat," she said. Mathias told her he had indeed already heard many similar stories from other women.

Though she wouldn't agree at that stage to be interviewed on camera, Mathias was especially intrigued by something her father said about how G. I. Smith had brushed off Donald Connors's concerns about the incident with his daughter. So Mathias went to see the former Tory premier. Smith was blunt about why he wouldn't agree to be interviewed about the incident: "If you do an item about Gerald Regan," he told Mathias, "the Liberals will have to find some dirt to throw at the Conservatives. And when they do that, that will discredit parliament. So I'm not going to help you."

Mathias also testified that he had interviewed Donna Johnson, the *Herald* reporter who said she had been attacked in Regan's motel room during the Maritime premiers' meeting, and Sheila Murphy, the CBC reporter Regan allegedly pushed on the bed in a hospitality suite. Both confirmed that the incidents had taken place but neither wanted to appear on camera to tell their stories.

Jennifer Oulton did agree to be interviewed on camera — so long as she wasn't the only one to come forward. Oulton, of course, was the page girl whose story the *Globe and Mail* had decided not to publish. Mathias came to see her in her apartment and she recounted not only the incident with Regan but the subsequent theft of the taped interview she had done with Bette Cahill.

Although only one of the women Mathias approached during his two visits to Halifax refused to be interviewed, not everyone confirmed the stories others had told Mathias. One woman said what had happened to her — which she described as a kiss at the end of a meeting with Regan — had been blown out of proportion. It was perhaps sexist, she told Mathias, but it certainly wasn't an assault.

Mathias told the court that Rose Dauphinee, the former Miss Canada, insisted nothing at all had happened. She was working as a public relations person for a local hotel, and he invited her to lunch, ostensibly to ask her some questions about the hotel. Over soup, after he disclosed his real purpose, she cut off any further discussion with an immediate outright denial. Mathias didn't believe her. For starters, he explains, she dismissed the allegation too quickly and then immediately changed the subject. "She wasn't curious about who had said these terrible things involving her. I thought there must be more to it than that."

Mathias was planning to follow up his inquiries about Dauphinee on his next visit. Just as he was intending to pursue another allegation — the first case he'd uncovered in which Regan allegedly forced someone to have sex with him.

Mathias told the preliminary inquiry that he had found Carly

Sinclair, the student who'd been working as a waitress at Billy Joe MacLean's motel and who had claimed Regan was her father, in a library in Halifax where she was now working part-time while she attended university.

She agreed to talk with him at the library but Mathias was concerned about discussing such delicate matters in public, so he persuaded her to find a private room in the library where they could talk. When he explained why he was interested in talking to her, Mathias says her face "collapsed" and she began to cry.

"Oh my God," she moaned. "What have I said?"

Remembering his own rule that he was interested only in cases where Regan had forced himself on a woman, Mathias says he gave her an out: "I'm not here to hurt you," he reassured her. "And I will vanish and never bother you again if you can tell me your conception was the result of a loving act."

"But it wasn't," she said.

Mathias eventually found out, as he later testified, that Carly believed Regan had raped her much older sister Elizabeth. Carly somehow also became convinced she was not really Elizabeth's sister but her daughter, and that Regan was her real father. There were a number of reasons why she might have come to such a conclusion: in those days in rural communities in Nova Scotia and elsewhere, families sometimes raised their daughter's illegitimate offspring as a sibling, creating the convenient fiction to hide their shame. Elizabeth was old enough — in theory at least — to have been her mother. And Carly would have almost certainly known — from family talk — about the birth of Elizabeth's actual illegitimate son in 1960. She may also have heard Elizabeth make comments about her alleged incident with Regan. She may have simply put all the pieces together and come to the conclusion her birth was a result of Regan allegedly raping Elizabeth.

In December 1980, Mathias asked *the fifth estate*'s unit manager to book a flight to Halifax for him so he could follow up those leads. But then Haggart suddenly countermanded that request, telling Mathias to cancel his travel plans. He wasn't going anywhere.

Shortly after Mathias began his investigations, Regan's lawyers had written a letter to Al Johnson, the CBC's president, complaining that they'd heard Mathias was looking into the page girl incident.

The alleged attack had never happened, they insisted, and was, in fact, part of a smear campaign being waged by the former premier's political enemies to discredit him. When Regan's lawyer later realized just how wide-ranging Mathias's investigation had become, he wrote Johnson a second letter, this time claiming that *all* of the allegations Mathias was looking into were unfounded and were part of the same smear campaign.

Johnson ordered the Mathias investigation halted while he figured out for himself what was going on. Although such interference in programming decisions was unprecedented, Mathias's superiors had no choice: they ordered him to produce a report, documenting his research to date and where it was leading.

Given the president's unusual interest in this case, Mathias says he became concerned information about the women might end up in the hands of Regan or his lawyers. So the report he wrote was incredibly circumspect. He didn't name Regan, referring to him instead as John Doe, and gave each of the women pseudonyms in alphabetical order from Alison to Zena and then on again from Abby to Maria — thirty-seven in total.

"Mr. John Doe has been the subject of rumours for many years and for a long time I ignored them," he began, explaining that he had only decided to go ahead when Doe "made clear his intentions" to seek the Liberal leadership. "At no time have I ever investigated Mr. Doe's private life in the sense of any behaviour based on consent," he added. "My investigation is focused sharply on the misuse of his authority to facilitate indecent assault and sexual harassment."

He noted he was only in the middle of the first phase — finding the victims and hearing their stories — of what he regarded as a three-stage process that would ultimately culminate in "corroboration of the victims' stories in a journalistically (and probably legally) satisfactory matter. . . . At the risk of appearing to preach to the converted," he added, "please allow me to reiterate that [*fifth estate* executive producer Ron Haggart, David Zarisky, a producer assigned to the project], and I feel very acutely the responsibility not to trade lightly in Mr. Doe's reputation and family honour. We all feel that the onus upon us to do our work well completely outweighs any superficial advantages that may appear to exist in a fast journalistic in-and-out."

So far, Mathias reported, he had spoken with ten of the women and, with the exception of Dauphinee, none had denied the incidents. But he said he still needed to dig deeper into those incidents as well as follow up on the other leads in order to know for certain whether there was a story worth reporting. "Mr. Doe must finally be judged by a large number of serious and fully proven incidents that indisputably demonstrate a pattern of behaviour."

Mathias's report was an unstated plea for more time to develop his investigation. Johnson, however, was uncomfortable with what he saw as the CBC digging about in the political muck and mire.

He ordered the investigation spiked.

Mathias's superiors, including Mike Daigneault, the TV news and current affairs director, lobbied Johnson, arguing the story was legitimate and in the public interest. "How can you say this is all speculation and rumour?" Daigneault demanded. "Here we have one of our own reporters [Sheila Murphy] who was exposed to this." Daigneault told colleagues he believed he was winning that journalistic argument until he was blindsided by what he regarded as a surprising legal opinion.

On December 18, 1970, Gerry Flaherty, the CBC's assistant general counsel, weighed in with a cautious legal opinion that suggested asking questions the wrong way about Regan's behaviour could be slanderous. After reading Mathias's report and interviewing him, Flaherty wrote to Daigneault:

> If it is decided to pursue the investigation of this matter further, one cannot minimize the risk that in attempting to elicit further information and evidence concerning the politician's activities, one might slander the politician. . . . Repetition to any person other than to the politician himself of the information already gathered concerning the various incidents could be damaging to the politician's reputation and could support an action for slander. Any further investigation of the alleged incidents would have to be conducted with extreme caution to avoid repetition of allegations concerning the politician as a means of eliciting further disclosures. It would not be slanderous to merely invite an interviewee to disclose any information he or she wishes to concerning the politician so long as the question is not posed as

to imply that the expected response will for instance reveal evidence of an indecent assault or lesser sexual harassment.

Daigneault considered Flaherty's opinion "outrageous" and said so. "If that's true, there's virtually no investigative reporting we can do," he complained. "We might as well give up."

But the ground had now shifted on him. Johnson no longer argued the issue on journalistic merits. He simply asked the same question over and over: "Who's going to pay the bill if he sues?" In the end, Johnson ordered Daigneault's boss, Peter Herrndorf, to tell Daigneault to tell Mathias to drop the investigation completely. Daigneault told Mathias later he briefly considered defying the order, but Johnson then threatened to fire Herrndorf — as the person ultimately responsible — if Daigneault allowed Mathias to go forward. The issue was even more complicated than that. Daigneault and Herrndorf were both new in their jobs and they had ambitious plans to move the CBC's National TV newscast to ten o'clock from its eleven p.m. slot. Johnson opposed that too. Were they going to achieve any of the larger goals they had established for themselves or were they going to get fired over one unfinished story that — when all was said and done — might never make it to air anyway?

Finally, reluctantly, Daigneault passed the word down to Mathias. The Regan investigation was dead.

But it would not be forgotten.

EVEN AS MATHIAS was looking into allegations of sexual misbehaviour by Gerald Regan, the RCMP was looking under another rock from the Liberals' eight years in office. The mounties were trying to figure out whether the age-old Nova Scotia practice of tollgating — in which companies wanting to do business with the government paid a "toll" to the party in power for the privilege of getting contracts — amounted to illegal influence-peddling.

During what it later described as "the most extensive commercial crime investigation in Nova Scotia history," RCMP investigators collected more than twenty-eight boxes of memos, correspondence, and financial records from the offices of three Liberal party fundraisers, various provincial government departments, and more than fifty private companies. They followed the money trail from the companies through more than a dozen personal and corporate accounts with links to the Liberal party. On February 10, 1981, they charged the three members of the Liberal party finance committee , during the Regan years — Irvine Barrow, a confidant of Regan's who was now a senator, the insurance executive J. G. "Suitcase" Simpson, and Charles MacFadden, a businessman — with conspiring "together and with various officials of the government of the province of Nova Scotia and with another person or persons unknown" to trade their influence with the government for contributions to the Liberal party.[*]

Simpson pleaded guilty and was fined $75,000.

During the April 1983 trial of Barrow and MacFadden, more than fifty-five Crown witnesses, including officers from twenty-three different liquor companies who handled their firms' dealings with the Liberal Party of Nova Scotia, laid bare a system in which companies paid the party a fee per case of liquor sold through the province's liquor commission. The companies understood that if they didn't pay the fee, their products wouldn't be listed for sale by the province's retail liquor monopoly. "It was the general scuttlebutt in the industry that in Nova Scotia you paid to get your products listed with the commission," testified Schenley's president, Donald McNaughton. "We were under the general belief and impression that, unless fund raisers gave their approval, listing requests would not be taken seriously." "Tollgating was the normal way of doing business in the province," agreed William Davidson, the executive vice-president of Hudson's Bay Distilleries. Jerry Gilmore, the vice-president of Gilbey's, which paid fifty cents per case of twelve bottles of liquor sold, says his firm paid its toll "regular as clockwork." Between 1970 and 1978, in fact, Gilbey's funnelled $327,000 into Liberal party accounts. In all, the Crown alleged, the party had raised more than $4 million this way.

Despite the apparent dot-to-dot linkages between contributions

---

[*] The mounties did try to look into Conservative party fundraising practices as well, but the Tories had conveniently thrown out all but one of their records before 1970. That file showed that Oland's Brewery had contributed $240,000 to the party between 1963 and 1970. One mountie testified during the trial that the Tory fundraiser Donald Ripley had burned the records. In his book, *Bagman*, Ripley said he made the remark facetiously but then added: "When I met Bob Stanfield at a social occasion [later], he held out his hand and said in a voice that he obviously wanted overheard, 'Mr. Ripley — awfully pleased to hear about your fire.'"

and contracts, a who's who of what author Jack Batten described as "clearly reluctant" Liberal prosecution witnesses — including two former premiers, Gerald Regan and Henry Hicks, the former party president Garnet Brown, two former ministers in charge of the Liquor Control Act, Glen Bagnell and Fraser Mooney, and the former Regan aides Michael Kirby, David Thompson, and Bob MacKay — all "took pains to emphasize that nothing improper should be drawn from such connections." Testified Regan: "At no time did Senator Barrow or Mr. MacFadden attempt to influence the decisions the government would make with respect to governmental matters."

In the end, the courts found otherwise, convicting both men. In fining Barrow and MacFadden $25,000 each, Batten wrote, Judge Denne Burchill, "wearing his customary frown, said he thought the convictions and the media attention were almost sufficient penalties for two men of the age and station of the accused."*

But that wasn't the end — or the worst of it — for Regan. During the RCMP investigation, the CBC went to court to force the mounties to release information it had used to justify seeking its search warrants in the case. Included in the documents was information about the secret trust fund that had been topping up Regan's salary since his days as an Opposition leader. Though Regan and party officials were at pains to distinguish between the Hawco fund, whose income had been raised legitimately, and the funds in other trust funds that had been fattened with illegal kickbacks, the distinction was lost on many. That was unfortunate for a man still dreaming of becoming prime minister of Canada.

But when Pierre Trudeau finally announced his retirement, Gerald Regan was not among those who lined up to try to replace him.

There were a number of good reasons for that beyond the revelations about trust funds. The truth was that Regan's tenure as a federal cabinet minister had been rather undistinguished. As he had been during his first stint in Ottawa in the sixties, Regan seemed uninterested in the current hot-button topics that drove federal politics, such as repatriating the constitution or fighting referendums on Quebec sovereignty.

---

* MacFadden paid his fine. Barrow appealed and the Supreme Court of Canada eventually overturned his conviction.

As Trudeau's minister of international trade, Regan did get to promote his own favourite issue — freer trade with the U.S. — but his
efforts in that area often generated more interest from the American
press than from Canadian journalists. While the *Wall Street Journal*
praised him lavishly for taking political risks "to pursue so forcefully
the free trade issue," the Canadian media pilloried him for taking his
family on fifteen free trips on government jets. In 1983, the CBC
reported that Regan had taken his wife and two children to independence celebrations in Antigua, stopping along the way in West
Palm Beach, Florida, to pick up and then drop off his wife's mother
and her husband. The trip cost taxpayers $15,000.

Other than such unwelcome blips, Regan barely registered on the
federal political radar. The parliamentary press gallery, when it spec-
ulated on who might eventually succeed Pierre Trudeau as prime
minister, for example, invariably dismissed Regan as an also-ran, if it
included him at all.

With good reason. Regan, whose command of French one reporter politely described as "about as good as Joe Clark's," couldn't
even count on the support of Liberals in his own province for a
leadership run. Allan MacEachen, who'd remained in Ottawa and
become one of its most powerful political figures, was considering a
run for the leadership himself. Despite Regan's eight years as premier,
most Liberals from Nova Scotia could be expected to fall in line
behind the wily Cape Bretoner who'd consistently delivered federal
dollars for projects in his native province.

To make the situation worse for Regan, he couldn't look for his
future back home anymore. Nova Scotians seemed more than content with Regan's successor, John Buchanan, whose Tory government
had already been re-elected once and looked to be a shoo-in for a
third term.

So Gerald Regan remained in Ottawa, going through the motions,
playing out the anti-climactic final act of the political career he had
once dared to imagine would one day take him to the prime minister's office.

But Gerald Regan was no longer in control of his own political
destiny. The government of which he was a member seemed almost
as accidental — and as transitory — as the Clark government that
had defeated Trudeau's Liberals in 1979. Rather than accept their

initial loss at the hands of Clark's Tories and begin rebuilding their party with new faces and new ideas, the Liberals employed parliamentary gamesmanship to defeat the Tories and force another election. They won it — with a leader who'd already announced he wanted to retire — but the party had no new ideas to bring with them back into office. Although the Liberals chose John Turner, their former finance minister, as their "new" face to counter the new Tory leader, Brian Mulroney, in the 1984 federal election, the voters weren't buying it anymore.

AS IF FIGHTING the rising Tory tide were not problem enough for Regan, he faced another and personally far more dangerous challenger during his re-election bid. It came in the unexpected form of Mike Marshall, a slight, self-effacing young man who had set himself on a self-appointed holy mission to hold Regan accountable for his treatment of women.

He distributed 6,000 copies of a leaflet — "a letter to the Honourable Gerald A. Regan from one of his constituents" — door-to-door in the constituency during the campaign. Though plenty of people were aware of the allegations of sexual misconduct against Regan, this was the first time anyone had raised them in print. "You now stand before me soliciting my support . . . because you share the Turner Team's strong commitment to protecting women's rights," Marshall wrote. "I am writing to you asking whether your public commitment to protecting women's rights is backed up by your own personal commitment."

Marshall not only sent copies of this letter to the media, he followed it up with publicly distributed letters to Prime Minister Turner, asking him to "assure me that you have at least investigated my very, very serious charges," and to Ron Giffin, the attorney general of Nova Scotia, claiming there'd been a cover-up of one alleged incident — the page girl case — by members of the legislature and urging him to make sure "the RCMP Police have been given their freedom to investigate this matter in the way that it should have been all along." Neither replied. Marshall later wrote a letter — also published as a pamphlet — to a local justice of the peace, saying he was "considering" filing criminal informations. He says he gave a copy of that letter to the Halifax City Police. On September 2, 1984, Marshall wrote again to Turner and Giffin, outlining what he said were more than a dozen incidents involving Regan, and renewing his call for an RCMP investigation into a "high-level, tri-partisan cover-up." He also called on Regan — who'd complained obliquely in news reports about "hate mail" being circulated against him — to "take me to court."

And . . .

"And nothing," Marshall laughs today. "Nothing happened."

Not then anyway.

THERE IS LITTLE in Mike Marshall's background to explain why he cast himself as the avenging angel for women he believed had been wronged. Marshall, the son of a Saint Mary's University philosophy professor, grew up middle-class in Dartmouth, an insular place with a "different reality" where "we never heard the stories everyone in Halifax took for granted."

He was a teenager in 1969 when Regan, then the Opposition leader, staged the filibuster that helped propel him into the premier's office. A few months later, Marshall remembers listening to a kitchen table conversation between his mother and a female neighbour, "a Catholic, Macdonald Liberal who was regaling my mother with all kinds of talk about Regan's antics at party meetings after the filibuster." The "antics," Marshall says, included details about his alleged behaviour with women. "No one, including the neighbour, thought of it as any big deal." Neither did Marshall. It was just gossip, strange if salacious, and he quickly dismissed it.

After graduating from Dartmouth High School in 1972, Marshall lived briefly in England but then decided he preferred Nova Scotia. He landed a low-level job at the Nova Scotia Hospital in Dartmouth, which helped finance his hobby/passion — setting up a small independent record label, which released a few recordings by local artists — and gave him the time to indulge his other passion, for politics.

Having dabbled on the fringes of the Labour Party in England, Marshall focused on the NDP at home. During the mid to late seventies, the New Democratic Party became "the main thing in my life. I was a campaign manager, a candidate, I even scheduled my vacations so I could work in by-elections." But he was a right-wing, "pinstripe socialist," out of touch with mainstream party thinking, and he soon drifted away.

By the late seventies, in fact, he'd found a new focus for his political interests. He studied political science at Dalhousie University, dabbling in journalism at the Dalhousie *Gazette* where he helped produce a 1970 parody issue that included a take-off on Gerald Regan's supposed interest in young women. The piece, Marshall says today, attracted virtually no reader response.

Marshall himself, however, had begun to re-think his own casual indifference to such stories. The most important, life-transforming experience of his university years, he says now, was his decision to become "a born-again Catholic. I'd been a Catholic but I'd fallen away from the church," he explains. "Being born again," he adds, "is one of the reasons I went ahead with Regan."

After listening to — and sometimes even passing on — Regan gossip, Marshall came to see himself as a hypocrite. He remembers hovering at the edges of one ceremony at which Regan, then the federal minister in charge of women's issues, was presenting a cheque to a women's group. "I was at the back of the room with the white wine and the white cheese listening to these prominent feminists making jokes about Regan and his ways with women. I said to them, 'Why are you making jokes? Why aren't you doing anything about this?' And then I thought, 'Why aren't I?'"

He vowed to do just that the next time he got the chance. Soon after, Regan was speaking at a public forum at Mount Saint Vincent University, a Nova Scotian university primarily for women. "At the end, there was a question period and I lined up at the microphone. My plan was to stand up and ask him about these complaints about him and women." But the meeting ended before he got to the microphone. He laughs. "I was half-glad I didn't get to ask my question," he says. "My throat was dry and I was really nervous."

Marshall finally decided on a less public approach, writing his private letter to Regan on July 19, 1984. "Now that the election has finally been called, soon you or your supporters will be coming round to my door, soliciting my vote and wondering if I have any questions," the letter began. "Well as it happens, I do. And since I have neither mail slot nor phone at home here (I live behind a storefront), I might be a little hard to find. So I am writing to you instead, hoping that you can still my concerns."

When his friends found out his plan, they warned him: "'This is dangerous,' they said. 'You'll be killed.'" So he decided to send copies of his letter to media outlets. Just in case. Marshall laughs. "Journalists assumed I must have the smoking gun," he says. "Obviously, they thought, 'If he's going to write this kind of letter, he must have some really, really, really juicy stuff.'"

The truth, as Marshall himself quickly realized, was that he didn't know very much at all. "I only knew then about three victims, and none of the incidents were what would be considered serious." He didn't even know when he wrote his letter that the CBC and the Toronto *Globe and Mail* had already investigated similar allegations against Regan.

Despite the flurry of media attention his private letter generated, no one reported anything this time either. That's when Marshall decided to publish the letter as a pamphlet "to preserve it for history."

Despite a continuing media blackout of his activities — there was only one oblique reference to the pamphlets in a CBC news report, which was repeated in a Halifax *Daily News* story the following day — Marshall's pamphleteering not only became the coffee-shop talk of the campaign but it also generated an avalanche of new leads and stories. "I became a kind of repository for Regan stories," he says now.

Marshall insists he had no partisan motivations — "the NDP were upset with me because they figured they'd be blamed for this when they had nothing to do with it" — but it's clear some of Regan's political foes wanted to use Marshall to discredit him.

One day, for example, someone left an envelope on the counter at the photo shop where he worked. It listed the name of the page girl, including her current address, phone number, and the names of other family members. As Marshall was puzzling over the material, a woman customer telephoned to say she was calling on behalf of a local stockbroker friend, who wanted Marshall to know the envelope was for him. The stockbroker was Donald Ripley. Later, he says, he was called outside the store by "an extremely nervous" former Tory MLA, who handed him a sheet of paper with a long list of names and places he said represented still more alleged incidents. The MLA was G. H. Paddy Fitzgerald, a former law school classmate of Regan's who'd had his own checkered career. He'd served as Speaker of the legislature before being convicted of income tax evasion, and later served time for raping a client in his law office.

Even as Marshall gathered new information and churned out more public letters, he continued to trudge door-to-door delivering his pamphlets. He developed blisters on his feet. "The pain just killed me." After a night of canvassing in a rainstorm, he caught pneumonia and became seriously ill. "I had to give it up after that," he recalls. "I just couldn't go on. By the time of the election, I was too sick to care even about the results."

Regan lost, but Marshall claims no credit for that. "I knew enough about politics to know he was going to lose anyway," he says, adding he's "always been frustrated that everyone painted this as a battle between me and Regan. That was never why I did it. From my point of view, the whole issue was really about people knowing and not doing anything. That's what upset me."

In the end, Marshall never did lay an information with a justice of the peace and he doesn't believe anyone in authority, including the police, ever bothered to look into the substance of his allegations. He calls their failure to do so "willful blindness. They knew."

After Regan's defeat, Marshall abandoned his quixotic quest and eventually even threw away his remaining copies of the pamphlets. He didn't expect he would need them again.

He was wrong.

IN JUNE 1993, Marshall's days as a pamphleteer seemed far in his past. He was forty-one now, and worked part-time as the Canadian Bible Society's resident expert on religious music and part-time at the Music Industry Association of Nova Scotia. His only writing these days was a book-in-progress, a philosophical examination of history through the interaction of religion and institutions.

Gerald Regan too had largely disappeared from public view since his 1984 election defeat. He'd settled into the life of an elder statesman, serving on corporate boards and taking on occasional tasks for his former colleagues in government. Mike Marshall couldn't remember the last time someone had even mentioned his name.

Then, one day, out of the blue, Philip Mathias called him from Toronto. Mathias and Marshall had gotten to know each other in 1984 after Marshall sent his first open letter to members of the media. Mathias was one of those who assumed Marshall knew more than he did. "He seemed like a nice young fellow," Mathias recalls. "But I didn't tell him much about what I knew. I wasn't sure I could trust him."

But, in 1993, Mathias was looking for advice and Marshall seemed as good as anyone to ask. "He said, 'Mike, you're a Christian. Do you think it's right after all these years to bring this [Regan] up again?'" Marshall recalls. "I assumed one of the victims had made a complaint." In fact, Mathias was at that point debating whether to turn over his John Doe file to Donald Ripley.

Marshall didn't discover that until nearly four months later when he got another call, this time from David Bentley, the publisher of *Frank* magazine, who told him the RCMP were finally investigating Regan. Soon after, the RCMP investigators themselves called. "They said they wanted to talk about my pamphlet," Marshall says. "I told them I didn't have it anymore. They said, 'That's OK. We have a copy.'"

10

"Many Straws Floating Down the Stream"

Staff Sgt. Brent Fraser would be the first to admit he wasn't singled out to coordinate Operation Harpy, the RCMP's task force on Gerald Regan, because of vast experience in investigating allegations of sexual misconduct. He had none. Or because of any expertise in handling politically sensitive investigations involving prominent individuals. He had none of that either. Surprising as it may seem now, Fraser was tapped to handle one of the most far-reaching, complicated, and sensitive RCMP criminal investigations ever, simply because he was available. And he wasn't the only member of the task force with few specific qualifications for such an investigation.

Fraser, a cheerful bear of a man, had bounced from detachment to detachment in rural Nova Scotia and Newfoundland — from Sydney to Stephenville to Goose Bay to Belle Island to Grand Falls to Gander to Twillingate to Lower Sackville to Enfield — during the course of a twenty-four-year career as a mountie, and had eventually risen to the rank of staff sergeant.

In September 1993, Fraser was settling into his most recent appointment — running the Halifax airport detachment — when Lorne Hall, the commanding officer of the Halifax Subdivision, telephoned to tell him he had been seconded to head up a special task force. Given that the airport detachment's main job was to enforce airport regulations, Fraser admits he "wasn't that busy" and was grateful for the chance to tackle something more challenging.

Though he'd worked for a while in drug enforcement and what the mounties called their major crimes unit, Fraser's only previous experience overseeing a task force investigation was more than a decade old. That operation — a drug case — had been wrapped up in a few days. He had very little experience with sexual assault cases, even less with decades-old allegations involving important public officials and none with an investigation that would drag on for more than a year.

Fraser's key investigators seemed cut from the same east coast mountie tunic as their boss. Since joining the force in 1970, a thirty-nine-year-old Newfoundland native, Sgt. Jerry Pretty, the first investigator assigned to Fraser's team, had also played career hop-scotch across Newfoundland and Nova Scotia. His most recent appointment had been with the mounties' Halifax-based drug squad. Although he'd spent a brief stint just before that in the mounties' Windsor, N.S., detachment, Pretty says now that the name "Gerald Regan" meant almost nothing to him when his boss called him aside in late September to tell him he'd been assigned to the Regan case too. He was just a sixteen-year-old Gander school boy when Regan became premier in 1970.

Sgt. Ron Nause, who would join the task force two months later in November, had spent his entire policing career in Nova Scotia and Newfoundland too. Though he'd worked with Fraser during post-ings in Newfoundland and Lower Sackville and had, in fact, been specifically requested for the task force by Fraser, Nause was under no illusions about why he'd been assigned to the task force. He'd become a pencil pusher — one of two officers in the Halifax Staffing and Personnel Office assigned to handle succession planning — so he could easily be spared.

IT WASN'T THE FIRST TIME Regan's name had surfaced during an RCMP investigation. He'd been questioned, of course, during the tollgating probe the mounties' commercial crime squad launched shortly after he left office but he was never charged in connection with that case and appeared only as one of many reluctant Liberal prosecution witnesses.

During an earlier investigation into what became known as the Hamilton Harbour dredging scandal, however, Rod Stamler, the RCMP inspector looking into allegations of political corruption, discovered Regan's name in a 1973 diary entry made by Harold McNamara, an executive later convicted in the scandal:

March 23: . . . summing up it has been suggested to Moore we might help out in drive for new hockey rink in Regan's area. Moore will bring down a small donation (5 grand). Called John Connolly [a senator and Liberal fundraiser] and tracked him down in Toronto. He will call Regan Monday and tell him what good Liberals we are & how good to build in Mulgrave. Will then call me back. Wouldn't be a bad idea to go & see Regan, I believe.

According to the investigative reporter Paul Palango's account of the incident in *Above the Law*, an exposé of how politicians attempted to control the mounties in the seventies and eighties, Stamler passed his information along to his brother mounties in Halifax. Curiously, no one followed up on what seemed like at least the hint of possible chicanery in awarding contracts for the Strait of Canso project. When the diary entry finally became public during McNamara's 1978 trial, Regan brushed it aside, telling reporters "he had no record of talking to Connolly nor did he think McNamara's company had contributed money to the Mulgrave arena project."

Stamler couldn't have been surprised by the lack of interest that Nova Scotia officials seemed to show in pursuing the matter. A few years earlier, he had wanted to file charges in Halifax against a number of well-connected dredging company executives over allegations of bid-rigging in connection with the raising of the Irving Whale, an oil-filled barge that had sunk off Prince Edward Island. Stamler filed his report to the federal justice department, which passed the recommendations on to the Nova Scotia attorney general. "The attorney general's staff was displeased with Stamler's recommendation," Palango reports, "but at first didn't say why. In discussions with federal justice officials about the case, a senior representative said the province wasn't interested in pursuing the matter. When pressed, he indicated that if the justice department persisted with its demand,

Nova Scotia might consider setting up its own provincial police force the next time the contract with the RCMP came up for renegotiation. But the justice department would not back down. Finally, the Nova Scotia representative conceded that the province would not prosecute the case because it might prove to be embarrassing to members of the Halifax Club. The justice department threw in the towel."

As startling as that may seem, it was, in fact, business as usual in Nova Scotia until very recently. The province's tightly interconnected business-legal-political power structure tended to look out for its own, and the forces of law and order — including the mounties, who depended on the provincial government for their policing contract with the province — knew better than to question or to challenge.

Police officers knew about the high-stakes poker games where local politicians liked to gamble and certainly the role that Ada played in the political life of the province but they also knew better than to try to do anything about either. The cozy relationship between the police and the political power structure, which was reminiscent of the worst of the American Deep South, was finally exposed in the late eighties, thanks to the fallout from the wrongful murder conviction of Donald Marshall, Jr.

Marshall, a poor, seventeen-year-old Micmac, was convicted of murdering a poor seventeen-year-old black man named Sandy Seale in Sydney in 1971. The police investigation wasn't merely sloppy; it was tainted. The Sydney police department's chief detective bullied and threatened teenaged "eyewitnesses" to change their original stories and incriminate Marshall. The Crown prosecutor didn't interview those witnesses, or even tell Marshall's defence lawyers of the existence of their initial contradictory statements. It probably wouldn't have mattered. Even though they had access to whatever funds they needed for Marshall's defence through the federal Department of Indian Affairs, his lawyers didn't trouble themselves to do any independent investigating or even ask for disclosure of the Crown's case. Despite his protests of innocence and one eyewitness's public recantation of his testimony outside the courtroom in the middle of the trial, Marshall was quickly convicted and sentenced to life in prison.

When someone else came forward just ten days later to say he had actually seen a man named Roy Ebsary stab Seale, the mounties were called in but their investigation was desultory and uninterested. No one cared. Marshall was only an Indian, after all, and he had been convicted of killing only a black man. The RCMP report concluded the initial decision was correct: Marshall killed Seale. That no one bothered to tell Marshall's lawyers or the Crown handling Marshall's appeal that someone had come forward with such startling new information only seemed to confirm the pattern.

It wasn't until after he'd spent nearly eleven years in jail that Marshall himself accidentally learned the identity of Seale's killer. He convinced his new lawyer to ask the mounties to take one more look at the case. They did and this time more professional investigators not only quickly discovered the Sydney police had pressured witnesses back in 1971 but also found the knife Ebsary had used to stab Seale.

When the new investigation led the federal minister of justice, Jean Chrétien, to ask Nova Scotia's Court of Appeal to review his conviction, the judges of the province's highest court almost reluctantly quashed Marshall's conviction while blaming him for his initial wrongful conviction. And the provincial attorney general's office then played hardball with Marshall's lawyers over compensating him for the time he'd spent in prison.

Marshall's wrongful conviction — and the establishment's cavalier response to it — stirred such emotion among Nova Scotians that in 1986, after Ebsary's final appeal against his subsequent conviction in the case failed, John Buchanan's government appointed three independent judges from outside the province as a royal commission to look into the Marshall case. But the commissioners, led by Chief Justice Alex Hickman of Newfoundland, surprised the government by refusing to limit themselves to the Marshall case. "In the process of investigating the specifics of his case," the judges wrote in their 1989 report, "we were confronted with a number of more general but no less troubling questions. . . . Is the criminal justice system inherently biased against minorities and the poor?"

To help them figure that out, the judges decided to examine how the system had treated two cases involving high-profile and well-connected political figures from the Buchanan administration — Roland Thornhill and Billy Joe MacLean.

During the mid-seventies, while he was an Opposition MLA,

Thornhill, a stockbroker, got into financial difficulties and borrowed heavily from a number of banks. Shortly after the Tories beat the Liberals in 1978, Thornhill, Buchanan's new minister of development, negotiated a deal with four banks to write off his outstanding debts of more than $140,000 by paying just twenty-five cents on the dollar. The Criminal Code says that any government official who receives a "benefit" without the written consent of his superior is guilty of an offence. Thornhill had no such consent. Despite that, the mounties initially refused to even investigate the matter. When they did finally launch an inquiry and investigators quickly concluded they had a prima facie case against Thornhill, the province's deputy attorney general, Gordon Coles, ordered them not to even talk with local prosecutors until they'd filed their final report with him. Then, despite the mounties' conclusion that charges should be laid, Harry How — the attorney general and Thornhill's cabinet colleague — issued a statement saying there were no grounds to lay charges.

In the MacLean case, the RCMP's initial investigation into allegations that MacLean had filed fraudulent expense claims was halfhearted at best. And Coles took charge of the investigation "in a way that seemed designed to protect MacLean from investigation rather than to determine whether there was substance to the allegations."[*]

Juxtaposing what happened to Marshall at the hands of the justice system with its white-gloves treatment of Thornhill and MacLean, the commission concluded that, in Nova Scotia, "status is important and that one is not blind to influence in enforcing the law."

It recommended establishing a director of public prosecutions to insulate the prosecution service from political interference as well as making it clear to the police that they have the power to lay charges without permission from their political masters.

By the summer of 1993, when Donald Ripley approached the New Minas RCMP with his vague allegations about Gerald Regan, much of what the Marshall Inquiry had recommended was already in place. John Pearson, a Crown prosecutor from Ontario, had been

---

[*] Largely because of a public outcry, MacLean was eventually charged in connection with his phony expense accounts. Thanks to a plea bargain deal, he pleaded guilty to four counts of uttering forged documents valued at $22,000 and was fined $6,000. MacLean later claimed it was simply an accounting mix-up.

appointed as the first director of public prosecutions[*] and there were clear guidelines to keep politicians from mucking about in police business.

But there was precious little to show for the effort. On February 21, 1991, over a year after the Marshall Inquiry report was published and only days after Thornhill lost his bid for the Conservative party leadership, the RCMP finally charged him with seventeen counts of illegally accepting a benefit, forgery and fraud.[†] The Crown dropped one charge even before the preliminary inquiry began and then — after Judge Hughes Randall dismissed thirteen of the sixteen remaining charges at the end of the preliminary hearing — Pearson announced the Crown was dropping the last three charges too because there was "no reasonable chance of obtaining a conviction."

Then the prosecution service's handling of the May 1992 Westray mine disaster that killed twenty-six miners became a national embarrassment. The provincial department of labour initially filed fifty-two charges against mine officials under the province's Occupational Health and Safety Act; Pearson ordered those charges dropped so the mounties could proceed with more serious criminal charges. But the initial criminal charges were so badly drawn, they were thrown out and had to be rewritten.

Even though there were obvious political overtones to the Westray case — senior politicians had championed its development and the president of the mining company was close to numerous senior politicians — critics say Pearson never seemed to understand the case's larger dimensions. In the words of a senior Crown attorney quoted in an article about the case in *Saturday Night*, the absence of sufficient resources was "a disgrace. I have on numerous occasions given my opinion that the Westray Case was the first substantial test of the prosecution service [since the Marshall Inquiry]," the Crown attorney Robert Hagell wrote to Pearson in June 1993, a month

---

[*] Pearson arrived at his post in 1992 fresh from controversy over his handling of the infamous Ottawa budget-leak case, which occurred while he was a Crown prosecutor in Ontario. Then, after taking the Nova Scotia job, he embarrassed himself by initially failing to pass the provincial bar examination.

[†] His lawyer? Toronto lawyer Eddie Greenspan, who would soon get a call for legal help from Regan too. The Regan case would, in fact, be his third high profile case involving Nova Scotia political figures. In 1990, he represented former Regan cabinet minister Leonard Pace when he was called before the Canadian Judicial Council to account for statements he made when the Court of Appeal acquitted Donald Marshall, Jr.

before the mounties began investigating Regan. "The premier, cabinet, and many government officials had a direct interest in this file. . . . You apparently failed to recognize the importance and complexity of the case. . . . The lack of proper support . . . has . . . fatally flawed any prosecution. . . . Concern for the cause of the death of twenty-six miners," he added angrily, "does not seem to be of concern to those in control of the justice system today."

Given that emotionally freighted backdrop, everyone — from the mounties on the case to their bosses at headquarters in Ottawa to the senior prosecutors back in Halifax — knew they couldn't afford to blow the Regan investigation too.

That may help explain why the mounties paid attention to Donald Ripley's vague complaints in the first place. The woman officer who first listened to Ripley's complaint did try to brush him off. He wasn't a victim himself, she noted, he had no specific allegations to offer, and most of what he was complaining about had happened — if it had happened at all — a long time ago. But Ripley was persistent, and insistent. He threatened to go to the press if the mounties refused to follow up. So the officer dutifully took down his vague, rambling allegations and noted that someone named Philip Mathias of Toronto could provide more details. Quickly recognizing both the potential sensitivity of the charges and the reality that investigating them was beyond the abilities of the small New Minas detachment, her boss sent the file — along with a copy of Ripley's newspaper column about "John Doe" — to the Halifax Subdivision, which asked the Milton, Ontario, detachment to interview Mathias.

Chief Superintendent Ralph Falkingham, the RCMP's newly appointed officer in charge of criminal investigations for Nova Scotia, initially failed to grasp the significance of the allegations against Regan. "Where's New Minas?" was the first question he put to his subordinates the day they first raised the allegations with him. His second question: "Who's Gerald Regan?"

By the time Fraser met with Hall on September 15, 1993, to discuss setting up the task force, however, he certainly knew better. Hall could already feel the political heat from Falkingham, his new boss, who had written Hall on September 9, attaching a copy of the Milton interview with Mathias and making the point that the investigation was "very obviously politically sensitive," and that headquarters in Ottawa will "no doubt" be interested in its progress.

Hall gave Fraser copies of Ripley's complaint, Mathias's subsequent interview, and the Ripley column that had started it all, asked him to read them, and then meet with him again in a few days to discuss plans for the task force. Hall said he didn't think the investigation should take any longer than three months.

Fraser and Pretty met for the first time to discuss how to tackle the case on September 28, 1993. The task force didn't yet have its own office so they met in a drug squad interview room in the mounties' Halifax offices. They agreed the first step would be to re-interview both Ripley and Mathias so they could develop their own take on the men behind what still seemed to Pretty "vague" allegations and "vast amounts of information that would need to be organized." At this point, says Fraser, he considered Ripley "the complainant" and Mathias "the keeper of the notes."

On the afternoon of October 5, Fraser and Pretty travelled to Kentville to interview Ripley, who had become increasingly paranoid and eccentric since his glory days as a stockbroker. Ripley, in fact, insisted on reading a handwritten three-page statement before answering any of their questions. In the statement, Ripley claimed he didn't know John Doe was Regan when he wrote the column. "I first assumed the story was about a Roman Catholic Church person of some importance as Mathias was distressed because a church person first tried to have Mathias drop the matter," he said.* He was concerned about people in positions of authority getting away with sexual assault, he claimed, because of "personal experience. When I was about sixteen, I was coming home from church on a Sunday night and some military police were beating an Indian they were arresting. It was every bit as bad as the Rodney King case as far as looking back. I interfered. I was badly beaten and spent the night in

---

* Ripley's unwillingness to admit he knew it was Regan when he wrote the column may have stemmed from the fact that others had immediately made the connection and complained to Jeremy Akerman, the *Metro Weekly*'s editor and an ally of Regan's. When Akerman confronted him, Ripley insisted he believed John Doe was a churchman. After his interview with the mounties, Ripley faxed Akerman a copy of the transcript of the portion of the interview containing his statement with a note: "See, I am not the S.O.B. you paint me to be."

the adult jail. An old wolf tried to sexually assault me and, without the help of another prisoner, I would have been raped." He says the incident "left a bitter taste of the Canadian justice system." That view, he added, was reinforced by a 1967 incident when someone "made an unwelcome, aggressive sexual advance on me during a political meeting. I told several people then, and since then. In 1967, I was put upon to keep the matter silent for political purposes." When he heard later that the man was being considered for a judgeship, he tried unsuccessfully to prevent the appointment. "I admit to bias against sex crimes," he told the officers.

Dumbfounded, Fraser asked Ripley if he wanted them to pursue his allegations against the judge or his suggestion that the magistrate who sentenced him on the assault case when he was sixteen had been involved in a "fine-stealing scam." Ripley said he didn't; he only wanted them to understand his motivations in the Regan case.

In the end, Ripley had little of substance to offer about Regan himself.

But Philip Mathias did. He'd kept the files of his 1980 investigation in boxes in his basement at home. In his first interview with the officers from the Milton detachment, Mathias had been coy, teasing them with what he knew but not turning over any of his files. "My approach was that I wasn't going to give them any documents or anything I considered evidence but that I would give them the leads to conduct their own investigation." Mathias tried the same tack with Pretty in October. He even wanted Pretty to agree that nothing he told him or gave him would be shown to anyone else except the Crown prosecutor. "Pretty wriggled and squirmed but I insisted and, eventually, he agreed. He promised he wouldn't show it to anyone else." The trouble was that Pretty couldn't — and admitted in testimony he knew he couldn't — give Mathias any such assurance. Under rules of disclosure, virtually everything the mounties turned up in their investigation would have to be given to the defence too. "He lied to me," Mathias later testified. But Mathias concedes Pretty was very good at getting him to open up. "He was quiet, persistent; he gets stuff out of people gently but he gets it out of them," Mathias says with a professional's admiration for the interviewing technique. "I think he'd be very good at interviewing women and getting them to say what had happened to them."

He had certainly been good at getting Mathias to talk. Back in Halifax, Pretty spent a week carefully combing through the 130-page transcript of his interview with Mathias and identified forty-one separate incidents that would need to be investigated.

But there was a complication. Regan's son, Geoff, was running as a Liberal candidate in Halifax West in the October 26, 1993, federal election that was less than two weeks away. If the press found out what the mounties were investigating, no one could be certain what impact it might have on the younger Regan's electoral prospects. Fraser and Pretty agreed the best way to keep information about what they were up to from leaking out before the vote was to hold off conducting any more interviews until after election day.

The possibility of a leak was real. Reporters from the CBC and *The Toronto Sun* — most likely tipped to the story by Mathias, who was worried that the new Liberal government in Nova Scotia and its likely counterpart in Ottawa would find a way to derail the investigation again — had begun sniffing around, asking questions about the outcome of an investigation that hadn't yet begun.

On October 25, the day before the federal election, Mathias telephoned Pretty to tell him he'd had a call from David Bentley, the publisher of *Frank*, which was planning to publish a story on the Regan investigation in its edition the next day. Although it wasn't considered a reliable source on its own, a story in *Frank* would almost certainly prompt urgent demands for official comment from mainstream media outlets.

The question of how the police should handle press queries about people being investigated has always been a dicey one. The Marshall Inquiry report recommended the province's attorney general issue a clear written directive to all police departments "requiring absolute confidentiality and secrecy of the identity of persons being investigated other than on a need to know basis within the police force and the department." The RCMP's own policy manual says investigators shouldn't comment to the media about individuals under investigation, and that news releases be issued only when charges have been laid.

But there are inevitably exceptions. One, in fact, occurred within months of the publication of the Marshall report, when the RCMP announced it had reopened its investigation of Roland Thornhill. In

September 1991, the mounties also issued another press release, this time to explain they'd finished their investigation of already widely reported corruption allegations against the former Nova Scotia Tory premier, John Buchanan, and "there was no evidence established to support any criminal wrongdoing." Although releasing the information appeared to violate the policy, the mounties in both cases were responding to information already in the public domain from other sources.

But that didn't make Sgt. Bill Price's dilemma any easier. Price, who'd been appointed the mounties' Nova Scotia media relations coordinator in 1992 and had gotten his baptism of fire during the police investigation into the Westray disaster, knew he would be hearing from the media about the *Frank* story. He'd known about the investigation since early October but had been asked to deflect any questions to protect Regan's son from embarrassment in the middle of his campaign.

But now, with the story about to be in print, Price knew he'd have to say something. But he didn't know what.

ROB GORDON, a Halifax CBC-TV reporter, had heard the rumours *Frank* was about to break the Regan story, but he says he was, in fact, following up on his own, slightly different lead when he and a camera operator showed up at RCMP H Division headquarters on Windsor Street in Halifax just after noon on October 27, 1993. "A couple of days before that, I'd gotten a tip that, if asked, the mounties would confirm the investigation. I'd tried to track down the mountie I usually deal with, but I hadn't had any luck then." On October 27, the day after the election and the day of *Frank*'s publication, Gordon finally found time to visit headquarters himself to see what he could learn. "Just as we arrived, I saw Price and Assistant Commissioner [Allen] Burchill [the senior mountie for the entire province] coming out of the building."

Gordon and his cameraman approached, cameras rolling.

"Sgt. Price," Gordon began without even a preliminary hello, "Can you confirm that the RCMP are investigating Gerald Regan in connection with sexual assaults?"

Price turned and whispered in Burchill's ear. "I asked him what, if anything, he wanted me to say," Price would explain later.

Gordon says he saw Burchill nod and then Price turned back to him. "I can confirm that we have received a complaint and we are investigating it. It involves sexual misconduct, but I can't tell you any more than that at this time."

(Price's disclosure would become one of the key elements of Regan's claims that police and prosecutors were out to get him. Regan's lawyer, Eddie Greenspan, filed an abuse of process motion, claiming the mounties not only showed bias by announcing the investigation in violation of their own directives and before they had interviewed any of the women Mathias had named but also — interestingly — that the mounties had no choice but to lay charges once they announced they were looking into charges. His rationale? If the RCMP decided not to lay charges, they would almost certainly have faced a civil suit from Regan for falsely suggesting he might have been involved in sexual misconduct. While the judge in the case eventually decided that Price hadn't acted out of malice he was "nonetheless troubled by this serious error in judgment.")

Price's disclosure wasn't much but it was more than enough. By that evening, every newscast in the country was carrying the story — and Regan's terse denial: "I have no comment on such nonsense," he informed the CBC.

In the nine years since Halifax voters had permanently retired him from elective office, Gerald Regan had seemed to settle comfortably into post-political life. He had joined a Halifax law firm, been appointed to a half a dozen corporate boards of directors, and spent a good deal of his time travelling the world as an international business consultant. From Thanksgiving to the end of March, his weeks revolved around the pleasant ritual of Monday night hockey games with a bunch of other over forty-five-year-old lawyers, businessmen, salesmen, doctors, real estate agents, and ex-politicians who all shared Regan's obsessive love for the game of their youth. "Gerry may be in Calgary on business on Monday morning," explained George MacDonald, a prominent Halifax lawyer who was also the team's goaltender, "but he does whatever he has to do to get back in time for the game that night."

Regan's children were grown — and successful. Besides his son Geoff, the new MP for Halifax West, his daughter Nancy was the host of ATV's *Live at Five*, Atlantic Canada's top-rated supper-hour

TV news program; Gerry, Jr., had become a pilot; Miriam worked for the real estate developer Ralph Medjuck, a friend of her father's; the youngest son, David, was employed by the federal Department of International Trade, and the youngest daughter, Laura, was a model in New York.

Though no longer seeking election himself, Regan hadn't totally abandoned politics either. He'd become a kind of elder statesman, who would be called upon from time to time to head up this committee or serve on that task force. Less than a week after news about the RCMP investigation broke, in fact, Regan was scheduled to hold a press conference to release the report of a task force he'd headed into the future of the port of Halifax. The press conference, in the legislature's historic Red Room, was crowded with reporters, but few seemed remotely interested in what he had to say about the port. Chasing him from the room at the end of the press conference, journalists showered him with questions about the investigation. Finally, near the exit, an obviously shaken Regan stopped and turned to the cameras. "I've made the only comment on the other matter that I want to — that I am greatly shocked, and as far as I'm concerned, it's a lot of nonsense."

And then he was gone.

GISELLE SUTHERLAND didn't think it was nonsense. She testified at Regan's preliminary inquiry that in most ways, she'd put her fifteen-year-old encounter with Gerald Regan far behind her. She was not the naïve, teenaged babysitter whose breast he allegedly had palmed while she held baby David in her arms or the terrified girl he'd tried to kiss on the drive home later that night. She'd moved away from Halifax, married, divorced, remarried, raised three children, and eventually settled in Ottawa, where she had a successful career as an interior designer for the National Capital Commission, responsible for the furnishings in Ottawa's official residences.

Though she didn't ever tell her parents what she said Regan had done to her, she did talk about it with her sisters shortly after it had happened, warning them not to babysit for the family. Now, one of her sisters had called to tell her she'd heard the mounties were investigating Regan. She watched the item on the news herself. Regan appeared angry, belligerent — the same attitude she remembered him displaying in the car that night so many years ago. She testified she knew for certain now that she wasn't the only one he had attacked. Perhaps she could help those others by coming forward too. "I have a very good life," she thought to herself, "loving friends, a family, a husband, an excellent career. If there's any credibility I could lend to this, if it helps stop that kind of behaviour . . ." She talked it over with her husband and then called Sgt. Price.

"I saw you talking about Regan on television," she began. "When I was fifteen something similar happened to me." She also told him about another sister, now living in British Columbia, who'd babysat for the Regans and "may have had problems too."*

AT FIRST, Constable Ken Brown of the RCMP's Guysborough, Nova Scotia, detachment thought he would be dealing with a domestic disturbance when he got the call to go to the home of a Mrs. Jennifer Norton. The woman had been cryptic on the telephone. There was something she needed to talk about, she said, but she couldn't discuss it on the phone. When he got to her house, he quickly discovered that, while there was an alleged assault involved, it wasn't a domestic situation at all. Mrs. Norton had heard the news reports that the RCMP were finally investigating Gerald Regan. She had some information for the investigators, she told him, and she wanted to know who she should call. Norton was her married name. Her maiden name had been Oulton. Some people, she explained, might remember her as "the page girl."

NEWS OF THE MOUNTIE investigation brought back memories for Alma Connors too. As soon as she saw the TV report, she immediately sat down and wrote an anonymous letter to the head of the task force. In it, she referred the mounties to an incident described in one of Mike Marshall's pamphlets, in which Gerald Regan had allegedly attacked a babysitter. Though the incident Marshall described had actually happened to her daughter, in her letter Alma only wrote obliquely that something similar had happened to someone in her family. But the person had been advised not to lay charges at

---

* She hadn't.

the time, Alma explained, "because it would have only brought disaster to the victim rather than the perpetrator." She couldn't tell the mounties her real name, she wrote, because the complaint could only be made by the member of her family "who still bears the scars of that encounter over twenty years ago."

She was referring, of course, to her daughter, Tammy, whose night of babysitting for the Regans back in Bedford in 1971 had ended so disastrously that "my stomach still turns over whenever [the incident] comes up."

What Alma couldn't know then was that the mounties already had her daughter's name from Phil Mathias[*] and information about the assault from Mike Marshall's pamphlet, and that they would soon be in touch.

JERRY PRETTY LATER TESTIFIED that he was beginning to feel overwhelmed. In addition to trying to track down all the women whose names Mathias had provided, he now had to sort through the growing pile of letters and phone messages generated by news reports about the investigation. Everyone, it seemed, had a tip for him. Including several of his own colleagues. Const. Derek Williams, who worked at the Halifax International Airport detachment, called him one morning to say that his sister-in-law had once been best friends with a woman named Catharine Schnare. He understood that Regan had gotten her pregnant when she was just fifteen or sixteen, that she'd gone to the United States to have an abortion and that Regan's government had handed out contracts to her father's construction company to keep the family quiet. "She's street-smart," Williams told Pretty. "She'll either tell it like it is or she'll tell you to go pound sand."

Pretty decided to pass that information on to Sgt. Ron Nause, who'd just joined the task force, and ask him to check it out. Meanwhile, he would focus on the most serious of the Mathias allegations: that Regan had raped Elizabeth Sinclair and that she'd had a baby, Carly, who was then raised as her sister. Pretty found Sinclair, now a

---

[*] Mathias had explicitly promised Connors he would not reveal details of what she told him during their conversation in 1980. He explained later that he believed telling the mounties how to reach her did not violate the agreement because Connors herself could still "tell the mounties to go to hell. It was her choice."

fifty-one-year-old mother of two grown children, in Edmonton, where her husband was a self-employed businessman. Sinclair had read about the investigation in the newspapers, so she wasn't totally surprised when Pretty telephoned. She admitted Regan had raped her in a gravel pit on a drive from Halifax to Windsor in the early fifties, but she emphatically denied Carly was her daughter by Regan or anyone else. Pretty decided not to press the issue at that point. Pretty eventually determined that Carly was not Sinclair's daughter but believes she may have become convinced of that because of rumours she'd heard about Regan attacking her sister and the fact her sister was already a teenager when she was born.

Was there anyone else she knew about who'd had problems with Regan? Pretty asked. Yes, Sinclair allowed, as she later testified. There was a girl she'd been friends with back in school, a Janice Corkum. Corkum had told her once that Regan had tried to rape her too. But she hadn't kept in touch with her since then and didn't know where she lived now.

By 4:30 that same afternoon, Pretty managed to locate Corkum as well. He left a message on the answering machine, asking her to call him back. Corkum couldn't figure out why the mounties would be calling her but she did know Regan was under investigation. She'd heard it on the seven a.m. radio news the day after the story broke. "I looked at my husband and I said, 'Guilty,'" she testified. "And he said, 'Yes.'" Still, when Pretty explained he was investigating some allegations about Gerald Regan, "I was shocked," she told the court later. "How could he know [how to find her]? I'd told so few people about what happened."

"Does the name Elizabeth Sinclair mean anything to you?" Pretty asked.

"I knew there was no point in lying then." Like Sinclair, Corkum was married as well, with four grown children, three daughters and a son. She and her husband of thirty-two years lived in Halifax, but were looking forward to moving back to the Annapolis Valley when he retired in a few years.

Yes, she told Pretty, Regan had tried to rape her, but he hadn't succeeded. It had happened in his car on the way home from skating one night in 1956. He'd only relented, she said, after she threatened to tear up his wedding photos. She too offered Pretty another alleged incident to investigate; she thought Regan might have attacked her older sister in a gravel pit near Mount Uniacke. Her sister was dead by that point and Pretty was unable to find any evidence to support Corkum's suspicion.

Despite her surprise that the mounties had found her, Corkum says now, she was "pleased that someone was finally going to do something." She agreed to meet with Pretty the next day to tell her story.

THOUGH HE'D BEEN on the job barely a week, Ron Nause's platter was filled to overflowing too. He had decided to work on a half-dozen files at a time, methodically checking each one until he ran into a dead end — no one at home, nothing to report — and then moving on to the next. It took him several days and several dead ends to find the woman whose name Pretty had gotten from Williams. He telephoned her office, told her he was investigating Regan and understood she'd had an "uncomfortable experience" with him. Could he ask her a few questions? They met that morning in his car in the parking lot behind her office in the Burnside Industrial Park in Dartmouth. Before Nause could ask his questions, however, she had a few of her own.

"How did you get my name?"

Nause talked vaguely about informants, trying not to be too specific.

"What constitutes sexual misconduct?" she wanted to know.

There isn't actually any offence called sexual misconduct, Nause explained, but if she was prepared to outline exactly what had happened to her, he could probably help her figure out whether what Regan did was a sexual assault.

"What happens if I agree to give a statement?"

Nause outlined the process. Schnare thought about it for a while. Should she, in the words of Const. Williams, tell the mounties to go pound sand or should she tell it like it is? "OK," she said finally. She would come to the task force's new headquarters in Bedford the next day and give her statement.

JERRY PRETTY TESTIFIED that he knew right away that Janice Corkum would not be an easy interview — or complainant. She was "emotional" and "troubled," but then again perhaps she had reason to be. The nearly thirty years since her alleged youthful encounter with

Gerald Regan had not been kind to her. "He ruined my childhood," she told the court flatly. "I'm very bitter about that." After the incident she claims happened with Regan, her school marks plummeted and she failed Grade Nine. Later, she was forced to take a full year off school and then had to be allowed to complete Grade Ten at home. She began to suffer what she called panic attacks. She was afraid to get in a car. She had to sit in the back row of the movie theatre so she could get out easily if she felt an attack coming on. Shortly after the birth of her first child, she reached the point where she couldn't even function — "I'd start out for the shopping centre and then I'd turn back" — and began to see a psychiatrist. From 1963 to 1981, she says, she saw the psychiatrist on "dozens" of different occasions, sometimes as often as two or three times a week.

She testified that she didn't associate her problems with the Regan incident at the time. But she added that she would turn away from the television set or leave the room whenever he appeared on the news. Sometimes, to protect her, her husband would hide newspapers with stories featuring Regan so she wouldn't have to read them. "He became the man without a face to me," she would eventually tell Regan's preliminary inquiry. "I didn't want to remember his face."

Eventually, Corkum had told her daughters about what she claimed Regan had done to her. But only slowly. And in bits and pieces. And only after they became teenagers. "I wanted to warn them of things they should be careful of," she recalled. "I told them there would be evil they would meet out there when they were young and naïve, that just because people were friends or they knew them didn't mean they wouldn't do something bad. I had gone through an experience and, if anything happened to them, I wanted them to come and tell me about it." The children, of course, wanted to know more. "I ended up telling them the whole story," she testified.

But not easily. And now, in front of a stranger, a police officer, Corkum said she found the idea of talking about that incident — and having to use embarrassing words like penis and penetration — almost too much to bear. In fact, it took nearly an hour for Corkum to feel comfortable enough for Pretty to even turn on the tape recorder. Greenspan would later question Pretty's failure to record the beginning of this interview, among others, suggesting police could have "suggested" what they wanted the complainants to say or "contaminated" their recollections of the events to make them more sinister.

Even when the tape was running, there was much she wouldn't, or couldn't, or at least didn't say in that first forty-minute interview — including the fact that she claimed Regan had attempted to penetrate her, something that the defence would later use to question her credibility. But for all his own concerns about what it would be like to deal with her, Pretty believed from the beginning that Corkum was telling the truth.

CATHARINE SCHNARE'S FIRST statement was equally vague and short on detail. Though she described Regan's kiss — "there's kisses and then there's kisses; he really kissed me, he frightened me" — she didn't call it a French kiss, which might have raised it to the level of a sexual assault. She did say Regan didn't touch her "private parts." And Nause didn't ask her on tape about the reports he'd heard from Const. Williams that she'd had an abortion in the U.S., and that her father had been paid off to keep the matter quiet.*

Part of the difficulty, Nause would explain later, is that police officers have to be extremely careful about how they phrase questions. Nause, in fact, had taken a course in the techniques of interviewing witnesses. "The trick," he explained in court, "is to ask open-ended questions to get the person to recall what happened in their own words, and not to ask restricting or leading questions" that might encourage the witness to answer what the officer wants to hear instead.

While that seems eminently sensible, not to mention fair, such vague, tell-me-whatever-you-remember questions can be decidedly unhelpful to someone who is trying to bring back a myriad of specific, concrete recollections — What time did it occur? Where exactly were you when it happened? Where was he? What kind of cake was he eating? How did he kiss you? Where were his hands? — of an incident that happened nearly twenty-five years before. It's even worse when you're trying to reconstruct it out of the blue in the context of giving an official statement about an intimate encounter

---

* During the preliminary inquiry, Schnare said that she too had heard those rumours but that they weren't true.

to a stranger, and without having a clue which details might be important to the police in deciding whether to lay charges.

Schnare and Corkum wouldn't be the only ones who would later want to make changes and additions to their first statements. And that, of course, would become fodder for the defence's contention that the investigators had conspired with the complainants to elevate initial recollections of what were simply misunderstood — even unwanted — kisses to the level of criminal offences.

When Schnare left Bedford RCMP headquarters after giving her thirteen-page statement that day, Nause admits, he still wasn't sure whether he was even dealing with a criminal offence. But he did have yet another lead. In 1985, Schnare said she had been a beauty consultant, putting on cosmetics shows in people's homes. While she was setting up her table before one show, she says she overheard her hostess's niece talking about having been attacked by Regan. Nause took down the name and added it to his own ever-expanding list of women he would need to contact.

When he did track her down, the woman denied she'd been involved in any incident with Regan. Schnare later told the preliminary inquiry that she may have mistaken the person's identity, but she insisted someone at the party had made the comment. "I didn't haul this woman's name out and make up this story."

EACH NEW INTERVIEW seemed to lead the investigators to more potential complainants, the police officers eventually testified. Take the Berlin Street babysitters, for example. Mathias's original collection of files didn't include reports about any of them. But after Giselle Sutherland gave her three-hour statement to another mountie in Ottawa, she called Sgt. Pretty to pass on the names of two other neighbourhood girls she believed had taken care of the Regan youngsters. One told the mounties about Susie Woods. Someone else mentioned Patricia MacDonald. And someone else suggested they contact a woman named Margaret Simpson.

Simpson was now forty-one. She was thirteen in 1968 when Regan had driven her home from a babysitting job. When they got to her house, she claimed — according to Crown allegations in court — Regan had leaned over and, while asking how much he owed her, put his hand on her leg and began to ease it up her slacks. Stop, she commanded. He did. As soon as she got in the house she told her mother what had happened. Although it didn't seem quite enough to justify filing criminal charges, the mounties added the case to their babysitter file. In a criminal trial on one of the other allegations, prosecutors might be able to use her as a "similar fact" witness to show a consistent pattern of behaviour.

To the investigators, Regan's behaviour had indeed begun to seem consistent — and consistently predatory. Pretty for one began to see the former premier's behaviour — as he described it during Regan's preliminary hearing — as like a certain kind of serial rapist. Regan would allegedly lure vulnerable, available, and almost always young women — babysitters, legal clients, office workers, reporters, job seekers — into situations where he could "capture" and then take advantage of them. His modus operandi seemed almost ritualistic, Pretty said later in testimony. He would pounce without preliminaries, paw and grab and force his tongue down his victim's throat. He rarely ever spoke during an attack but, then, once it was over — sometimes because he had ejaculated prematurely — he would often behave as if nothing untoward had occurred. Most of the time too, the mounties noted, the women made a point of saying that Regan would back off if the victim resisted. After a while, Pretty began to find he could guess correctly what each would-be complainant would say next.

There were occasional unexpected twists, however, including a case of two women, aged seventeen and sixteen at the time, related by the prosecutor during a pre-trial motion. The women claimed Regan had attacked them after meeting them at a dance in New Glasgow in the summer of 1960 — but they also claimed he told them his name was Gerry Grant. After dropping off one of the women on the way home from the dance, the man drove the other young woman down a gravel road where he allegedly assaulted her. He was, she remembered, a big, strong man who pushed her down on the car seat and kissed her hard, forcing his tongue down her throat. He grabbed her breasts and tried to get her dress up over her underwear. Because she was wearing a garter belt and nylons, however, he couldn't manage to pull her panties off. She said she screamed when she felt his penis on her thigh. Soon after that, he stopped suddenly, casually offering to drive her the rest of the way home if she would agree to go out with him the next night. The following day, the man picked up the younger woman at her place of work on the pretext he would drive her home too. Instead he took her to a secluded spot where he ripped her dress off while trying to assault her. During the struggle, she says, he ejaculated on her stomach.

That was the last either of them saw of the man until, a few years later, one of the women claimed she saw the man she remembered as Gerry Grant on television. He was a young, up-and-coming politician, and his name was Gerald Regan. "I recognized him right away," she told police. So did her friend. And they were willing to testify to that fact, they told the mounties.

Although police eventually decided not to charge Regan with those assaults either, they did note what prosecutor Adrian Reid would later call the "similarity in the M.O." to other allegations involving Regan. Police also discovered that, at about the time those assaults occurred, there was a man by the name of Gerry Grant who boarded in a rooming house in Windsor very near where the Regans lived.

THAT'S NOT TO SUGGEST all the leads the mounties followed led police to potential complainants, or even any evidence at all. In some cases, in fact, an investigation into an allegation seemed to take on an almost surreal life of its own. Consider the case, described in court by Sgt. Nause, of the mounties' quixotic quest for evidence of so-called Sri Lankan sex weekends, during which Regan was supposed to have enjoyed pre-pubescent girls as one of his perks of power.

In November 1993, the director of sports and community services in the provincial Department of Recreation during Garnet Brown's tenure there told Sgt. Pretty he'd heard rumours the president of Anil Canada, a Sri Lankan–based company the previous government had lured to Nova Scotia with a variety of grants and loans in the late sixties, had repaid the government's continuing generosity by flying Regan to Sri Lanka so he could have sex with children as young as ten years old. The mounties spent a considerable number of hours tracking down information on the company, finally interviewing a former Anil director who was in hospital at the time. The bewildered man told investigators he'd had no contact with Regan, no knowledge of any such trips, and even less understanding of why they were bothering him.

And then there was the case of Doris L.N.U. (Last Name Unknown), also narrated by Nause at the preliminary inquiry. The task force began trying to track her down in mid-December 1993 on the basis of a tip that Serena Renner, a former secretary to Garnet Brown and later the NDP, had initially passed on to Philip Mathias.

Renner said she'd heard rumours Regan had had an affair with a black woman named Doris. After the woman had had a child by Regan, Renner said, the premier supposedly set her up with accommodation in a public housing project in Sackville, just outside Halifax. There were suggestions the woman might have worked at a Greek restaurant near the legislature. Sgt. Nause, who got assigned the file, dutifully contacted the owner of the since-closed Acadian Grill, a popular Greek-owned luncheonette across from Province House. But the owner said no black women had ever worked for him. Someone else suggested a woman named Doris might have worked at a drycleaning firm next door on Granville Street. So Nause carefully checked the firm's payroll records. He uncovered a Doris, but she wasn't black and she hadn't had an affair with Regan. Another investigator then interviewed a policeman who'd done foot patrols in the area at the time. He remembered a black woman who might have been named Doris who worked at Willman's, a popular fish-and-chip shop in the city's north-end — far from the officer's beat and farther and farther from the original rumour. When Nause questioned Willman's owner, the only black woman he could recall employing was actually of mixed race and her name was Betty, not Doris. And she'd only worked for him for two weeks. Nause interviewed her anyway. Perhaps not surprisingly, she'd never worked in a drycleaner's, never worked with a woman named Doris, and had no idea what the RCMP could possibly want with her. By then, it seems, neither did the mounties. They finally abandoned their search for Doris L.N.U.

There were other cases where the police believed an assault had, in fact, taken place and could even identify the victim, but decided not to pursue the case for other, unrelated reasons — including, in several cases, the fact that the alleged assault had taken place outside Nova Scotia.

That was the reason they decided not to follow up Kelly Allan's allegation that Regan had assaulted her in a Toronto hotel hospitality suite during a federal Liberal fundraising dinner in the mid-seventies.

The situation was the same in the case of Wanda Allison's allegation that Regan had tried to rape her in a Calgary hotel suite on May 5, 1990 — just three years before the RCMP investigation began and more than thirty-five years after the first allegation they were investigating against Regan. This story was recounted by the Crown during the defence abuse of process motion.

At the time of this alleged assault, Allison was a thirty-eight-year-old executive with a Calgary-based firm. Regan, sixty-two, sat on the company's board of directors. At the end of a reception on the eve of the firm's annual meeting, Regan allegedly approached Allison and asked her to drive him back to the Westin Hotel where he was staying. He said he wanted to review with her a report she'd prepared on compensation, which the board was supposed to discuss the next day. They could talk in his room, Regan suggested. Once inside, he offered her a drink. But then, what she would describe to police as "a wrestling match began. . . . I did what I did many times in my life, quite frankly, which was to maintain this guy's ego and not hurt his feelings and not tell him to go to hell." But Regan was apparently not easily dissuaded. "I do this all the time," he allegedly told her. "I'm on the road a lot. I get lonely. It's just sex." With that, he pulled her backwards on to the bed. She says he held both her arms while he ground his crotch against hers. Then he grabbed her breast and placed his other hand up under her dress and began pulling on her pantyhose. Crying, she finally managed to slide away from him and make her escape.

After that incident, she claims, Regan stalked her. On one occasion, she asked another couple to walk her back to her own hotel room because she was afraid she might run into him. She and the couple did see Regan, she says, "hiding" in a doorway adjacent to her room. She went to another executive's room until he'd left. After she got back in her room, however, Regan telephoned her to say he was downstairs and he wanted her to come down and join him. "I want to dance with you," he said. He became angry when Allison refused. "I know exactly what you're doing," he told her. "Someone

else is going to your room. That's the only reason you're doing this."
And he slammed down the phone.

THE POLICE LATER TESTIFIED that some women they approached confirmed they'd been victims of Regan, but said they didn't want to
become involved in any prosecution. Although the mounties theoretically could have filed charges anyway under recent "zero tolerance"
policies in sexual assault cases, everyone knew these were unusual
circumstances — few of the women had come forward to complain
on their own — so the task force made a conscious decision not to
press any charges if the victim was unwilling to go forward.

Donna Johnson was among the unwilling. The newspaper
reporter, who said she'd been attacked in Regan's hotel room during
a Maritime premiers' meeting, told Pretty her encounter with Regan
hadn't adversely affected her career and, while she sympathized with
other women whose attacks may have been more serious, she said
she personally didn't want to proceed.

CBC reporter Sheila Murphy was even more adamant. Although
she said she'd been accosted twice by Regan in the mid-seventies, she
told the mounties she had no interest in laying charges. "What's done
is done," she told me later. "Whatever happened happened a long
time ago and if I wasn't offended enough to do anything about it then,
I'm certainly not going to complain now to fit in with somebody else's
agenda." Still, she says, the mounties seemed "unwilling to accept
that no means no. They called me at work. They called me at home.
When they first called, it was guys. Later, it was female officers who
called. I told them all, 'No.' Then when I came back to Canada [she'd
been posted abroad at the time the investigation began], they called
me again to see if I'd changed my mind." She hadn't. She says now
Regan's behaviour was so far from untypical of the times she believes
it would be unfair to judge him by contemporary standards. "The
night that the incident at the convention happened I was working
TV," she notes. "Afterwards I was driven home by the cameraman,
and he made similar kinds of advances. It may not have been nice —
and I certainly wouldn't have tolerated it today — but you can't apply
standards now to twenty years before. It's not fair."

According to Crown submissions in court, Kathleen Hennan
didn't want the mounties to file charges in connection with her

complaints, either, but not because of any sympathy she felt for Regan. In fact, when she first called Sgt. Pretty in December 1993 to tell her story, she'd called Regan "a dog." In the spring of 1961 when she was twenty-two, she said she had hired Regan to act as her lawyer in a contentious custody case. When she came to see him in his law office in Windsor, he closed and locked his office door. While she explained the problem — she was appealing for custody of her three-year-old daughter from her ex-husband, a man she was afraid was going to kill her — Regan took a few brief notes and then, while she was still talking, came around to the front of his desk and allegedly tried to put his hand up her dress. She slapped his hand several times, then screamed when he put his arms around her, finally managing to convince him to stop and let her leave. Because she still needed the help of a lawyer in her case and she wasn't sure where else to go, however, she conceded to police that she went back to see Regan several more times where the "pawing and mauling continued." These days, she lived alone and was in failing health so she didn't think she could cope with the pressures of a trial, but she encouraged Pretty to "keep going with it. Don't give up. And let people know you are open to receiving their stories so they will come forward with the entire truth about Regan." Pretty accepted her decision not to press charges and advised her to seek help from the province's Service for Sexual Assault Victims.

THE MOUNTIES, IN TRUTH, didn't need any more complainants. The three months they'd initially been given to wrap up their investigation had come and gone, and there was still more to do. They were having a difficult enough time just investigating the complaints they had — and dealing with what many of the women described as additional recollections of their various encounters with Regan.

On February 15, 1994, for example, Schnare amended the transcript of her initial thirteen-page statement to add to the sentence, "I mean he kissed me, he really kissed me," the phrase "he French-kissed me." Nause made a special trip to the law library after that, where he discovered a case in which French-kissing was considered a sexual assault.

And one complainant's mother changed a critical recollection in her initial statement. She'd originally said her daughter had told her

Regan hadn't touched her breast. Now, she said, she remembered
that her daughter told her Regan "had touched her breast but not
under her clothes." While the defence would later suggest that
mother and daughter must have talked it over and decided on a
single, more damning version of events, Nause testified he believed
the mother had simply "lightened things up" in her original statement out of embarrassment, and was now telling what she actually
remembered her daughter saying.

Meanwhile, Pretty had encouraged Corkum, who still seemed
reluctant to talk openly about the specifics of Regan's attack on her,
to write down any additional recollections she might have. She began
making notes in a steno pad she kept on a table near the refrigerator.
"When I was vacuuming," she explained during Regan's preliminary
hearing, "I was thinking about the investigation and I suddenly
remembered that he'd threatened to destroy the wedding photos.
So I wrote that in the notebook." On March 15, she met with
Pretty to give him the notes, which included two key additions from
her initial statement: that she'd felt Regan's penis in the area of her
vagina and that he had ejaculated on her clothes.

AS TIME WENT ON and the investigation spread and grew, so too did
the pressures on some of the women making allegations, including
Tammy Connors. After quickly making the connection between
Alma Connors's anonymous letter and the references in Mathias's file
to the assault on Tammy, Pretty had tracked her down and taken a
statement from her.

Later, Connors, who was now working for the province's
Correctional Services, learned that Bob Hayes, the athletic director at
Saint Mary's University, had telephoned her boss to ask if he could
speak to Connors. He wanted to talk to her, he said, about Gerald
Regan. Hayes was a friend of Regan's. He was also the man who'd
written the letter of reference that helped Connors, who'd been an
athlete during her years as a student at the university, get her job with
the province.

Connors reluctantly agreed to Hayes's request. Hayes, she later
told police, was "diplomatic and did not appear to put any pressure
on her in any way." He said he was a good friend of the former premier's and that the premier had been a good friend to Saint Mary's.

Regan, he said, had difficulty remembering any incident involving a babysitter. Having said his piece, Hayes didn't pursue the matter, but Connors became so concerned that Hayes had contacted her boss and what that might mean for her future job prospects in a province with a new Liberal government that she hired a lawyer who came with her the next time she spoke to the police.

FOR HIS PART, Regan didn't sit by silently and wait for the police to charge him either. He had hired George MacDonald, a highly respected Halifax civil litigation lawyer, to sue *Frank* for its original story that he was under investigation. Though MacDonald was a well-known Tory and the lawyer Donald Ripley had once hired to represent him in his battle with the Investment Dealers' Association, he also considered himself a friend of Regan's. But since MacDonald's specialty was civil litigation and since this case — other than the libel complaint — was likely to turn into a serious criminal matter, MacDonald suggested that Regan contact flamboyant Toronto lawyer Eddie Greenspan to handle the criminal aspects of the case.

Although Greenspan's caseload was already heavy, "I'm a sucker for a phone call for help." Besides, the Regan case seemed intriguing. "I talked to George and there was a grave concern even then that this thing wasn't normal," Greenspan recalls. "*The fifth estate* were roaming around and [the Regan family was] getting calls from friends of theirs who'd been approached by the mounties and then, right after, by *the fifth estate*. It was like they were working together. And these people were very upset by the way they were being approached. It was all very accusatory."

Greenspan agreed to take on the case, and he and MacDonald decided the first step should be to go and see the province's top mountie, Chief Superintendent Ralph Falkingham, to find out what was going on and to let the RCMP know their client wanted the chance to respond to anything that was being said about him before charges were laid.

CLARE RITCEY HAD just returned home from an afternoon of cross-country skiing with her husband and their two children near her home in Rocky Mountain House, Alberta, when the phone rang. It was Claude Vickery, a voice from her long-ago past. She'd known

Vickery when she lived in Halifax in the late 1970s. He'd married a friend of hers, a woman she'd met through her best friend, who had also worked in Gerald Regan's office.

Vickery, then a local television reporter, was now a producer for *the fifth estate*. He was, he explained, working on a story about allegations of sexual misconduct by Gerald Regan and he was wondering if she knew how he could reach another woman who'd also worked in Regan's office at the time.

Ritcey didn't, but when Vickery asked if she knew of any other incidents involving Regan, Ritcey (née "Clare-insky" Bennett) decided it was finally time to unburden herself of the secret she'd kept for more than sixteen years. After talking with her husband, she agreed to be interviewed on camera for the program. "I was thinking about my age [at the time of the incident] and my fear, and thinking of my own daughter who was very quickly maturing," she recalled later. "I decided if I could help her or any other young female, I would."

So did more than a dozen other women who agreed to tell their stories of their alleged encounters with Regan to the television program, many of them on camera. On March 29, 1994, the current affairs program broadcast what it called "the story of the powerful premier of a small province and the young women who were subjected to his unwanted sexual attention."* Those women included not only Bennett and Jennifer Oulton, the page girl, whose allegations would later both be included in the criminal charges against Regan, but also Heather Snow, Peter Nicholson's secretary, and Glenna Hanley, the single mother Regan had allegedly offered to help find a job. All appeared on camera, and all allowed their real names to be used.†

Although the women's allegations were the centrepiece of the program, *the fifth estate* also revisited its own 1980 investigation of Regan too. Host Hana Gartner pressed the former CBC president, Al

---

* On April 12, 1994, Regan's civil lawyer, George MacDonald, announced plans to sue *the fifth estate* for its report on Regan. And Tammy Connors's parents independently complained to the CBC about comments Philip Mathias had made about them during the program. Interviewed by the program about his earlier investigation, Mathias said Connors's parents "begged" G. I. Smith to do something about Regan. They said the characterization was inaccurate.

† Despite that, the real names of Oulton and Bennett still can't be reported here because of a ban on publication of the names of all the complainants against Regan.

Johnson, about his decision at the time to stop the investigation in the middle of Mathias's research.

> *Gartner*: Why did you decide to stop the investigation even before it was completed? They were just asking questions.
>
> *Johnson*: What was at issue here were the principles of journalism. What should the CBC — any journalism organization — be doing? If they were preparing to do a story of this kind, as far as I was concerned, in the very nature of what seemed to be underway, the CBC would end up as being the policeman, the investigator, the prosecutor, the judge, and the jury.
>
> *Gartner*: This was an extraordinary story. We're talking about a man who was the former premier and was a cabinet minister.
>
> *Johnson*: Excuse me, I don't care whether he was Mickey Mouse. That has nothing to do with it.
>
> *Gartner*: Did anyone close to Gerald Regan, anybody in the Liberal government, try to intercede, give you a call?
>
> *Johnson*: I knew you would come to this, and it's absolutely preposterous.

Alyson Morris had been too busy to watch *the fifth estate*'s story about Gerald Regan, but she read with more than passing interest the report about it that appeared in the next day's *Globe and Mail*. It had been twenty-five years ago, but Alyson testified she could still remember her own Gerald Regan kiss, still remember him driving his tongue down her throat. She was only fifteen at the time, a kid with a summer job washing dishes at the Mountain Gap Inn, a Digby resort where her father worked as a groundskeeper.

She'd never talked about what she alleged had happened that day, not with her parents or with anyone else. And, in large measure, she had put the incident behind her. Today, she was a professor at the University of Saskatchewan. She'd married a United Church minister, with whom she'd had a child, but they'd since separated. Her current romantic interest was a man named Mike Leslie, a federal civil servant based in Halifax. She and Leslie had known each other since they were in high school and then undergraduate students together in Nova Scotia in the late sixties and early seventies.

Perhaps not surprisingly, during a telephone conversation with

Alyson later that week, Leslie mentioned he'd watched *the fifth estate.* What was surprising was that Alyson, after so many years of silence, finally confessed she too had "had an incident with Mr. Regan."

As she testified later, she didn't offer many details, but she did begin to think, for the first time, that perhaps she should tell someone in authority about what had happened to her. Perhaps it would help the police to bring him to justice. But then she got busy with other things. It would be almost another full year before she finally acted on the thought.

ON MARCH 30, 1994, the day after *the fifth estate* broadcast its program, Fraser's task force submitted what it believed would be its final report on the Regan investigation. The report outlined twenty-two cases, categorizing the various complaints into groups: there were nine victims whose allegations the task force believed and who had expressed a willingness to testify against Regan; six women who were willing to confirm they'd been attacked by Regan but, for a variety of reasons, weren't willing to become complainants; four women who said they would be willing to appear as similar fact witnesses but didn't want to file charges themselves; and three cases in which the evidence didn't meet the legal test for criminal charges but whose cases police believed helped confirm Regan's "M.O." After sifting through all the possibilities and permutations, the task force recommended filing charges in connection with the following *alleged* incidents: the 1956 rape of Elizabeth Sinclair in the gravel pit on the trip from Halifax to Windsor; the 1956 attempted rape of Janice Corkum on the drive home from the skating rink; the 1965–70 sexual assaults of three babysitters; the 1969 sexual assault of Catharine Schnare, the live-in babysitter; the mid-seventies sexual assault of Aileen Santos, who'd been attacked while escorting Regan to the hospitality suite at the opening of the athletic tournament at Saint Mary's University; the 1977 sexual assault of Jennifer Oulton, the page girl; and the 1990 sexual assault of Wanda Allison, the Calgary oil executive. The investigators believed Susie Woods and Giselle Sutherland, who'd allegedly been attacked while babysitting, could be called to testify to provide evidence of "similar facts" during Regan's trial on some of the other cases.

The next stage in the investigation was to send the report to what are known as "readers," police officers whose job it is to make sure the investigation has been conducted properly and to identify any loose ends before filing charges. Sgt. Jim Brown, the chief reader assigned to the Regan file, did find some holes. He pointed out that in some cases, there were still witnesses who needed to be tracked down and interviewed. Jim Rose, Elizabeth Sinclair's cousin, for example, might remember Regan driving her to visit him and his wife in Halifax; the two legislative pages Jennifer Oulton said she had talked to after her encounter with Regan might be able to confirm that; and the teenagers Janice Corkum says Regan also drove home the night he tried to rape her could lend credibility to her story if they could be found.

The police did find the page girls, who gave statements supporting Oulton's story and they contacted Corkum, who offered some names of people who might have been in the car that night. None of the leads panned out. By the time the police tried to locate Jim Rose, however, he had died — a point Regan's lawyer would later use to attack the RCMP's investigation.

Sgt. Brown also urged the task force to try harder to pin down more specific dates for when the alleged offences were supposed to have occurred before laying any charges.

On May 19, 1994, Chief Superintendent Falkingham sent a formal memo to the Public Prosecutor, John Pearson, asking him to review the task force's lengthy report. "I believe there are sufficient grounds with respect to some of these complaints to charge Mr. Regan," he noted. "I invite your comments on whether you agree or disagree. If you are in agreement, I would ask that recommendations be made with respect to specific criminal charges."

Pearson, Susan Potts, the senior Crown attorney (sexual assault prosecutions), and Marc Chisholm, the assistant chief Crown attorney (trials) all reviewed the file.

On June 28, 1994, Pearson wrote back recommending the mounties go ahead with charges in only four of the nine cases — Sinclair, Corkum, Santos, and another babysitter — in which the women had told police they were prepared to proceed. He pointed out that it would be impossible for the Nova Scotia mounties to lay charges in the Wanda Allison case because it didn't happen in their jurisdiction.

But he did recommend that the mounties re-interview some of the women who'd refused to press charges "because the case would be significantly enhanced if some of the more recent incidents were proceeded with." While Pearson conceded there appeared to be enough evidence to proceed in the other four cases the mounties had proposed, "public interest factors tip the scale in favour of not proceeding with these matters as criminal charges." Those public interest factors included Pearson's view that the allegations involving Oulton, Connors, Schnare, and Patricia MacDonald were old and "minor in nature, especially when placed in the context of societal values at the time." He also argued that the mounties didn't need to file those charges in order to "sanction" Regan's behaviour; they'd achieve the desired results, he said, simply by going ahead with the more serious charges. Going ahead with the lesser charges, he suggested, might be regarded by the public as "persecution" rather than prosecution.

"We are mindful in providing charging recommendations that you're not obliged to accept our opinion and that the final charging decision rests with you," Pearson carefully pointed out, but then added: "We're also cognizant of the duties and responsibilities of Crown counsel to consider whether or not it is appropriate to proceed with charges once they have been laid. . . . I suggest that your investigators meet with Susan Potts to finalize the wording of any charges you decide to proceed with."

Within days of writing that letter, however, Pearson had resigned his post to return to Ontario, leaving his deputy, Martin Herschorn, in temporary charge of the prosecution service. Herschorn hadn't read the mounties' file at the time Pearson made his recommendations.

It's still not clear who in the prosecution service decided to revisit Pearson's opinion but it was obvious within weeks of the Pearson letter that the prosecution service had decided to take a new and different approach to the Regan case. And that Susan Potts, the first Crown prosecutor in Canada appointed to handle only sexual crimes, would play a lead role in working with the mounties on it.

Potts, who'd joined the prosecution service in 1986, had become the province's reigning specialist on sex assault as much by circumstance as by choice. In the spring of 1987, she had been assigned a high profile case involving a man accused of sexually assaulting a prostitute. Potts used new provisions in the Criminal Code to prevent the defence from using the woman's sexual history against her. The man was convicted. "It was my first jury trial and my first sexual assault case."

But far from her last. There are more than one thousand sexual assault cases in Nova Scotia each year. Because many victims prefer to deal with a female prosecutor, Potts — then one of only three women Crown prosecutors — was assigned more than her fair share of such cases.

In September 1988, Potts began a stint as a Crown prosecutor in the busy Bedford court. Just as she arrived, the community was rocked by two "unspeakable" sexual crimes — the "horrendous" rape of a chambermaid at a local motel and the "brutal" sexual assault of three people during the robbery of a convenience store in nearby Windsor Junction — that helped cement her reputation as a sexual assault prosecutor. During the sentencing of the assailant in the convenience store case — he pled guilty and was sentenced to twenty-five years in prison — Potts managed to break new legal ground by having someone who was counselling the *family* of a teenager sexually assaulted during the incident testify as part of the victim impact hearing. And she was so successful in making her case in the motel assault that the perpetrator — a first offender — was sentenced to fourteen years in prison. "Both of those cases," Potts was proud to note, "are regularly quoted in sentencing hearings." Her reputation was only enhanced when she became the first provincial Crown prosecutor to not only use videotaped evidence in child sexual abuse cases but also to employ protective screens to shield children from their alleged attackers when testifying in court.

Given her success in the courtroom, other prosecutors from around the province soon began calling for advice on various aspects of sexual assault cases. And, when the provincial attorney general announced plans in the summer of 1991 to adopt a recommendation from the Nova Scotia Advisory Council on the Status of Women and appoint a person in his department to deal exclusively with sexual assault issues, Potts says, "I knew I was going to apply."

Potts won the post. Her duties involved everything from training and advising the province's sixty-five local Crown prosecutors on how to best handle sex assault cases, to educating the public about issues around sex crimes, to helping develop new laws and policies, and to personally prosecuting a "representative sampling" of sexual assault cases.

Including the one against Gerald Regan.

Her involvement would change the nature of the case — and the charges — and make the prosecution even more controversial than it already was certain to be.*

STAFF SGT. BRENT FRASER wasn't surprised when Potts called him to say she'd been appointed to handle the file and would like to meet with him and the other members of the task force to discuss how to proceed. In fact, he was relieved. During the investigation, Fraser had consulted *Sexual Assault Legislation: 1927–1983*, the thick manual Potts prepared to assist prosecutors preparing cases such as Regan's in which the alleged incidents occurred at a time when other laws applied. He figured she knew her stuff.

When Fraser and Nause met with her at the Halifax Subdivision offices on August 22, 1994, Potts said she wanted to meet with all of the victims herself — including those Pearson had recommended against charging — in order to get to know them better and explain to them the court process. She even wanted to talk to some of those who said they weren't interested in proceeding with charges to see if they might have changed their minds since their initial interviews with police.

All of this, as the defence would be quick to point out, was unusual — and it flew in the face of key recommendations of the Marshall Inquiry report, which called for the separation of policing and prosecuting functions. The argument is simple: the police offi-cers' role is to investigate to determine whether they believe a crime has been committed; if they do, they have the unfettered right to lay charges. That insulates them from interference by prosecutors or their political masters. But the Crown has an equal, counter-balancing obligation to serve as a kind of check against abusive police power; it must examine the charges the police lay and decide

---

* Following criticism from the defence that she had exceeded her role by becoming directly involved in the police investigation, Potts was reassigned off the case just four months before Regan's preliminary hearing began. She was replaced by another senior Crown, Adrian Reid.

whether there is enough evidence or a compelling public interest to proceed.

Nothing is ever as neat as the policy manuals suggest, of course. The police often approach Crowns before deciding whether to lay charges in order to get legal advice or to scope out whether the Crown believes the evidence they've gathered justifies filing charges.

But Potts's involvement was unusual — and unusually effective. She and another young female prosecutor, Denise Smith, spent much of the fall of 1994 travelling to Ottawa, Calgary, and Washington to interview potential complainants.

Meanwhile, Sgt. Brown, the reader who'd been assigned to the Regan file, had used Pearson's June 28 letter as the basis for his "Executive Brief: Gerald Regan Investigation." In his September 30 report, he noted that Aileen Santos had decided she wasn't up to facing Regan in court and so there were — using Pearson's logic — only three cases left to prosecute.

But Susan Potts's efforts were beginning to bear fruit. At her meetings with the complainants, she would begin with what she called "rapport-building" conversations to put them at ease. She told Janice Corkum, for example, that she suffered from claustrophobia too. She'd outline her own background and explain how she came to be prosecuting the case. She'd ask questions about the incidents that had occurred to them and then lead them step-by-step through the legal process if they went ahead with charges. After meeting with Potts, three of the women the police had earlier identified in their report as nothing more than potential similar fact witnesses — Barbara Hoyt, Giselle Sutherland, and Susie Woods — agreed to become complainants.

Hoyt, who initially told police she didn't want to become involved in what she called a "witch hunt against Mr. Regan," changed her mind after talking with Potts in Sydney on February 16, 1995. As she would explain later, picking up on a theme Potts raised in the meetings, "the women who are accusing Regan of rape and attempted rape need someone to stand up for them." Potts, she added, had had "special training in asking questions" and seemed to know how to put people at ease.

But not everyone was swayed. Including Donna Johnson, now a Canadian Press reporter based in Washington. The prosecutor

desperately wanted to convince her to become one of the complainants, not so much because of what she said Regan had done to
her in the hotel room in Windsor during the Maritime Premiers'
Conference but because the incident seemed similar enough to the
1990 Wanda Allison assault in Calgary that the Crown might be able
to get a judge to admit it as similar fact evidence during the trial.
That was important not only because the M.O. had been similar in
both cases but also because the Calgary incident happened much
more recently, and Pearson had told the mounties that trying the
more recent allegations could enhance their case.

By the time Potts and her fellow prosecutor Denise Smith finally
interviewed Johnson in late February 1995 in a room in the Embassy
Suites Hotel in Washington, she had already resisted earlier efforts by
Philip Mathias in 1980 to get her to talk on camera about her experience with Regan, by *the fifth estate* again in 1994, and finally by
Sgt. Pretty that same year to get her to press charges. "Pretty was a
very good listener," she recalled, "very good at getting people to tell
their stories without putting them under any pressure."

So was Potts. "She and Denise [Smith] were very sympathetic.
They talked about how it was the right thing to do, that I could add
my voice in support of the other women." They also referred to the
Calgary incident and the importance of the jury hearing about it.
"But I didn't feel any undue pressure. No one twisted my arm."

By the end of the two-hour meeting, Johnson was leaning to
allowing the prosecutors to include her as a complainant. She would
talk to her husband, she said, and get back to Potts. But, after discussing it with him, she called back to say she still didn't want to
be part of the case. It would take another two years and another
prosecutor to finally change her mind.

By February 1995, it was no longer a question of whether the
police would lay charges, but simply how many charges would be
filed and what they would be.

In fact, it appears the decision to charge Regan may have been
made much earlier. According to Staff Sgt. Fraser's notes of a July 15
meeting between members of the task force and Susan Potts, they
discussed "where charges are laid and an appearance by Regan
in court." At that same meeting, Potts told the mounties it wasn't
"advisable" to bring the charges before Provincial Court Judge

Hughes Randall. "Political appointment," Fraser's notes say cryptically, adding: "Potts is to keep monitoring the court docket to see who is sitting when and what would be in our best interest." Those notes became the basis for Judge Michael MacDonald's scathing criticism of Potts in his April 2, 1998, decision on the defence's abuse of process motion. "This entry represents a blatant attempt at judge-shopping, pure and simple," MacDonald wrote. "It is offensive and most troubling. . . . Ms Potts's statement has the effect of tainting her entire involvement in the process."

On March 2, 1995, at eight o'clock in the morning, Pretty and Nause drove to Regan's Shore Drive home on the edge of Bedford Basin. They planned to arrest him there but there were no signs of life at the house. The long steep driveway was ice-covered and apparently hadn't been cleared for a while. They waited for an hour and then left. The next afternoon, the two mounties, dressed in plain clothes, showed up at Regan's law office to do the deed, only to discover Regan was out of the country, vacationing in Florida. Finally, Chief Superintendent Falkingham called Regan's Halifax lawyer, George MacDonald, to officially inform him the police did intend to charge his client and to make arrangements for his surrender.

Ed Greenspan was livid. He and MacDonald had met with Falkingham back in December 1993 and thought they had a deal that Regan would get a chance to tell his side of the story before police decided whether to lay any charges. He was even more livid after he spoke by phone with Susan Potts and Martin Herschorn. Potts not only told Greenspan the police planned to charge Regan regardless of what he had to say but she also said that she would be asking the court to lift Regan's passport as well. "I went off the dial," Greenspan admits. "Regan wasn't going anywhere and they knew it. They just wanted to embarrass him in a public courtroom."

On March 15, Greenspan flew to Halifax to accompany MacDonald, Regan, his wife Carole, and daughters Miriam and Nancy to the Bedford courthouse, where Pretty formally arrested Regan in an anteroom, and where Regan finally, just before the hearing began, got the chance to take a look at the charges against him. There were names on the list, he told Greenspan, he didn't even recognize.

He was charged with a total of sixteen offences involving eleven different women. The charges ranged from nine counts of indecent assault to one count under an old Criminal Code prohibition against having sexual intercourse with "a female person who was not his wife and was of previous chaste character and was fourteen years of age or more and was under the age of sixteen years." The dates of the alleged incidents ranged from 1956, when Regan was a young lawyer, to 1978, when his government went down to electoral defeat, and included not only three of the four cases Pearson said should go forward but also two cases (Sutherland and Susie Woods) the police originally intended to use only as similar fact incidents, and four more (MacDonald, Connors, Schnare, and Oulton) Pearson had specifically recommended against proceeding with.

Greenspan didn't know that yet. He wouldn't learn of the existence of the Pearson letter for more than a year, and even then he would have to fight Crown claims of solicitor-client privilege to finally see a copy of it. But even as he quickly riffled through the package of disclosure material the Crown provided him with that day — a collection of complainants' statements, plus a mixed bag of odds and ends, including a colour-coded floor plan of the Regans' Berlin Street house that Sutherland had prepared from memory and statements from Catharine Schnare's parents about their recollections of the day Catharine had called to ask them to come pick her up at the Regan house — Greenspan was already certain there was far more to the case than he would ever find in those documents, or in the charges themselves.

As they waited for Regan's case to be called, Greenspan began rehearsing arguments that, at this stage at least, were designed as much for the swell of reporters crowding the courtroom — and their readers and viewers at home — as they were for the judge. As always, Greenspan was eager to perform.

For Regan, however, it had to be an ignominious moment. The Halifax *Daily News* columnist David Swick described the courtroom scene: "Dignified and well dressed, [Regan] looked out of place surrounded by his fellow accused: drunks and petty thieves, sporting fresh haircuts and their best Nikes."

When his turn finally came, Greenspan deftly turned what would normally have been a perfunctory five-minute arraignment into a seventy-minute harangue. His essential argument — and one that would become the mantra for both Regan and Greenspan — was that the police and prosecutors were out to get Regan because he had once been a public figure. "The climate of unfairness in this case is staggering and overwhelming," Greenspan declared. "I am not guilty of these charges," Regan said outside the courtroom, his wife at his side, "and I have no doubt whatsoever that I would not be facing these ancient allegations if I had not been in public life." Greenspan's conspiracy theory included not only the police and prosecution but also the CBC. "*The fifth estate* and the police unfortunately got into bed together and now we are faced with these charges," he said.

By the end of the session, Greenspan had well and truly served notice he planned to play hardball with everyone, including the complainants. He even asked the judge to lift the usual ban on publishing the names of Clare Bennett and Jennifer Oulton since they'd already appeared on *the fifth estate*. In a tone that seemed calculated to send a chill through all of the complainants, Greenspan said he wanted to place ads in newspapers across the country to ask for public assistance in finding out more about their backgrounds.

At the end of the hearing, while other reporters hurried outside to prepare for scrums with Regan and Greenspan, Swick hung back. "It was moving," he wrote, "to see Carole lean toward her husband and put her hand on his shoulder. His head was bent. He was reading the case file, assessing the damage, and his wife had her arm draped down his back, her hand on his shoulder, and kept it there for several minutes. It was a sign of support, of love."

After the arraignment, MacDonald drove Regan to the Sackville RCMP headquarters where he was fingerprinted and photographed. He would be back in court May 30 for election and plea.

Flying back to Toronto that night, Greenspan finally got the chance to read the case book. He carefully examined the various statements the complainants had made to the police, looking for discrepancies he might be able to exploit in the courtroom. He found plenty. Janice Corkum's statements, for example, escalated the seriousness of the offences Regan was alleged to have committed. It was only after several interviews — and based on some notes she'd written up (which Sgt. Pretty, in his own notes, described as a "sudden episode of recall") — that Corkum "remembers" a feeling of flesh on flesh as Regan's penis touched her vagina. Greenspan was looking forward to cross-examining her.

"MANY STRAWS FLOATING down the stream tell which way the current runs." Brent Fraser re-read the sentence. It had only been a few days since he'd gone to the Bedford courthouse to file the formal charges against Gerald Regan but the words on the page in front of him in a letter from a woman who had signed herself, "Alyson Morris, Ph.D.," seemed eerily appropriate to this still-unfolding, seemingly never-ending Regan case.

The publicity following filing of the charges against Regan had led to yet another freshet of phone calls and letters containing still more allegations, still more victims.

Including this one from Alyson Morris, Ph.D. In addition to the quotation — which came from a privately published 1916 book entitled *God's Word to Women* — Morris's letter contained the details of an incident in which Regan allegedly assaulted Morris in 1968 while she was a fifteen-year-old student working as a dishwasher at the Mountain Gap Inn.

Alyson . . .

Alyson?

Fraser was sure he'd heard that name before in connection with this investigation. Oh yes, now he remembered. A sergeant had told him about a phone call he'd received from a man named Mike Leslie who'd described an incident with Regan involving a friend of his named Alyson. The incident was the one described in the letter.

Fraser added Morris's name to the list of those who would have to be contacted.

ON MARCH 21, less than a week after the first set of charges were laid, Susan Potts called Jerry Pretty with yet another lead. A former Halifax police officer named David Rent had called about an incident from the late sixties involving Regan and the daughter of one of his neighbours. At the time, he said, he and his wife had shared a Dartmouth duplex with an Italian family called the Palermos. After he laid out what he remembered about the incident, he told Pretty how upset he was with himself at just how relieved he felt when the young woman told him she didn't want him to do anything about it. At the time, he said, he couldn't help worrying about what prompting an investigation into the sexual conduct of someone as powerful as Gerald Regan might do to his career as a policeman.

Now, he told Pretty, he wasn't nearly so concerned. He wasn't sure if the Palermo case was one of the charges against Regan but, if it was, he said, he'd be happy to be a corroborating witness.

While Francetta Palermo wasn't one of their complainants, it turned out the mounties had recently learned of her case through another source. Leo Hobin had once been married to Francetta's younger sister, Anna Maria. She had told him about her sister's encounter with Regan. Though they were now divorced, Hobin not only told police about what he remembered of what he'd been told — which matched up with Rent's story — but also helped them track Francetta to British Columbia where she was working as a legal secretary.

On May 26, she flew to Halifax to meet with Pretty and Potts. The week before, Alyson Morris had made the flight to Halifax from Saskatchewan to give a statement too. Fraser began drawing up new charges to add to those Regan was already facing.

EDDIE GREENSPAN didn't know any of that yet. But the very idea that the prosecution would add new charges just two and a half months after filing sixteen other complaints against his client fit very well with Greenspan's developing thesis — that the police and prosecutors were out to get Gerald Regan for the crime of being a public figure.

On April 24, Greenspan released a nine-page open letter to John Savage, the premier of Nova Scotia, imploring him to appoint a special prosecutor to review the evidence against Regan and decide whether the case should proceed at all. Although he knew Savage was unlikely to agree to interfere in such a politically sensitive case, writing the letter gave Greenspan the chance to put his own best spin on the evidence against his client.

The mounties' massive investigation, he noted, had been spawned not by an alleged victim but by a complaint from a "well-known political enemy of Mr. Regan." The investigators then questioned witnesses "in a leading manner in an effort to have their stories conform to what the investigators wanted to believe was the truth." To compound that unfairness even more, he added, the prosecutors, who should have been assessing whether it would be fair to Regan to proceed on these ancient and minor allegations, had lost their sense of perspective on the case because "I understand that at least two of the prosecutors with the prosecution service participated directly and actively in the investigation."

Greenspan also used the letter to publicly attempt to undermine the credibility of many of the complainants. "The complainant in Count #9 initially says that while he was driving the car, Mr. Regan touched her breasts with both hands," Greenspan wrote of one allegation. "In view of the obvious improbability of such a story, the police officer, after prolonged questioning, is able to have the complainant accept that it could only have been with one hand." In another case, Greenspan said, one of the police officers suggested to a complainant's mother that her daughter's incident with Regan — which Greenspan characterized as "touching outside clothing and a kiss" — must have been "devastating." "I do not believe that in the twenty-five years that I have practised law I have ever seen a police investigation show such bias against a client," he wrote. "This kind of unfairness has, I believe, infected the investigation and the early stages of the prosecution. It has also hampered the investigation of the truth of these allegations. For example, I am now in possession of numerous affidavits, all credible and convincing, that [Elizabeth Sinclair,] the complainant in counts one to four, the most serious cases upon which this prosecution rests, is an unmitigated liar. For example, one of the allegations with respect to this complainant [count #2] is that Mr. Regan had intercourse with her when she was of 'previously chaste character.' On more than one occasion, this complainant alleges that she was a 'virgin' and indeed had never been kissed before when she was allegedly assaulted. Had the police done a proper investigation they would have learned that, prior to or at the time of the alleged assault, this client was known and seen to have been pregnant with an illegitimate child.*

"While certain of the allegations are quite serious," he conceded, "the majority of the complaints, even if fully believed, amount to little more than unwanted kisses, or what today under today's height-ened sense of morality might be considered sexual harassment." Besides, he added, "these charges call for Mr. Regan to account for

---

* While Sinclair did have an out-of-wedlock child and while its existence would become a key bone of contention during Regan's 1998 trial, the baby — contrary to Greenspan's letter — was born several years after the alleged incident with Regan.

conduct that reached back into the dim recesses of time to another era and another generation.

"Although he was a high-ranking government official who served his province and this country with distinction for many years," Greenspan offered, "Mr. Regan has no right to any special favourable treatment. On the other hand, he also has the absolute right to expect that he will be treated fairly and in the same manner as anyone else. While no one is above the law, no one is beneath the protection of the law."

While Greenspan conceded that appointing a special prosecutor to reconsider the Regan case might smack of political favouritism, he told the premier, "It is the special, even extraordinary, treatment which this investigation had already had which leads me to make this request, not so Mr. Regan will be given special treatment, but to ensure that he receives equal treatment."

As expected, Savage passed the hot potato on to Bill Gillis, the onetime Regan cabinet minister who was now Savage's attorney general. Gillis refused to go near the case. "We have an independent prosecution service and I don't think it's appropriate to intervene," he explained.

Still, Greenspan had accomplished much of what he set out to do. He'd shifted the focus from whether Regan did what he was accused of doing to whether police and the Crown had deliberately targeted him for persecution.

Gerald Regan certainly saw himself as the real victim in the case. And, perhaps in a sense, he was.

One would be hard-pressed to characterize Donald Ripley as a public-spirited individual concerned solely about justice for women. If not for Ripley's hatred for Regan, it's clear the police would never have known about the collection of allegations that became the starting-point for their investigation. And — because of who Regan was, and because of the Crown's and the mounties' own need to demonstrate that they have learned their lessons from the Marshall Inquiry's exposure of the tainted history of unequal justice in Nova Scotia — the case itself has also always clearly been about more than simply whether Gerald Regan did what he was accused of doing.

If he had never been premier of Nova Scotia, would authorities have spent the time and the money and the energy to pursue allegations dating back thirty and forty years, many of which — at least when considered individually — would constitute relatively low-end sexual assaults at worst?

The answer is . . . probably not.

Even though Greenspan had forced the police and the Crown to defend themselves, the question remained whether he could use these issues to convince a judge to throw out the charges. And, if not, whether he could convince a jury to acquit his client.

11

Time Out:
Gerry and Me 3

" I haven't sat in on the [preliminary] court proceedings and I haven't asked him to tell me anything," Arnie Patterson begins carefully. We are sitting in a west-end Halifax Tim Hortons sharing a coffee and talking about Gerald Regan. Patterson has known Gerry Regan since they were teenagers together. Young Gerry would travel to Dartmouth from Windsor during the summers to visit his cousin Jack, who happened to be Arnie's best friend. Arnie and Gerry and Jack often went to dances together, and they played and watched sporting events as a group too. "He was fun to be around, interested in the same things as the rest of us," Arnie says fondly. Later, when they became adults, Arnie and Gerry continued to share passions — for sports, and broadcasting, and, especially, for Liberal party politics. These days, the two men — senior citizens, grandfathers — are neighbours in the exclusive Shore Drive section of Bedford outside Halifax.

Arnie and his wife know — and like — Gerry and Carole and the Regan kids. "They're great kids," says Arnie with almost paternal pride, "and Gerry's a great father, a father-of-the-year kind of guy."

Arnie doesn't want to believe his friend could have done bad things with women. Like a lot of Regan's friends, particularly men of a certain age, Arnie believes Regan is probably a victim of his

political enemies and — more likely and perhaps also more importantly — our politically correct times. "I don't know the details —
and I don't want to know the details," Arnie tells me again, "but let's
face it. The times were different back then. Everyone did things then
they wouldn't do today. I mean, I'm Gerry's age, and I can tell you
I did things then I wouldn't do today." He stops, freezes me with
a look. "I'm sure you did too." Point made. "So is it really fair to
charge someone now for doing things that may not have been
considered so bad twenty-five or thirty years ago?"

"Arnie," I begin. I want to answer him carefully because I have
heard this argument before, and have even from time to time made
some variation of it myself. "When your kids were young and you
hired teenaged girls to babysit them, did you ever try to kiss and grab
one of them on the drive home?"

Arnie blanches. "No," he says finally. "Is that . . . is that what they
say?"

It is.

12

Proof Beyond a Reasonable Doubt

" **M**embers of the jury, have you agreed upon your verdicts?" The court clerk asked her rote question with a wavering, tell-me-don't-tell-me tone that seemed to capture perfectly the nervous, nerve-wracked mood among the more than three dozen men and women sitting in the Halifax Law Court's Courtroom 3-1 on the blustery afternoon of December 18, 1998. Everyone in the sterile, high-ceilinged, red-bricked courtroom — Gerald Regan, his wife Carole, their six grown children, their spouses, Sgt. Jerry Pretty, Eddie Greenspan, the Crown prosecutor Adrian Reid, their respective legal associates and support staff, the rows of suddenly no-longer-bored-been-there-done-that reporters, the clutch of curious between-hearings lawyers and the gaggle of faithful courtroom regulars, Greenspan groupies and Regan haters, many of whom had sat through every hour of every day of this six-week trial — craned to look at the six women and four men in the jury box, trying to read the tea leaves of their faces for some sign of the outcome, waiting with a kind of desperate unease for the pregnant pause between the clerk's question and the jury forewoman's answer to finally end.

The moment only seemed to last forever.

"We have," the jury forewoman said, her voice clear, quick, and confident, a telling counterpoint to the court clerk. The clock, high on the wall behind the ten-member jury showed the time: 2:25 p.m.

The five-year saga of the Queen versus Gerald Augustine Regan had finally come down to this simple yes/no, guilty/not guilty moment, to the answers the jury forewoman would now offer to the clerk's mantra-like questions, which would be repeated for each of the eight counts in the indictment.

"What is your verdict on the first count?" the clerk asked.

Everything that went before — the RCMP investigation, which had begun in 1993 and never really ended, even after police laid the first charges in March 1995, and had still not ended now; the indictment itself, to which so many charges had since been added, dropped, amended, stayed, and appealed it was sometimes difficult to keep track of the current status of any of them; the legal jockeying between Crown and defence, which began before the ink had dried on the first charges and had still not ended, even after the judge had issued his own final instructions to the jury the day before; the rancorous sixty-seven-day preliminary hearing, which had dragged out over nearly twelve months of testimony and argument and then ended abruptly and without resolution in April 1997, when the Crown opted to use a rarely used power to force the case directly to trial; the more weeks over more months of pre-trial hearings on defence motion after defence motion, which had ultimately served to whittle the case against Gerald Regan down to just nine charges involving four different women; and, finally, to this trial itself, which had dealt with eight of the charges clustered around the three most serious allegations: the alleged rape, indecent assault, and forcible confinement of Elizabeth Sinclair, the alleged attempted rape, indecent assault, and forcible confinement of Janice Corkum, and the alleged attempted rape and indecent assault of Francetta Palermo — was all now merely prologue.

The truth — or lack of truth — of the sometimes graphic, often conflicting, occasionally conflicted testimony of the trial's twenty-four witnesses, already reduced to 4,000 pages of typed transcript neatly piled on tables near the court clerk; the 129 official exhibits — an oddly eccentric collection of yellowed newspaper clippings, ancient school records, happier-time family photos, lifeless aerial pictures of long grown-over gravel pits, a recipe for Carole Regan's fish chowder that may or may not have been Carole Regan's, a receipt for a 1956 honeymoon sightseeing bus tour of Washington, D.C. — and even the impassioned closing arguments of Crown ("[The complainants are] here for the sole and single reason that what they're telling you is the truth") and defence ("I urge you to acquit Gerald Regan, I ask you . . . to raise that shield against injustice called reasonable doubt and say, 'No, this is not enough.' I ask you to acquit him and return him to his wife and children") suddenly mattered less than what the jury had made of it all. And — only slightly less important to the defendant, a man who had sought to live his life in the glare of the spotlight — what the public would ultimately make of whatever the jury made of it all.

Gerald Regan knew, as he had known from the beginning, that there could very well be two verdicts: the one rendered inside Courtroom 3-1, based on the evidence the judge permitted the jury to hear, and the other, rendered beyond here in the much less circumspect court of public opinion, based not only on that evidence but also on all of the other evidence, allegations, innuendo, inference, and assumptions Regan and his lawyers had fought so desperately for so long to keep from the jury, and from the public.

"The day it all comes out," Eddie Greenspan advised his client once, "is the day you should arrange to leave town."

It was too late for that now.

In one of the few setbacks the defence had suffered inside the courtroom, the trial's presiding judge, Associate Chief Justice Michael MacDonald, had the day before rejected a defence plea to extend a publication ban on everything heard in the jury's absence until at least after the jury had rendered its verdict.

"I have never asked for this before because I have never thought there would be an onslaught of information that would prejudice [the jury]," Greenspan explained to the judge shortly after the jury had retired to begin its deliberations. "I have grave concerns."

In the end, the judge's decision to reject the request lifted the curtain on virtually all of the details of the Crown's case against Gerald Regan for everyone in Canada — except for the ten members of the jury, the ones whose views mattered most.* They had been sequestered in a nearby hotel overnight, hermetically sealed off in rooms that had been stripped of television sets, radios, and telephones. Sheriff's deputies, who monitored their telephone calls home, had also been ordered to keep them as far as possible from other diners in the restaurants where they ate. The judge even ordered newspaper boxes along the path between their hotel and the courthouse covered or turned away so the jurors couldn't read the headlines.

The front page headline the jurors didn't see in the next morning's Halifax *Daily News* said it all: "What the Regan Jury Didn't Hear." There was a lot.

As is usual in criminal cases in Canada, the judge at the Regan preliminary inquiry, Jean-Louis Batiot, had issued an order on the opening day of the proceedings barring anyone from publishing or broadcasting any evidence presented. The purpose of such bans is to protect the defendant's rights at any future trial. But since our system also stresses the importance of justice being seen to be done as well as being done, publication bans almost always expire once a case is disposed of, regardless of the outcome. The problem in the Regan case was that there were so many separate but inter-related cases the bans had remained in effect even after some of the charges were stayed in the spring of 1998. While the media could report that Regan had been charged initially with eighteen sex-related offences and the judge, after much evidence and legal argument, had stayed nine of them, they couldn't report the details of even those allegations until the end of this trial. During the lengthy pre-trial arguments and the trial itself, journalists could only report what was said when the jury was present. The purpose again: to prevent the jury from being influenced, even accidentally, by reading about any testimony or exhibits the judge ultimately decided not to admit into evidence. In the Regan case, that meant journalists couldn't report

---

* The *Toronto Star* described Regan as "ashen-faced" after Justice MacDonald refused to extend the ban. Even though most of his family didn't know the extent of what would become public as a result — none of them had sat in on all of the sixty-seven days of the preliminary, and none of them, except Regan himself, was in the courtroom the day Adrian Reid outlined all of the other allegations the Crown had decided not to charge him with — they agreed among themselves not to watch the TV news reports or read the next day's newspapers.

that the prosecution had tried and failed to convince the judge to allow it to introduce what it called "similar fact" witnesses — six other women who were not part of the current charges but who also claimed Regan had attacked them in ways the Crown considered similar to the cases before the jury.

As soon as the jury retired to consider its verdict, the ban expired and the media was free to empty its notebooks. And the floodgates opened. Canadians learned that thirty-five women had claimed Gerald Regan had sexually assaulted them, that the allegations ranged from unwanted kisses to rape and stretched over four decades, up to and including the nineties, that many of the allegations involved teenaged babysitters, and that many of the women who had complained, most of whom did not know each other, described remarkably similar incidents.

The public still was digesting all of that when the jury forewoman informed Justice MacDonald early Friday afternoon that, after eight hours of deliberation, the jurors were ready to render their verdicts in R. vs. Gerald Regan.

Getting here had been a long, strange trip.

PRELIMINARY HEARINGS IN CANADA usually tend to be perfunctory affairs. The Crown lays out the fundamentals of its case against a defendant, the defence listens carefully but usually offers very little by way of direct response, preferring instead to husband its own arguments, evidence, and witnesses to present at the more important trial it realizes will ultimately take place. That's because the threshold of proof a judge in a preliminary hearing requires in order to send a case on to trial is so low it's rare for criminal cases to be dismissed at this initial stage. Defence lawyers know that, and — usually — act accordingly.

So the Crown prosecutor, Adrian Reid, could be forgiven for publicly predicting on the opening day of Gerald Regan's preliminary hearing on April 8, 1996, that the court would not likely need all of the seven weeks it had set aside to hear the case — then totalling seventeen charges involving thirteen women — even if Regan's defence counsel did decide to use the preliminary as a forum to challenge the Crown's case. "They have the opportunity to explore different options, what defences might be available to him later on in a trial context, possibly even including abuse of process," Reid told reporters. "That should take probably three weeks."

Retorted Eddie Greenspan acidly: "I wouldn't agree with anything the Crown said, including that. . . . I plan to call a lot of witnesses. I have no ballpark."

But he did have a game plan. He had already achieved some of it — including having the original lead Crown attorney, Susan Potts, whom he had privately described as a zealot, removed from the case.

Hostilities between Potts and Greenspan reached their peak — or bottom, depending on how you look at it — in August 1995, when a routine court appearance to set the date for the preliminary hearing turned into a personal public slanging match during which Regan became, in the words of one news account, "a bit player in his own sex crimes court case."

Outside court, Greenspan brandished pages of transcripts of interviews officials had conducted with complainants in which major sections had been blacked out. "I say the Crown attorney doesn't know the meaning of the word 'disclosure,'" Greenspan thundered. Shot back Potts: "We have given him everything. He knows when police officers went to lunch." The blacked-out sections, she said, were simply designed to prevent other women named in the documents — not complainants — from "harassment" by Greenspan, who, she pointed out, had already threatened to advertise nationally for information he could use to discredit Regan's accusers. Greenspan's behaviour in the Regan case was already so far over the line, Potts claimed, she'd twice had to write the Toronto lawyer to "remind" him of the code of professional conduct "in case he was not familiar with the way we operate in Nova Scotia." "I don't need anybody to tell me what the rules of professional conduct are, especially Miss Potts," Greenspan countered hotly, adding pointedly he'd been on the committee that drafted those rules. And so it went.

Greenspan claimed that during a June 21 meeting in Halifax with two of his associates, Potts had threatened to cancel the preliminary and go straight to trial if the defence refused to bow to her position on disclosure. Potts denied saying any such thing, but told the judge: "I don't want to take any chances of anyone putting words in my mouth," so she had decided, she said, to tape-record all future meetings with defence lawyers.

At the end of that August hearing — during which, almost incidentally, Regan chose to have the case against him heard by a judge and jury, and the judge set April 8, 1996, for the beginning of his preliminary — Potts attempted to give Greenspan a pile of what she described as additional disclosure documents. But Greenspan turned away when she approached him, so Potts tossed them on the defence table and walked away.

By December, with the preliminary inquiry just four months away and the two sides still routinely sniping at each other by letter and fax, the province's newly appointed director of public prosecutions, Jerry Pitzul, decided to try and lower the legal temperature.

As part of a broader shake-up of the province's still troubled prosecution service,* Pitzul "reassigned" Potts off the case and into what were vaguely described as "new responsibilities for the Savage government's Framework for Action on Family Violence." While Potts would continue on the Regan team in a "consultative role," Pitzul said, the main responsibility for carrying the case forward would now fall to Adrian Reid, the associate regional Crown attorney for Halifax, whom fellow prosecutors described as the prosecution service's "best trial lawyer" and a "dogged" cross-examiner. For most of the Pearson era, he'd languished in an administrative limbo, managing the scheduling of other Crown attorneys. "It's a proper deployment of resources," Pitzul told reporters carefully. "That's what has happened here."

Whatever it was, it did little to improve relations between Crown and defence. And little wonder. On the opening day of the preliminary, barely a few questions into his cross-examination of the first complainant, Tammy Connors, Greenspan accused Reid and a second Crown, Denise Smith, of coaching the witness to get her to add inflammatory details to her story, and he asked the judge to exclude both Crowns from the courtroom while he grilled Connors on what had prompted her to "change her story."

The irony in all of this was that the issue in dispute seemed, to the casual observer at least, relatively unimportant in the context of Connors's criminal allegation that Regan had attacked her sexually

---

* At the same time, Pitzul replaced the Crown's lead prosecutor on the Westray case — who'd come under fire from the judge in the case as incompetent — with a team of six Crown lawyers.

in 1970 while driving her home after a night of babysitting at the Regans' new Bedford home.

During her first statement to Sgt. Pretty on November 15, 1993, Connors had not mentioned Regan's alleged comment — "This will be our little secret" — when he dropped her off at her house. But when Connors met with the two Crowns to go over her testimony a week before Regan's preliminary began, Greenspan said, she "suddenly" recalled Regan had used those specific words. Greenspan, his voice dripping with disbelief, pointed out the words just happened to be the very same ones Phil Mathias had written in his notes after his interview with Connors way back in 1980. Had the Crowns "refreshed" Connors's memory so she and Mathias would be on "the same page" in court and, perhaps more importantly, so her recollections could then be used indirectly to bolster the much more serious charges involving Elizabeth Sinclair and Janice Corkum, both of whom also claimed Regan had tried to convince them to keep silent about what he'd allegedly done.

"This is fundamentally wrong," Greenspan told Judge Batiot. "The witness changed her statement and I'm entitled to [find out why]."

The judge eventually ruled against Greenspan's effort to send the Crowns out of the room and gently urged him to get on with his cross-examination. But Greenspan had effectively served notice he not only planned to target any and all changes in the complainants' statements but he also intended to attack the prosecution itself at every turn, making it plain there would be no professional courtesy extended to the Crowns occupying the table in front of him.

Clearly too, this would be no perfunctory three-week hearing.

BY THE TIME THE preliminary inquiry had begun, Greenspan's multi-pronged strategy was clear. He would use the hearing to build his abuse of process case against the Crown and the mounties, then use that to try to get all the charges tossed at the end of the preliminary or, more likely, later, during the pre-trial motions stage. Failing that, he would apply to have each case tried separately or, at least, in groups, so the more serious and less serious charges would be heard separately from one another.

In the meantime, in case none of that worked, he'd use the hearing itself as a kind of global discovery process — cross-examining each of the complainants in great detail to find out everything he could about them: their personal biographies, their family relationships, their friends, their jobs, even whether they'd ever consulted with a psychiatrist or counsellor.

At the same time, of course, he would question each of them in minute, sometimes excruciating detail about their versions of their alleged incidents with Regan. You claim Mr. Regan drove his tongue down your throat, he demanded of Jennifer Oulton at one point. How far? A millimetre? Two? Three?

He not only questioned the complainants closely about their statements to the police, but he also asked them about anything and everything anyone might have said before or after their formal, taped police interviews. He was trying to determine if the investigators had ever said anything away from the tape recorder to coach or coax the women to enhance their stories. Later, he put similar questions to the police officers to probe for inconsistencies or disagreements in their recollections.

In the cases of Oulton and Clare Bennett — whose allegations against Regan had been included in the *fifth estate* broadcast — Greenspan wanted to know everything the women had told CBC researchers about their complaints that hadn't been included in the broadcasts, as well as anything the journalists had told them about other women's stories that might have influenced them in telling their own stories. Greenspan subpoenaed the program's host, Hana Gartner, as well as a number of producers and reporters, to compare their recollections with those of the women. And he pointedly instructed the journalists to bring with them the tapes of their outtakes of their interviews so he could look at them too.*

They weren't the only journalists he intended to call to the stand. He subpoenaed Philip Mathias and Peter Moon, the investigative reporters who'd spoken at various points with Oulton.† He was

---

* The CBC resisted the subpoenas all the way to the Supreme Court of Canada, but Greenspan prevailed. The journalists were, in fact, scheduled to appear to testify the week after the Crown cancelled the preliminary and sent the case directly to trial. They never did testify.

† While Mathias did testify, Greenspan never did call Moon to testify.

especially keen to hear from Mathias, whose decision to talk to the police had touched off the investigation in the first place. Did Mathias have something against Regan? It was all part of Greenspan's broader strategy to link the police, the CBC, Mathias, Don Ripley,* and the Crown in a sinister plot to target his client.

During Regan's preliminary inquiry, Greenspan also pressed each of the complainants for details about any meetings they had had with Susan Potts to find out if anything she said during what Greenspan mocked as her "rapport-building" sessions with potential complainants had convinced them to become involved in the case or testify in a particular way, and to determine — since the Crown hadn't given the defence any notes of those meetings — who, if anyone, had kept a record of what was said at them. By demonstrating that no formal notes of those sessions existed, Greenspan hoped to make a case for calling Potts herself to testify. Subpoenaing a Crown attorney to testify is unusual, but Greenspan argued that "Sheriff Potts," as he called her, had become so intimately and wrongly involved in the police investigation she'd lost whatever privilege from testifying she might otherwise have enjoyed.†

Given all Greenspan's many and various objectives, it probably shouldn't be surprising that the preliminary inquiry would drag on and on, not only past the seven weeks initially set aside for it but through another two weeks of hearings that summer, then more days here and there that fall and winter with still no end in sight.

It also probably shouldn't have been all that surprising that Greenspan's courtroom strategy would sometimes be difficult for the uninitiated to fathom. Watching Eddie Greenspan perform in court for the first time during the preliminary inquiry — sometimes aggressively cross-examining a complainant on the same seemingly obscure point for hours at a time, refusing to stop until the witness, often in tears, finally relented and gave him the answer he was looking for; at other times, beginning what appeared to be a fruitful line of inquiry only to abandon it and move on to something entirely

---

* Greenspan did try to serve Ripley, who had moved to the U.S., with a subpoena to testify in the case. But Ripley eluded all their best efforts, including one attempt to serve him at his father's funeral in 1996.

† Greenspan was still trying to convince the courts to force Potts to testify when the Crown opted to send the case directly to trial. She never did testify.

different as soon as the answers became interesting — I sometimes found myself wondering if his scattershot approach demonstrated a lack of preparation or perhaps even skill.

It didn't. Greenspan's reputation as one of Canada's best — and most flamboyant — criminal defence lawyers is deserved. And hard-won.

"I always have one eye on the [preliminary hearing] transcript," he told me at one point during the hearings. "I'll ask the same question over and over if necessary until I get the answer I want. Sometimes, a witness will give me a smart-ass answer and think they've outsmarted me. They might be very happy with themselves, but at the trial, I'll be able to refer back to the transcript and show them exactly what they said." Without, of course, mentioning the hours it might have taken to get his answer. That would be the Crown's job.

During the preliminary, for example, Greenspan spent close to an hour pressing a combative Barbara Hoyt about Regan's alleged kiss the night she babysat the Regan children in Windsor. In her statement, she'd said at one point she thought it was a French kiss. If he could move her away from that, Greenspan knew he might be able to argue she too simply mistook a friendly peck for something more sinister, and convince the judge to dismiss the charge.

"So," he began in a mocking tone, "thirty-three years ago you got kissed!"

"A kiss I never forgot," she shot back.

"I suggest to you that [the RCMP's] questioning was very clever. They got you to say things. They got you to say he was 'slobbering' all over you. They got you to say there was lot of saliva in his mouth, you *think* it's a French kiss. Your description is that it was 'like this was Niagara Falls.' They got you to say all that, isn't that right?"

"No," she answered. "No one gets me to say anything."

He pressed her so hard and for so long about whether the kiss was a French kiss the prosecutors eventually objected that he was badgering the witness. Judge Batiot told Greenspan he could rephrase the question once more, but then he had to move on.

"I'm going to ask it real specific so you can answer it," Greenspan taunted her. "Would you adopt this quote: 'I think it was a French kiss'?"

"Can I see it in writing?" Hoyt replied, to courtroom laughter. "Let me just say we exchanged body fluids." But then, finally, she gave Greenspan exactly what he'd been looking for the past hour. "Here's my answer," she said. "Quote. I don't know if it was a French kiss or it was not a French kiss. End quote."

A year later, when the Crown decided to abort the preliminary and send the case directly to trial, it dropped the charge involving Hoyt without explanation.

Score one for Greenspan.

To say Eddie Greenspan loves being a lawyer is to wildly understate the depth of his passion. Back in 1968, Greenspan — according to his autobiography — laid it out for his bride to be. "They say the law is a jealous mistress," he told Suzy Dahan, "but in fact I'm married to the law. You are my mistress. No matter how much I love you, the law will always have to come first in my life." Sounding more like a lawyer than a suitor, he then added: "It is a condition of our marriage. It is the only condition. Do you agree?"

She did. Today, thirty years and two grown daughters later, Greenspan still lives for the law. "I don't play tennis, I don't golf," he says. "In all the time it was on, I only saw two *Seinfeld*s."

Greenspan is exceedingly well paid for his devotion. In 1986, he billed more than a million dollars to defend Helmuth Buxbaum, a nursing home operator accused of murdering his wife — even though Buxbaum was found guilty and sentenced to twenty-five years in prison. No one will say for sure how much he is charging to defend Regan — "If you want to know my fees," Greenspan joked with curious reporters, "get yourself charged with a crime and then come see me" — but the best estimates were that his fees would be well over a million dollars by the time the case was all over.

Though Regan raised some of that himself by selling off properties and liquidating investments, friends, including the former Stanfield-era Conservative cabinet minister Gerald Doucet, quietly raised hundreds of thousands from wealthy friends of the former premier, reportedly including Harrison McCain of the New Brunswick french fry empire. Most of the donors knew little of the details of the charges against Regan; they were persuaded to help out primarily because of past friendships and because Regan's supporters made a forceful case that Regan was a victim of political enemies and out-of-control prosecutors.*

However much Greenspan billed Regan for his services, it's clear he was worth it. It's also clear Greenspan isn't in it for the money.

He rarely eats in fancy restaurants; during the Regan case, he became a lunch-hour regular at an A&W fast-food restaurant near the courthouse. "Suzy and I go to Europe occasionally, but never for longer than a week at a time," he notes, then adds almost unnecessarily: "I call the office every day." He stops, considers. "This is my life, my hobby. My favourite place in the world is the courtroom."

To understand the forces that drive Edward Leonard Greenspan, you need to go back to Niagara Falls, Ontario — not to the postcard-picture, natural-wonder, touristy Niagara Falls but the stiflingly small, down-at-the-heels, tourist-trap town. Although it is a far cry from Windsor, Nova Scotia, Niagara Falls — like Windsor — is the kind of town that ambitious young men like Eddie Greenspan or Gerald Regan flee for their futures.

Eddie Greenspan was born in Niagara Falls in 1944, the oldest of the three children of Joseph and Emma Greenspan. By the time he was ten, he says he already knew he wanted to be a criminal lawyer — not like his dad, but like his dad *wanted* to be. Joseph Greenspan's ambitions had been derailed many years earlier when his father — Eddie's grandfather — became ill; Joseph had to abandon the dream of law school for the reality of a life as the head of the family scrap business.

But his life also turned out to be far shorter than it should have been. When Eddie was thirteen, his father died. He was forty-two years old at the time.

Fuelled by a son's ambition to fulfill his late father's dashed dreams and goosed by a fatalistic sense that he too would probably die young, Eddie Greenspan became known as a driven young man in a hurry, and very quickly established a reputation for himself as one of the country's brightest and best-known criminal lawyers.

---

*   The fact the case dragged on as long as it did apparently depleted the initial defence kitty even before the main trial itself began. During the summer of 1998, fundraisers were forced to go back to donors for more money to keep Regan's defence on the rails. Because most of those who contributed were writing cheques from their personal rather than corporate accounts and paying in after-tax dollars, there was a good deal of resistance to these second requests for money.

In part, Greenspan has built that reputation by taking on high-profile cases — from the high-society Demeter murder case in Toronto in the seventies to the theatre impresario Garth Drabinsky's high-flying business battles in the nineties. He is not always successful — Demeter, a wealthy building contractor who hired a hit man to murder his wife so he could collect a one-million-dollar insurance policy, was eventually convicted — but no one would ever accuse him of doing anything less than his absolute best for his client. That may explain why he is so sought after by prominent criminal defendants.

Even though he's based in Toronto, Greenspan's Nova Scotia clientele during the past decade reads like a veritable who's who of accused at the bar: an appeal court judge accused of making inappropriate comments in the Donald Marshall case; a former Conservative cabinet minister accused of influence-peddling; a prominent shopping-centre owner appealing a conviction for abusing a skateboarder; the Government of Taiwan in the *Maersk Dubai* case; and, of course, Gerald Regan.

Greenspan can be a master of self-promotion. He wrote and starred in an award-winning CBC radio series recreating famous legal cases. His autobiography — *Greenspan: The Case for the Defence* — was published in 1987 before he'd celebrated his fortieth birthday.

Partly because of his out-sized ego and partly because his father's early death kept him from learning much about his father's life, Greenspan religiously keeps virtually everything ever written about him to pass on to his children. And, because of his flamboyance as well as his courtroom successes, there's plenty of copy to save.

As any reporter who has ever covered one of his cases knows very well, he's always at least as good copy as his client or his case. But Greenspan never loses sight of the real goal, which is to get his client acquitted. Perhaps the most important factor in Greenspan's success as a criminal lawyer — one many who know him will tell you is also the direct result of his father's early death — is his willingness, eagerness, perhaps even obsessiveness to work longer and harder than anyone else.

That was certainly in evidence in the Regan case.

"I don't accept anything as a given, even from a client," Greenspan told me once. To prepare for arguing the Regan preliminary, for example, he drove the highway from Halifax to Windsor, stopping at every side road he could find, talking to people about how the road had changed, looking to see if he could find the spot where Elizabeth Sinclair said she was raped. He drove around Windsor too, carefully inspecting the area Janice Corkum claimed was the local lovers' lane where she says Regan tried to rape her. Later, he got Regan himself to take him on a tour of Province House, so he could see the premier's office, where Jennifer Oulton says Regan came on to her, the washroom she said she went to after the incident, even the safe where she said she frequently went to get liquor for the members.

"I must be prepared," he explains.

Greenspan learned the importance of preparation early in his career when he articled in the Ontario attorney general's office where he "started off reading thousands of pages of transcripts" in preparation for appeals. Even today, he claims to spend so much time studying the transcript of a preliminary inquiry he knows them "better than anyone" by the time the actual trial starts. "You have to," he says simply. "You have to be able to find things when you want them."

But those things have to be there to be found.

That's where planning comes in.

By the time his flight landed back in Toronto on the March 1995 night after Gerald Regan was first charged, Greenspan had already read through the collection of Crown briefs concerning each charge against his client and was beginning to formulate how he would deal with each of them.

Given the age of most of the allegations and the often vague date ranges — the charges alleged that the attempted rape of Janice Corkum, for example, took place sometime during a thirteen-month period between November 17, 1956, and December 31, 1957, while the attack on the babysitter Patricia MacDonald was supposed to have occurred sometime in a nearly three-year time period between 1965 and 1968 — Greenspan knew right away he would not be able to construct a complete alibi defence for his client.

But he recognized at the same time the very fact of those imprecise dates and the staleness of the allegations could become a key — and useful — building-block in his claim of abuse of process.

So too would the nature of many of the charges. Eliminate the accusations of rape and attempted rape and what was left? A lot of complaints — most of them dating back to the sixties — that Regan had kissed someone who preferred not to be kissed, or, at worst, grabbed one quick feel of a breast over clothing. Even if they were all true, did any of them really even constitute a case of sexual assault?

Throughout the proceedings Greenspan wouldn't concede his client had actually done any of the things he was accused of doing, of course, but when he talked about some of what the trial judge delicately described as the "less serious charges" against Regan, Greenspan minimized even the allegations, transforming the Crown's criminal charge of sexual assault into an "awkward, boorish pass" or a simple "unwanted kiss." Trying to fit such alleged behaviour into the context of the times in which it's supposed to have taken place, Greenspan employed fifties style words like "masher" to describe the actions his client was accused of committing. The 1954 *Funk & Wagnalls Standard Dictionary* describes a masher as "one who persistently annoys unprotected women unknown to him." Greenspan insisted that even in today's far less forgiving social and sexual climate, most people would consider Regan's alleged behaviour — if true at all — to be at the very low end of the sexual harassment scale, meriting little more than an official reprimand and an admonition not to do it again; certainly not the full, oppressive weight of the justice system slamming down like an anvil.

The rape and attempted rape allegations were clearly of a different order. No one ever tried to minimize those. Greenspan, on behalf of his client, simply argued they never happened.

But at this stage of his preparation, as he read the files, Greenspan began to zero in on those cases — Jennifer Oulton, the page girl Regan had allegedly kissed once in his office, Barbara Hoyt, the Windsor babysitter he'd allegedly kissed on a drive home, Catharine Schnare, the live-in babysitter who claimed Regan had kissed her in the kitchen one morning, and Susie Woods, the Berlin Street baby-sitter Regan had allegedly jumped on while she was lying, fully clothed, on the Regans' bed watching television — he believed he might be able to get dismissed at the preliminary.

He knew, of course, that that was still, at best, a long shot. But, even if he couldn't convince the judge to dismiss those charges outright, perhaps he could combine the age and seriousness of those allegations with what he was learning about what he considered a wildly out-of-control RCMP investigation and the Crown's unusual role in the police investigation itself in order to get those charges — and perhaps the others too — thrown out as an abuse of the legal process.

Unlike some defence lawyers, Greenspan says he makes it a habit to ask his client for his side of the story: What's your position? Tell me what you can about this allegation. Who is this person?

In this case, Regan not only denied most of the incidents ever took place; he told Greenspan he didn't even know who some of his accusers were. But he did remember, he told Greenspan, the incident with Cathy Schnare. "But it was innocent, not criminal — a little kiss on the cheek," Greenspan insists. "She was like one of the 'little girls' in the family and so he gave her a kiss on the cheek. That was all. She just misunderstood. And, you have to remember, she did come back and she stayed with the family after that, so it obviously was not that bad an event."

In her initial thirteen-page statement to Sgt. Nause November 24, 1993, Schnare said Regan kissed her but she did not characterize it as a French kiss and specifically made the point he never touched her "private parts." Three months later, however, she amended her written statement to add: "I mean he kissed me, he really kissed me, he French-kissed me." And then on March 18, 1996, two and a half years after her initial statement and less than a month before the beginning of the preliminary, Schnare dropped a bombshell in a phone call to the Crown prosecutors. Regan, she said, had touched her breast during the incident.

Greenspan's task in the preliminary was simple: "I had to get her off the breast." Did Sgt. Nause encourage her to embellish her original story in order to make an innocent kiss something more sinister — and criminal? Did the mounties or the Crown ever suggest they'd have a better case if she could say he touched her breast?

But Schnare insisted no one had prompted her. She'd just been too embarrassed to talk about the specific details of the assault when the mounties initially approached her, she explained in her testimony, but "when I decided to go ahead with it, I realized I had to tell everything. His hand," she insisted, "was on my breast."

And Greenspan couldn't get it off.

That's not to say he wasn't able to accomplish anything during his preliminary hearing cross-examination of Schnare. In order to develop his theory that the mountie investigation had gotten off the rails, Greenspan would need to show how the investigation had become an "inquisition." The Schnare case, he believed, helped him. After Schnare initially told Sgt. Nause Regan had only kissed her, why didn't the mounties just walk away from the incident? Why did they continue to pursue the investigation at all?

Greenspan's theory: the police had decided Regan was "dirty" and they set out to construct a case to prove it rather than allowing the evidence to speak for itself. Though what Greenspan delicately called "Regan's reputation" with women would often seem like an obstacle for the defence to overcome, Greenspan turned it into a positive in this case. During his cross-examination, he got Schnare herself to raise — and shoot down — the wild rumours that had long circulated in her community that Regan had raped her, that she'd gone off to Boston to have an abortion, and that Regan had then arranged to pay off her father with lucrative government contracts. She'd heard those rumours, too, she told the court with a laugh, but none of them was true.

Greenspan, however, had what he needed. He could use the fact of those groundless rumours — which he later established the mounties had already heard when they first approached Schnare — to show why he believed the mounties might have became "obsessed" with transforming an innocent encounter between Schnare and Regan into a crime. "The cops got hold of all these juicy rumours and they smelled payoffs, so they decided he must be guilty of something and then they set out to prove it — even though none of it, not the rumours, not the incident itself, none of it was true. They were just totally out of control."

The role of the mounties would become central to Greenspan's aggressive defence on the most serious charges as well.

In the case of Francetta Palermo, Greenspan argued that Susan Potts or Sgt. Jerry Pretty must have somehow encouraged the former Halifax policeman David Rent to escalate his initial recollection that Palermo's mother had told him about the alleged incident between Regan and Francetta, which would have been hearsay and inadmissible in court, into a statement that Francetta herself had told him about it, which could be used in court to bolster Palermo's credibility.

The only evidence to support Greenspan's argument was a brief note Pretty had made for his file after Susan Potts first called him to tell him Rent had called her. The note said Rent talked to the mother. Rent's own statement several months later said he'd spoken to Francetta herself.* Greenspan not only hammered away at the discrepancy during his aggressive questioning of Sgt. Pretty at the preliminary but he also publicly described Rent as "a damnable liar" even as he announced he'd be subpoenaing him to testify.†

It was, Greenspan knew well, one of the ironies of the publication ban that, while journalists couldn't write about the testimony itself, they could — and would — report at length on Greenspan's theatrical asides and outbursts. Ban or no ban, Greenspan knew how to get the spin he wanted on the case into the media. Even though he insisted he would have been happiest if reporters weren't allowed to report anything, the truth was that Eddie Greenspan always gave good copy.

Perhaps too good.

On April 11, 1997, just over a year after the "three-week" preliminary had begun, with the hearings themselves about to stagger into a sixteenth week of testimony and with no end in sight, the public prosecution service issued a terse press release. "The Crown has moved to end the preliminary inquiry in the case of R. vs. Gerald Regan and go directly to the trial court," it said.

At the same time, the Crown quietly dropped one sexual assault charge involving Barbara Hoyt and added one involving Donna Johnson, the reporter who said Regan attacked her in a motel

---

* Potts says she may have inadvertently told that to Pretty; Pretty says he may have simply taken the information down wrong. In either case, Rent testified he always claimed to have talked to Palermo herself.

† Rent didn't actually end up testifying until the trial itself and then he was called as a Crown witness.

room at a 1976 premiers' conference. No reason was given for either decision.

"We feel the balance at this point favours moving on to the trial and showing some greater respect for the rights of the complainants, who have been sitting for a very long time," Adrian Reid told reporters.

The timing of the termination of the preliminary hearing raised troubling questions Greenspan was more than happy to point out to reporters. For one thing, he had finally won a lengthy legal battle to force CBC reporters to testify at the hearings. For another, he had recently renewed his attempts to force Susan Potts to testify at the preliminary about what had been said during a dozen "pre-charge" interviews she'd had with the complainants. Judge Batiot had earlier denied his application, calling it "premature" and suggesting the defence might be able to find out what it needed to know by questioning police officers instead. But the police officers had testified they couldn't remember what was said at the meetings and had no notes about them so, on March 26, 1997, Greenspan had filed an application asking the judge to "revisit" his decision. "They had to know she was going to be called and they had to know that this was the only way they could insulate her from public scrutiny," he alleged.

Perhaps even more telling, he said, was the fact the defence had recently won another ruling from Judge Batiot forcing the RCMP to turn over more material — including the letter from John Pearson to the mounties recommending that they not go ahead with some charges and some notes Staff Sgt. Fraser had taken during a 1994 meeting between Potts and the task force. The Crown had claimed the material involved privileged solicitor-client communications. The judge disagreed.

Fraser's notes indicated Potts, an officer of the court, might have been trying to find a judge who might favour the Crown before the police filed their charges. When the public discovered that, Greenspan told a press conference, it would not only "shock the conscience of the community" but it would also lend weight to his claim there had been a massive abuse of process in the prosecution of Gerald Regan.

Now, with the preliminary "cut off at the knees," as one local defence lawyer put it, he would get his chance to prove abuse of process. "That will be the first thing," Greenspan told reporters. But certainly not the last.

WERE THE POLICE and the Crown really out of control, as Greenspan alleged? The problem is that there are many ways of interpreting almost everything the defence raised.

Take the issue of "judge-shopping," for example. It can certainly be argued, as Greenspan did — and as the judge later agreed — that Susan Potts overstepped her proper role by agreeing to monitor the court docket before the Regan charges were laid "to see who is sitting when and what would be in our best interest." On the other hand, the notes indicate Potts's real concern may not have been so much to find a judge favourable to the Crown as to prevent the charges from being presented to a judge too closely connected to Regan. The only judge mentioned by name in Fraser's notes, Provincial Court Judge Hughes Randall, was, in fact, a Liberal who had been appointed to the bench while Regan was premier. Given Nova Scotia's well-documented history of patronage appointments to the bench and its equally well-known reputation for two-tiered justice, one could just as easily argue that Potts was simply trying to avoid the appearance of any partisan taint by steering the first court appearance away from any judge with a political connection to Regan.*

Or, more substantively, consider the issue of prosecutorial discretion. Greenspan says the Crown didn't use any, accepting virtually anyone who said "Regan attacked me" as a complainant in their case. There's some evidence to support that view, including the startling reality the mounties didn't even conduct face-to-face interviews with Palermo or Morris — who both contacted police after the first charges were laid — until the week before they added them to the charges against Regan. And the police didn't — in those and several other cases — spend a lot of time checking out the women's stories until after charges were laid. Despite that, the Crown willingly went ahead with all of those prosecutions.

But the Crown was quick to counter that this was a case in which "victims were dripping off the walls." During the abuse of process

---

* In the end, the question of which judge handled the initial routine reading of the charges was largely beside the point anyway, since that judge wouldn't necessarily end up presiding at the preliminary or even at other procedural hearings.

hearing, Adrian Reid outlined more than a dozen other cases, which the police and the Crown believed were strong enough to justify laying charges but which they had decided not to pursue. "There could have been many more charges," Reid concluded.*

On the question of whether the Crown had overstepped its role when it became involved in interviewing potential complainants before any charges were laid — perhaps the most important, and most contentious, legal issue in the abuse of process hearing — both sides produced expert witnesses who each, not surprisingly, disagreed with each other's conclusions.

In the end, Justice Michael MacDonald,† the judge who would preside at the trial itself, sided with the defence. By interviewing the complainants before any charges had been filed, he concluded, the prosecutors didn't "dispassionately protect the process" or provide the appropriate checks and balances on police power. Instead, he wrote, "they became part of [the police investigation]." While not questioning their motives — "it appears to me that all Crown counsel were well-intentioned throughout" — he determined that "their involvement became subjective by nature. [What should have been an objective review of the case] becomes a joint endeavour and a joint decision. That I believe is what happened in the case at bar."

Having reached that conclusion, MacDonald had to figure out what to do next. Rather than simply throwing out all the charges, MacDonald decided to rely on advice contained in the letter the then-director of public prosecutions, John Pearson, had written to

---

* While the defence's abuse of process motion was legally effective in convincing Judge MacDonald to stay nine of the criminal charges against Regan, it may have backfired in the court of public opinion. The defence argument gave the Crown an opening to put on the record just how many other women had made allegations against Regan. The sheer number and details of those allegations, in turn, became an important and highly damaging element in the media coverage at the end of the trial.

† MacDonald was one of the Nova Scotia Supreme Court's youngest judges — he would have been only a year old when Regan allegedly assaulted Elizabeth Sinclair and Janice Corkum — but he was hardly inexperienced at handling difficult, high-profile cases. He'd just finished presiding over a complex three-month extradition hearing for six Taiwanese officers Canada wanted to send to Romania to face charges in connection with the alleged murders of three Romanian stowaways aboard the container ship *Maersk Dubai*. MacDonald found evidence implicating the officers in the deaths but ultimately decided he had no jurisdiction to do what the federal government had requested. Eddie Greenspan represented the Government of Taiwan during the hearings. Before being appointed to the bench in 1995, MacDonald was a Sydney trial lawyer for sixteen years. He was also a prominent Liberal, who served as the official agent for the federal Liberal MP David Dingle's 1993 election campaign.

the RCMP in response to the task force's March 1994 final report. That was the letter the Crown initially wanted to withhold on the grounds of solicitor-client privilege. When he finally got to read it, Greenspan had called it "dynamite."

For the Crown's case, it was exactly that.

That letter, which was written before any Crown interviews with complainants, contained what MacDonald described as an "objective analysis" of the police evidence. In conducting his own case-by-case analysis of the charges, MacDonald relied on its conclusions, which included recommendations on ten of the thirteen cases before him.

Pearson had argued the police should proceed only on the most serious charges, which included Sinclair, Corkum, and one other from the task force's original report. MacDonald agreed, and added the Palermo case to the list. Although it didn't come to the attention of the police until after the Pearson report was prepared, the case also involved attempted rape, MacDonald wrote, and that meant "a strong societal interest for a full and fair prosecution . . . outweighs the cumulative effect of any abuse so far in the process."

MacDonald also went along with Pearson's conclusion that, in the interests of "fairness," the Crown shouldn't proceed with the "less serious" charges involving Schnare, Connors, Oulton, and MacDonald. Justice MacDonald stayed all of them, as well as the charges involving Susie Woods and Giselle Sutherland — whom the police had initially intended to call upon only as similar fact witnesses anyway — and those involving Alyson Morris and Clare Bennett, whose similarly "less serious" allegations surfaced after the Pearson report.

Pearson had recommended re-interviewing Donna Johnson, whom police initially identified as an unwilling complainant, and she had in the end become one of the charges against Regan. But Justice MacDonald stayed it too, criticizing the Crown's motives in pursuing the charge as a backdoor way of attempting to introduce otherwise inadmissible similar fact evidence. He ruled it "would offend the community's sense of fair play and decency to have it proceed."

The Justice said he had "particular concerns about the way in which this charge was created." He concluded the Crown only filed it in order to justify calling Wanda Allison as a similar fact witness.

Allison was the Calgary oil executive who claimed Regan assaulted her in a hotel room in 1990. "The Crown therefore felt it needed [Johnson] as a complainant so [Allison's] 'story could be told.' . . . To proceed on this basis," MacDonald wrote in his decision, "would be totally improper."

In all, MacDonald stayed nine charges involving nine women.* His April 2, 1998, decision was a major pre-trial victory for the defence. But it wasn't the last.

After another hearing, Justice MacDonald agreed with the defence that one other charge was different enough from the others it should be tried separately. (As this book goes to press, it is still before the court.) That not only cut the number of allegations Regan would need to defend himself against during his first trial to eight counts involving just three incidents but it also made it unlikely the judge would allow any of the other complainants whose allegations were of the "less serious" sort to offer potentially inflammatory similar fact evidence in a climate that might influence a jury trying to consider those other very serious rape and attempted rape charges.

The defence didn't achieve all it had hoped.† It had asked the judge to order a separate trial on the attempted rape charges involving Palermo as well.‡ During a trial, Greenspan believed he would be able to paint Sinclair and Corkum as friends who had concocted their allegations against Regan and, more, that he would be able to use Corkum, whom even the prosecution considered a "problem-atic" witness because of the number of times her story had changed, to raise questions about the much stronger Sinclair's credibility on the witness stand. With Palermo in the mix, Greenspan worried a jury might be less inclined to view Corkum and Sinclair as schemers out to get his client and assume instead that — because there were three complainants, one of whom didn't know the other two — there must somehow be "something" to all of these complaints against Regan and want to convict him of "something."

That made it even more critically important for the defence to

---

*   The Crown appealed all of the stays. That appeal was scheduled to be heard in May 1999.

†   The defence also lost battles to be allowed to ask questions about any of the complainants' sexual histories, and to inspect the records of any discussions they may have had with psychiatrists or psychologists.

‡   The day before she testified, Greenspan asked Justice MacDonald again to sever Palermo's case from the others. The judge said no.

win the final pre-trial battle involving the admissibility of similar fact witnesses.

The Crown wanted the jury to hear the stories of three of the women whose cases had been stayed — Johnson, Connors, and Bennett — and two others whose allegations had never become the subject of criminal charges: Kelly Allan, the Liberal party worker who — as the Crown told the court in argument — claimed Regan attacked her after a 1976 fundraising dinner in Toronto, and another woman, Jane Evans, who — as the Crown told the court in argument — claimed Regan had forced himself on her during a drive home from skating in Windsor in the mid-fifties.

The judge refused to let any of them testify. In the case of the complainants whose cases he had stayed, MacDonald said his stay was the equivalent of an acquittal, even though he himself made the point in his April judgment that the Pearson recommendation not to file charges in those cases was "not based on a perceived weakness with the evidence. In fact, [prosecutors] felt that these . . . charges could be sustained." In the case of Kelly Allan, MacDonald decided the Crown — which had had trouble contacting her — had waited too long to notify the defence of their intentions to call her as a similar fact witness. He did allow Jane Evans to testify, but he said the attack she described after an evening of skating was not similar enough to the charges for her to be regarded as a similar fact witness. She could only testify, Justice MacDonald said, to the fact Regan did drive young women home from the skating rink from time to time. Her testimony, in the end, probably helped the defence more than the Crown. Evans said Regan not only drove her and a friend home from the rink but that he bought the girls a hamburger. "He was very kind to the young people around," she testified.

Adrian Reid would have to demonstrate to the jurors what he called "the dark side" of Gerald Regan's private life largely on the strength of what three women claimed Gerald Regan had done to them decades ago.

It would not be easy.

All three incidents happened — if they happened at all — a long time ago: the most recent allegation was nearly thirty years old, the oldest from forty-two years before. There was no physical evidence any of the assaults had ever taken place. There was no direct corroboration either, and the indirect corroboration that did exist often raised as many questions as it answered. Although the central core of the women's stories — that Regan had attacked them sexually — never changed, none of them could pin down a precise date for their alleged attack and they were often hazy about many of the decades-old details. Perhaps worst for a jury trying to determine whether the evidence in each individual case demonstrated beyond a reasonable doubt that Regan had assaulted the woman, every story came with its own inherent contradictions and complications.

TAKE ELIZABETH SINCLAIR, for example. On the one hand, she was the Crown's strongest complainant — a well-dressed, matronly fifty-six-year-old woman who exuded a kind of motherly believability. When he first saw her, an unhappy Eddie Greenspan confided to a colleague that he reminded her of the popular former U.S. first lady Barbara Bush.

Sinclair told the jury about the summer day forty-two years before, when she claimed Regan had taken her to a secluded gravel pit near Mount Uniacke, locked the car doors, and brutally attacked her. "He was on top of me," she told the jury, pausing for a long moment while she rested her head in her hand, "then I felt a terrible pain." She had been raped, she said.

But during cross-examination, Greenspan immediately began picking at the scabs of her story. He pointed out that Sinclair and Sgt. Pretty had driven up and down the same highway in 1994 looking for the gravel pit where she claimed the attack occurred, and didn't find it. "I am going to suggest to you," he said, his voice rising theatrically, "that there is no pit, there never was a pit, and you can drive up Highway 1 till the cows come home, lady, and you will never be able to point to a pit because there was no pit and there was no rape. Is that correct, yes or no?"

"No," Sinclair replied flatly. While the Crown later introduced aerial photos from the fifties to show various locations along the road where a now long-since overgrown pit might have been,* Greenspan continued to hammer home the point that she hadn't

---

* After the papers reported Greenspan's "there-was-no-pit" declaration, several people telephoned the prosecutor's office to offer information on gravel pit locations in the area during the fifties.

been able to positively identify the location as a way to undermine her overall credibility with the jury.

There was no question the case turned on her credibility. There was little else to support her story. Her parents were dead, as was Bertha Rhodenizer, the woman she said had accompanied her on the first part of the trip to Halifax, as were Jim and Jean Rose, the cousin and her husband she said she'd gone to visit.

In truth, Jim Rose had only died in August 1994, six months after Sinclair first told Sgt. Pretty her story. Why hadn't he interviewed the man before he died? Pretty told the jury he had no reason to expect Rose would die, so he simply didn't "prioritize" it at the time — he wasn't allowed to tell jurors about all the other allegations he was investigating during that period — but Greenspan skillfully used his questions to suggest Pretty's real reason for not interviewing Rose earlier was the fact "you weren't prepared to gamble" he might say Regan never drove Sinclair to Halifax in the first place. Although Pretty called that suggestion "preposterous," Greenspan had managed to create yet another question for the jurors to ponder when they asked themselves if the Crown had proved its case beyond a reasonable doubt.

Greenspan even managed to raise questions about Sinclair's claim she'd overheard Rhodenizer and Regan talking in the car on the drive to Halifax about Regan's plans to go to Liverpool to broadcast a baseball game the next night.

It seemed to make sense. Liverpool fielded a team in the popular H&D League. Regan was a Halifax-based sportscaster for CJCH, and he regularly broadcast play-by-play accounts of games involving the league's Halifax and Dartmouth teams. The Crown introduced newspaper clippings to show Liverpool had played plenty of home games that summer against teams from Halifax or Dartmouth. It seemed logical Regan must have broadcast at least one of them.

But when Greenspan called Regan himself to the stand, in part to undermine that apparent logic, Regan produced his own collection of newspaper clippings — a selection of radio program guides from the summer of 1956 — that he claimed showed all the baseball games his station broadcast that summer. They all began at 7:05 p.m. Liverpool's games, on the other hand, Regan testified, all started at six or 6:30, depending on the month of the summer, so they'd be over before dark because the town's ball field didn't have artificial lights. That meant, he explained triumphantly, that he could not have been planning to go to Liverpool to broadcast a game the next night as Sinclair had alleged.

During his cross-examination, Reid introduced still more newspaper clippings, these ones showing that the Liverpool franchise was in financial trouble that summer. In mid-summer, in fact, the paper reported that league officials and the media had gotten together and agreed to do whatever they could to spark fan interest — including broadcasting more of the team's games. Wasn't it likely that CJCH would have altered the rest of its broadcast starting time to include a few Liverpool home games, Reid asked, or perhaps even join a game in progress? But Regan refused to go along with either of Reid's suggestions.

What would the jury believe?

More important, what else was there to support her story? Sinclair testified she'd told only two people about what she said Regan had done to her — Janice Corkum, with whom the defence hoped to show she'd conspired to concoct her story, and her husband, whom she testified she'd told about the rape just before they married in 1964. His testimony did indeed confirm that but, in the process, it raised another question. Why did Sinclair tell her husband-to-be that Gerald Regan had raped her, but not confess at the same time that she'd had an out-of-wedlock baby in 1960, which she'd given up for adoption?

And that, in turn, raised perhaps the biggest hurdle the Crown would need to overcome — how to explain Sinclair's clearly tangled childhood family life.

The problems began with how the police discovered Sinclair in the first place. They'd been tracking down rumours — originally from Mathias but later "confirmed" by Elizabeth's sister, Carly — that Carly was Elizabeth's daughter by Regan. She wasn't — and the Crown produced a birth certificate to prove it. But there were other, more puzzling, more troubling complications. During their investigation, the mounties also discovered that, in the early seventies, Elizabeth's mother had told some of her friends that Gerald Regan was the father of Elizabeth's illegitimate baby. Again, he wasn't. The Crown produced his birth certificate too.

But the defence used these bizarre rumours to good effect, painting Sinclair's family life, in the words of the *National Post* columnist Christie Blatchford, "as a cross between *Peyton Place* and *The Jerry Springer Show*," and Sinclair herself as a product of a rumour-filled, untrustworthy upbringing.

On the stand, Sinclair was at a loss to explain why her sister and mother would make up such stories, simply that they had. Greenspan, however, was quick to suggest his own theory. "You were pregnant, you were in trouble and you made this up," he told her. She'd made up the whole story about Regan, Greenspan claimed, in order to cover up the fact she'd gotten pregnant by Clare Weir, a local hockey player her mother didn't approve of. It sounded better, he suggested, for her to claim Regan had raped her than to explain to her husband-to-be the real reason she wasn't a virgin. Just as it had sounded better for her mother to claim to her friends that a prominent young lawyer about town had gotten her daughter pregnant, rather than the ne'er-do-well hockey player who'd really done the deed.

To bolster his theory, Greenspan produced a birth certificate of his own. Though Sinclair had never testified whom Janice Corkum had been babysitting the night the two girls confided in each other about their separate encounters with Regan, Corkum claimed the child's name was John Sweet and that he was two or three years old at the time of the conversation, which she said took place sometime in 1957. But the child's birth certificate showed he wasn't born until 1958. If he was really two or three, as she claimed, that would have meant the babysitting confession didn't take place until at least 1960 — the same year Sinclair had her baby by someone else.

There were, as the Crown tried to show, other possible explanations for this discrepancy. Corkum, who babysat frequently, could have been mistaken about the name of the child she was looking after that night. Or she could have been mistaken about his age. And Reid also introduced evidence — including photos of Sinclair with Clare Weir and a touching love letter she'd written him from the hospital before their baby was born — to show Sinclair had never tried to hide her relationship with Weir from people in Windsor or the fact that he was the father of her child.

In the end, Reid's most powerful rejoinder was simply to ask the jurors why Sinclair would lie. She had, he pointed out, already paid a horrific price for coming forward. Because of the family secrets that had tumbled out of the closet, she and her sister no longer spoke, not even when they had met at her mother's funeral a few years before. She also had to tell her husband her long-kept secret about the baby she'd given up for adoption before they met. Finally, she'd been forced to come face to face with her own emotions about that event: she was now, she told the jury, actively looking to find her thirty-eight-year-old son. Why would she put herself through all of that, Reid asked the jurors, if she was not telling the truth?

But the jurors, of course, did not have to decide she was lying about anything — simply that the Crown hadn't proven the truth of it beyond a reasonable doubt.

IF THE CROWN WAS HAPPY with Sinclair's testimony, it knew from the outset that convincing a jury of Corkum's credibility would be a harder sell. Even Sgt. Pretty conceded during the preliminary that she was the most troubled — and troubling — of the complainants he dealt with.

It wasn't that the Crown didn't believe her. It did. But would a jury? During the preliminary, she'd had frequent confrontations with Greenspan from the witness box, once even accusing him of "mouthing dirty words" at her while she testified. During her testimony at the trial, she was, as Christie Blatchford put it, "a handful, the sort of witness who makes the criminal courts so wholly fascinating and who, by everything she does and says, snaps to attention anyone who may have been dozing."

She told the jurors she'd known Regan as a church-going friend of her parents. Regan's new bride, Carole, she testified, became good friends with her mother. They'd often see each other at the Catholic Women's League; sometimes they exchanged recipes. In fact, Corkum said, she still had one of those recipes she'd copied over from her mother's collection into her own red notebook — a recipe for Carole Regan's Seafood Chowder that included a notation in Corkum's own neat handwriting at the bottom: "Great Chowder!" it said.

Then she described the winter night she said Regan had tried to rape her in his car on the ride home from skating. Afterward, she testified, Regan told her: "It makes me feel so warm to see you frightened like that. You look so cute huddled by the door like that."

It was a compelling, horrific, and incredibly detailed account. But there were problems with it, as Greenspan was quick to point out. Especially in the details. The reality was that while Corkum never wavered in her contention that Regan had tried to rape her, her story had expanded and evolved several times since her first relatively cryptic statement to Sgt. Pretty in November 1993. She explained that that was because she didn't initially realize how important it would be to provide precise details and because she was still embarrassed to talk about the specifics of what had happened to her. Later, when she began to make notes about other things she remembered, she said she was simply following Sgt. Pretty's advice to write down memories as they came to her. They came to her while she was vacuuming, she testified, and one night, in bed. And they were significant. The most important of the new memories was that she said she recalled seeing Regan's penis and the feel of his flesh on her flesh as he touched her vaginal area, trying to enter her. She hadn't said any of that in her first statement to Sgt. Pretty. By the time she testified at Regan's preliminary, she had remembered something else that wasn't in her first statement — that he'd ejaculated. By the time the case came to court, Regan had not only ejaculated once during the attack, she said, but had masturbated to climax again after it.

Greenspan, not surprisingly, used each of those changes as another club to beat up on her credibility. And Corkum, who often seemed unable to avoid serving up to Greenspan what Adrian Reid would refer to as generous helpings of "shark food," seemed almost anxious to make Greenspan's job easier. At one point, for example, Greenspan pressed her on the fact she'd given two different versions of the path she'd taken through her house after Regan let her out of the car. Corkum, whose family had moved seven times in the seven years they lived in Windsor, confessed she was no longer sure which house she lived in at the time of the attack. She had two distinct but still real recollections of how she'd gotten to her bedroom, she said, depending on which house she actually lived in at the time.

Not content with having raised questions about her recollections of the incident itself, Greenspan called Carole Regan to the stand to testify she was never friends with Corkum's mother and could only vaguely recall her as "quite a large woman" she saw once working in the kitchen at a church tea. She also said she not only didn't learn to make seafood chowder until after 1958 but also that variations of her recipe — which she'd only learned to prepare because it was a good Nova Scotia dish for a politician's wife to claim as her own — had been published frequently over the years in newspapers and magazines. Anyone could have copied it out. What's more, Carole Regan claimed the recipe in Corkum's notebook wasn't even hers. "I have never put cornstarch in seafood chowder in my life," she told the jury. "I'm sorry. I just don't do that."

For his part, Gerald Regan testified he didn't remember Corkum at all and had never been in her house as she'd said. While both Corkum and her older brother, a Saint Mary's University professor, testified Regan had had a relationship with Corkum's now deceased older sister — she dumped him, the brother testified cryptically, after she "decided she didn't like him because he did something she didn't like" — Regan said he had never dated her and had only seen her a few times around town.

Although the Crown had deliberately kept the time frame for the alleged attack on Corkum as loose as possible — stretching all the way from the date of Regan's wedding on November 17, 1956, to the end of 1957 — Corkum's own testimony seemed to narrow the possibilities considerably.

Greenspan used that testimony to set a clever trap for her. Like a master bricklayer, Greenspan constructed it modest brick by modest brick, seemingly unconnected question by unconnected question, inconsequential fact by inconsequential fact, guarded answer by guarded answer until he had finally created what he hoped the jury would come to see as an impenetrable brick wall of impeccable logic. *His client could not possibly have committed this assault.*

You say you were fourteen at the time? he asked Corkum.

She agreed.

And your birthday was November 4?

And you say this incident happened after a night of skating?

Greenspan then produced a 1956 newspaper clipping that showed the Windsor skating rink didn't open that year until November 27.

So it must have happened after that, he suggested, but certainly before the rink opened the next fall because you would have been fifteen by then. Correct?

You testified you were so upset by what you say Regan did to you that you missed some school after the incident? Well, here are your school records. Yes, here it is, you did miss a week of school early in December of that year.

And you say your marks fell off after Regan tried to rape you? Well, here again are your school records and they do show your marks going down in December.

So . . .

So, since there were public skating sessions on Sundays and since you missed a full week of school in early December, this incident must have happened on Sunday, December 2, 1956. Correct?

But here Corkum demurred. "I'm not convinced it's got to be that week," she told Greenspan. "I hesitate to agree. It doesn't feel right."

Greenspan simply bulldozed past the caveat.

Instead, he produced yellowed, original copies of the *Hants Journal* newspaper from the late fall of 1956. They indicated that, on December 2, 1956, the day Greenspan insisted Corkum had claimed the incident occurred, Gerald Regan was actually in Florida. "Florida is wonderful but I'll take Nova Scotia anytime," Regan had written in a postcard to friends, which the newspaper quoted from. He and Carole were on their honeymoon, the paper reported, and not expected back in Windsor until December 4 or 5.

Now, Greenspan moved in for the kill. "On your logic," he concluded with a theatrical flourish, "you say this happened on December 2, and the fact of the matter is that Mr. and Mrs. Regan are not in Windsor. Is that not right?" It was not so much a question as a righteous demand for acquiescence.

"It appears you're right," the woman answered wearily.

But Greenspan still wasn't satisfied. He wanted to add one final brick, to cut off any chance of escape. "No matter how you cut it," he thundered, "the Regans are not in Windsor on the second or the third. Correct?"

"Correct," the woman answered.

As Blatchford summed up the moment in the next day's *National Post*: "Mr. Greenspan, whose usual state appears self-satisfaction, was clearly pleased with himself."

Greenspan called both Gerry and Carole to testify about the details of their honeymoon. After their marriage in Ottawa, they testified, they'd taken the leisurely, scenic route down to Florida, stopping along the way to indulge in such touristy pursuits as taking a bus tour of Washington, D.C. Carole kept the receipt from the tour in a scrapbook of honeymoon memories, and Greenspan entered the receipt as evidence — along with hotel receipts and even a photo showing the young couple enjoying a night on the town in Miami Beach. After basking in the Florida sunshine for a while, they'd driven slowly back to Ottawa, stopping along the way in Virginia to visit a friend of Gerry's and in New York where they saw the Rockettes at Radio City Music Hall. After picking up their wedding gifts at Carole's mother's in Ottawa — staying a day longer than they'd planned, Carole testified — they drove back to Windsor, arriving the night before a local Liberal constituency meeting Regan wanted to attend. The meeting, according to yet another newspaper clipping entered as an exhibit, took place December 7, 1956 — five days after the skating session Greenspan insisted was the one Corkum had claimed she attended the night Regan supposedly tried to rape her.

And, if that wasn't reasonable doubt enough, Greenspan led Carole and Gerry Regan on a trip down memory lane through the first winter of their marriage — during which they said they'd spent several weeks in Ottawa and Montreal, and Gerry himself had travelled to Moscow to attend an international hockey tournament.

The message was clear: Regan wasn't even in Windsor for most of the time in which Corkum claimed Regan tried to rape her.

The Crown tried its best to counter that — showing, for example, that even if one accepted the Regans' account of their travels, there were still plenty of other dates during the time frame of the charge when Regan was in Windsor and could have assaulted Corkum. Reid also questioned the Regans' account of their honeymoon. Wasn't it curious, he noted at one point, that Carole had carefully preserved so many mementos of the happy couple's honeymoon up to and including their time in Florida but, mysteriously, there were no similar, dated souvenirs from places like Radio City Music Hall — which they also claimed they'd visited — in order to document the dates of their trip back to Canada. Perhaps, Reid suggested, they'd come home sooner than they claimed. Perhaps they were in Windsor on December 2.

Perhaps. But the real question was, Had the defence raised enough of a reasonable doubt about all of that to keep a jury from convicting Gerald Regan of trying to rape Janice Corkum?

For her part, Corkum — at the end of Greenspan's grueling deconstruction of her life and memories — was reduced to almost pleading with the jurors to believe her: "I may have some of these facts wrong. I knew when I gave the information to the police in 1993 that was a possibility. The only thing I can say is that, in fact, what happened to me when I was fourteen did happen. Mr. Regan picked me up and took me to the dark woods where he sexually abused me and physically abused me. He changed my life and he ended my childhood and I'm not going away until there is something done about it."

FRANCETTA PALERMO, now a forty-seven-year-old Victoria divorcée with two grown children, should have been the Crown's most compelling complainant. She didn't know the other two women, so Greenspan couldn't suggest she'd gotten together with them in some sort of conspiracy against Regan.

While her recollections of the buildings in which she'd worked for the Liberals seemed, at first blush, frustratingly hazy, they did end up fitting perfectly with what the police later confirmed as the facts. She said she'd worked for the Liberals for a few months in an old office building she couldn't specifically identify near the waterfront and that, sometime later, the party moved to a new office building, also downtown, though she couldn't remember its address. It turned out that the party had indeed moved its offices in July 1969 from a rundown waterfront building to the new nearby Royal Bank Tower. Better still, though Regan would testify he didn't remember her and the party's executive director, Len Giffen, would testify he couldn't recall hiring or firing her — or even knowing who she was — Giffen's own date book for 1969 showed he had met with her father in mid-March (she claimed she'd gotten the job through his lobbying efforts) and then with Palermo herself the day before Regan's fourteen-hour legislative filibuster, which was, coincidentally, two days before Palermo said she began working for the party. Better than that even, there appeared in this case to be evidence she'd told others about the attack shortly after it happened. Both her sister, Maria, and her downstairs neighbours, David and Linda Rent, testified

Francetta had told them about the alleged attack shortly after it happened.

But Greenspan continued to argue that Rent, a retired police officer, and his wife were simply trying to help the police "get" his client and had therefore concocted their stories to suit the Crown's need. He was also able to show that Maria's testimony at the trial was different on several points from what she had first told police. On the stand, Maria's version was almost identical to Francetta's, but she told investigators in 1996 she remembered her sister telling her back in 1969 that the attack had taken place on Regan's desk instead of on the floor in the office. She also said her sister had told her only that Regan had tried to put his hand up her skirt and that she'd pushed him away, not that he had ejaculated on the floor. In her testimony, Maria conceded she had talked to her sister after her first statement, but insisted the conversation had simply brought back her own memories. "As she told me, it sounded familiar and I actually said, 'Oh yeah, how could I have forgotten?'" On the stand, Greenspan zeroed in on Francetta, accusing her of getting her sister to change her story to match her own. "You called her, had a conversation with her because you were unhappy with what you heard she was saying," Greenspan postulated, adding in an incredulous tone of voice: "You two get together, you talk and now, all of a sudden . . . she now tells the story your way?"

Greenspan had already done much to undermine Palermo's credibility with the jury — on a matter, ironically, that had nothing to do with the alleged assault. It concerned an incident two years earlier in 1967 when Palermo forged a school record to get into Grade Ten. She told the jury she'd done it to avoid being forced to go to school with kids two years younger than herself. The problem was not so much that she'd altered that document but that she'd lied about it under oath at the preliminary inquiry, and only finally confessed her transgression during the trial when it appeared Greenspan might get access to her school records.

In cross-examination, Greenspan confronted her with her testimony from the preliminary showing she'd lied about the incident on five different occasions. He referred her to the court transcript of each of those occasions. And each time, he went through his mantra: "That was a lie. That was a falsehood. That was a perjury." Finally, he finished off with a flourish: "Unless a record established you as a liar, you had no intention of correcting your lie," he declared. "That's the kind of person you are!"

Is that what the jury would believe?

IT WAS PERHAPS FITTING that the final witness in the case of The Queen versus Gerald Augustine Regan would turn out to be Gerald Regan himself.

Defendants don't have to testify in their own defence. It's up to the Crown to prove them guilty, not the other way around. And judges inevitably instruct juries not to hold it against defendants who exercise that right not to testify.

But Greenspan knew that in a case like this, which would almost certainly turn on whom the jurors believed, Regan's testimony could be critical to the ultimate outcome. The jury would not only want to hear him say he didn't do it they'd also want to watch him while he said it.

And Gerald Regan, Greenspan told the jurors as he opened the defence's case, wanted to let them do just that. "He wants to give up that very fundamental right to remain silent in order to tell you in his own words and out of his own mouth that he did not commit these crimes, that he is innocent," Greenspan said.

Perhaps surprisingly, Greenspan was concerned about how his client would come across to the jurors. Because of his years in public life, Regan carried himself with an easy confidence that sometimes came across as arrogance. In the weeks before his testimony, Greenspan spent countless hours with his client, coaching him as much on his demeanour as on what he would say, teaching him to be "humble." Nothing was left to chance.

On the stand, Regan was everything Greenspan could have hoped for in a witness. And more. Even though he was almost seventy-one years old, had been a premier and a federal cabinet minister, Regan was almost deferential in his answers to questions from Greenspan and Reid, frequently ending a reply with "sir."

Whereas Carole, in her testimony, had simply confirmed the couple had had six children, Regan added a reference to "the seventh child we lost as a baby," when Greenspan asked him the same question.

While Carole testified they'd become engaged on July 19, 1956,

Regan said that didn't sound quite right to him because he thought he had broadcast a baseball game that night.

"You're not going to challenge her on that?" Greenspan asked lightly.

"I'd better not," he replied.

When Greenspan led him through his years as a sportscaster, or his courtship of Carole, or his honeymoon — all, of course, in an effort to counter the Crown's case against him — it was almost as if the two men were having a private conversation.

But when they reached the critical moment, Greenspan's questions — and Regan's answers — would change cadence, taking on a passion and an urgency that had previously been absent.

"Did you rape Elizabeth Sinclair forty-two years ago in a gravel pit?" Greenspan demanded.

"I did not rape Elizabeth Sinclair," Regan replied firmly.

Later, Greenspan asked: "Did you try to rape Janice Corkum?"

"I certainly did not."

"Did you sometime in 1969 attempt to rape Francetta Palermo?"

"I certainly did not."

AFTER A DAY OF CLOSING arguments — Greenspan had made a powerful, emotional plea to jurors that left Regan and several of his children (as well as at least one juror) with tears in their eyes while Reid ended up delivering a rambling address that seemed to lose focus and steam rather than building to a climax* — and another half-day of instructions from the judge on the legal issues, the case against Gerald Regan was suddenly, almost anti-climactically, in the hands of the jury.

They were not really a jury of Gerald Regan's peers. There were two firefighters, a retired coast guard employee who said he was a Reform party supporter, a homemaker, a banker, a locomotive engineer, a bookkeeper, a telephone company marketer, a technician, and a care worker. The ten jurors — there had originally been twelve but one, a woman, was excused early in the trial for medical reasons and another, a man, was dismissed with no reason given mid-way

---

* Reid apparently had gone without sleep for most of the previous two days while preparing his address to the jurors but then, rather than presenting it as written, ended up trying, extemporaneously, to counter the points Greenspan had made in his clearly effective presentation.

through the prosecution's case — included six women and four men. The oldest, at fifty-nine, was more than a decade younger than Regan; the youngest, a twenty-three-year-old woman, told the judge she "didn't even known who [Regan] is," when she was chosen.

Three hours after they began deliberating — and while most of the fifteen journalists who had covered the trial were still busy writing their stories about the evidence the jury didn't hear — the jury forewoman sent Justice MacDonald a handwritten note asking for clarification on three points.

- How much weight can/should we put on testimony of witnesses when making a decision? Should we go with gut feelings?
- Can we use testimony as evidence and can it outweigh actual physical evidence, i.e. exhibits?
- How exactly do we determine reasonable doubt, i.e., definition/ explanation?

MacDonald told them they should use their common sense and the evidence, not their gut feelings. While allowing that reasonable doubt was a difficult concept for juries to get their heads around, he offered them this advice: "Even if you believe Mr. Regan is probably guilty, that is not sufficient to convict. If you are sure that Mr. Regan is guilty, you must convict him."

Outside the courtroom, Greenspan saw the questions — and answers — as a positive sign. "If your gut tells you they're guilty, you must acquit," he explained, echoing the judge's comments. "You can only convict on the basis of evidence, so I'm heartened by those questions."

Early the next afternoon, after three more hours of deliberation, the jury sent MacDonald two more questions that seemed to indicate they were close to a decision on at least one case:

- We need clarification on how use of the Rents' testimony should be treated differently than the other witnesses' testimony. Does this piece of evidence, standing alone, excluding other evidence, not carry some relative value or weight as do other pieces of evidence?
- Does the verdict on count 7 infer the same verdict on count 8?

The only value of the Rents' evidence, MacDonald told them, was "to refute the suggestion that [Palermo] told her sister a different version of this story." And they had to find Regan guilty or not guilty on both count 7 — the attempted rape — and count 8 — the indecent assault together.

Forty minutes later, they sent word to the judge they were ready to render their verdicts.

"NOT GUILTY," the forewoman said in response to the court clerk's question on count 1, the alleged rape of Elizabeth Sinclair. She repeated the same two-word answer to each of the next seven questions. With each new not guilty verdict, Carole Regan, sitting in the front row of the spectator section behind her husband, silently crossed herself.

When the forewoman said her seventh "Not Guilty" — to the charge of attempted rape of Francetta Palermo — there was the sudden sound of breath being exhaled at the defence table, where no one had seemed to even move a muscle through the reading of the first six verdicts.

It was over.

Gerald Regan was free.

As soon as the jury forewoman uttered her final "Not Guilty," Regan stood and turned to embrace his wife, kissing her on the cheek. Then he hugged his lawyer while Carole turned to comfort Laura, the Regans' youngest daughter who — like their other two daughters and several other members of the family — had begun to weep. So too did Gerald Doucet, the one time Tory cabinet minister who had not only raised funds for Regan's legal defence but who had attended almost every day of the trial and preliminary inquiry. Regan embraced him too.

Sgt. Jerry Pretty surveyed the scene briefly from a seat near the back of the courtroom, then, without a word, quietly slipped out the door and out of the building.

Adrian Reid left the courtroom quickly too, without even a glance at Greenspan or the no longer accused Gerald Regan. Reid's co-counsel, Denise Smith, offered a perfunctory congratulations to Greenspan but she too seemed in a hurry to get away from the still celebrating Regan family. Outside the courtroom, Reid told a crush of reporters that the system had worked, that the Crown had presented an important case fairly and vigorously but that it had simply not been able to convince a jury of its case beyond a reasonable doubt. Yes, he said, the Crown would consider whether there were grounds to appeal the verdict.* Yes, he said too, the Crown still intended — at this point at any rate — to go forward with the remaining charge against Regan, still planned to appeal Justice MacDonald's decision to stay those other charges.

And then he too was gone.

It was like an election night. The losers conceding, the winning party's strategists explaining how they'd done it, and then — finally — the victorious party leader, surrounded by his beaming family, thanking his workers, his supporters, and, most of all, his family for his success.

Gerald Regan knew all about electoral victory and defeat. Once, long ago, he'd told me that victory and defeat were "equal imposters; sometimes you lose when you should win, sometimes you win when you should lose." Today he was a winner.

"I want to say that, speaking for my family, that we're tremendously relieved at the verdict," a smiling Regan declared to reporters as he stood outside the courtroom, his wife beside him, his family behind. "I want to thank my wife and the rest of the family for the tremendous support they've given me. It's been a long ordeal. I just want to thank God that we've come this far."

How far that really might turn out to be became clear very quickly. In the corridor outside the courtroom after the media scrum, Mark Ilich, an Ottawa economist who'd watched the trial's final days, shouted after Regan: "I think you know every Canadian knows you're guilty," he yelled. "And you can take that to your grave!"

The headline on the front page of the Perspectives section of the next day's Halifax *Daily News* was almost openly dismissive of the verdict: "Meet Our O.J.: Gerald Regan" read the headline over an opinion piece by the popular local columnist David Swick. "It's the verdict Nova Scotians expected because we don't expect our

---

* The Crown announced in January 1999 it would not appeal the verdict.

justice system to give us justice," Swick wrote. "We expect powerful, wealthy people to be found not guilty. Not guilty, by the divine right of kings and premiers."*

While the jury was deliberating, Rick Howe, the host of CJCH Radio's open-line program, had asked his listeners to call with their predictions on the outcome. "The phones lit up and they didn't stop for two hours," Howe recalled later. "To a person, they said they believed he was guilty, but that he would get off." On his next show, Howe asked listeners what they thought of the verdict. "People called back to say, 'We told you so.'"

Christie Blatchford, whose *National Post* reports on the trial — part conventional straight reportage, part very personal opinion column — had helped make many of the issues in the case more real for her readers,† wrote a retrospective column after the verdict, in which she told her readers she'd begun her coverage of the trial with an open mind, but had come away at the end believing the stories of the three women who said Gerald Regan had raped or attempted to rape them.

The Toronto Sun, while endorsing the verdict — "[Regan] has been found not guilty by a jury of his peers of any criminal wrong-doing and that is good enough for us" — was quick to add: "But we also do not intend to abandon all common sense. . . . Many people also know that in both provincial and federal politics, Regan had a reputation as someone women were well advised not to be alone with in a room." In the editorial, the *Sun*, which had been generally sympathetic to Regan in its trial coverage, added: "We believe that when more than twenty women — many of whom were teenagers at the time — all come forward with stories of inappropriate conduct by one man — a powerful figure in Canadian politics to boot — then that is something the public should note."

An *Edmonton Journal* editorial went even further: "It is more than reasonable to conclude," it argued, "that Gerald Regan reached the high office of Canadian premier despite a lifetime of disgusting

---

*   In January 1999, Regan's lawyer, George MacDonald, wrote a letter to the newspaper threatening to sue over the comments in Swick's column and another one written by Parker Barrs Donham.

†   During her coverage of the trial, Blatchford says four women who had not previously talked to the police contacted her to claim Regan had come on to them too.

behaviour toward many young girls and women."

Gerald Regan had been found not guilty of rape and attempted rape in a court of law but it was clear he had not won the benefit of the doubt in the court of public opinion.

Not guilty, but not innocent either.

It is hardly the epitaph Gerald Augustine Regan — the boy with a "lot of crust," the ambitious young man who set out to be prime minister, the man who did ultimately earn the nickname "The Preem" and dreamed big dreams for himself and for his province — would have chosen for himself.

Or did he?

Bibliography

Batten, Jack. *The Dean of Canadian Lawyers*. Toronto: Macmillan of Canada, 1984.

Beck, J. Murray. *The Politics of Nova Scotia:* Vol. 1 and 2. Tantallon, N.S.: Four East Publications, 1985, 1988.

Belliveau, John Edward. *The Headliners: Behind the Scenes Memoirs*. Hantsport: Lancelot Press, 1984.

Bruce, Harry. *Frank Sobey*. Halifax: Nimbus, 1985.

——. *Corporate Navigator: The Life of Frank Manning Covert*. Toronto: McClelland and Stewart, 1995.

Calhoun, Sue. *Ole Boy: Memoirs of a Canadian Labour Leader*. Halifax: Nimbus, 1992.

Cameron, Silver Donald. *The Education of Everett Richardson*. Toronto: McClelland and Stewart, 1977.

Cameron, Stevie. *On the Take: Crime, Corruption and Greed in the Mulroney Years*. Toronto: Macfarlane, Walter, and Ross, 1994.

Camp, Dalton. *Gentlemen, Players & Politicians*. Toronto: McClelland and Stewart, 1970.

Carnes, Patrick. *Out of the Shadows: Understanding Sexual Addiction*. Minnesota, U.S.: Hazelden, 1992.

Chrétien, Jean. *Straight from the Heart*. Toronto: Key Porter Books, 1985.

Greenspan, Edward L., and George Jonas. *Greenspan: The Case for the*

Defence. Toronto: Macmillan of Canada, 1987.

Haliburton, E. D. *My Years with Stanfield*. Hantsport: Lancelot Press, 1970.

Hawkins, John. *Recollections of the Regan Years*. Hantsport: Lancelot Press, 1990.

Kavanagh, Peter. *John Buchanan: The Art of Political Survival*. Halifax: Formac, 1988.

Levin, Jerome. *The Clinton Syndrome: The President and the Self-Destructive Nature of Sexual Addiction*. California: Prima Publishing, 1998.

Loomer, L. S. *Windsor, Nova Scotia*. Windsor: West Hants Historical Society, 1996.

Palango, Paul. *Above the Law*. Toronto: McClelland and Stewart, 1994.

MacEwan, Paul. *The Akerman Years*. Antigonish: Formac, 1980.

Newman, Peter. *Distemper of Our Times*. Toronto: McClelland and Stewart, 1968.

Raddall, Thomas. *Halifax: Warden of the North*. Toronto: McClelland and Stewart, 1971.

Ripley, Donald F. *Bagman: A Life in Nova Scotia Politics*. Toronto: Key Porter Books, 1993.

——. *The Roos of Bay Street*. Halifax: Ripley Book, 1991.

Simpson, Jeffrey. *Spoils of Power*. Toronto: Collins, 1988.

——. *Discipline of Power*. Toronto: Personal Library, 1980.

Special Senate Committee on the Mass Media. *Mass Media, Volume I: The Uncertain Mirror*. Ottawa: Information Canada, 1970.

Stevens, Geoffrey. *Stanfield*. Toronto: McClelland and Stewart, 1973.

Vaughan, Garth. *The Puck Starts Here*. Fredericton: Goose Lane Editions, 1996.

Index